Gender and Diversity

Gender and Diversity

India, Canada and Beyond

Edited by
Malashri Lal
Chandra Mohan
Enakshi K. Sharma
Devika Khanna Narula
Amrit Kaur Basra

RAWAT PUBLICATIONS
Jaipur • New Delhi • Bangalore • Hyderabad • Guwahati • Kolkata

ISBN 978-81-316-0714-5

Published by
Prem Rawat for **Rawat Publications**
Satyam Apts, Sector 3, Jawahar Nagar, Jaipur 302 004 (India)
Phone: 0141 265 1748 / 7006 Fax: 0141 265 1748
E-mail: info@rawatbooks.com
Website: www.rawatbooks.com

New Delhi Office
4858/24, Ansari Road, Daryaganj, New Delhi 110 002
Phone: 011 2326 3290

Also at *Bangalore, Hyderabad, Guwahati* and *Kolkata*

Typeset by Rawat Computers, Jaipur

Printed at Chaman Enterprises, New Delhi

Contents

II
Gender Perspectives

III
Life-Story / Her Story

IV
Practical Applications

Preface

It was indeed quite a creditable academic achievement for the Centre for Canadian Studies, University of Delhi to have organized an International Conference on *Gender, Diversity and Cultural Pluralism: Canada and India*, on 17–18 January 2012 at the India International Centre, New Delhi. The University of British Columbia, Vancouver, Canada and Women's Interlink Foundation, Kolkata (West Bengal) graciously joined with the Centre for Canadian Studies, University of Delhi as partners in the development of Canadian Studies in India. This magnificent event was financially supported by the Department of Foreign Affairs and International Trade (DFAIT) Canada, along with the Advocacy Program, the Canadian High Commission, New Delhi.

The conference was inaugurated by the Hon'ble Vice Chancellor, Professor Dinesh Singh. In his address Professor Dinesh Singh highlighted the development of Indo-Canadian Studies especially in the area of Literature, Social Sciences and Higher Education. Professor Braj Sinha, President, Shastri Indo-Canadian Institute (SICI) congratulated the Centre for holding this conference and assured academic support on behalf of SICI. Mr Simon Cridland, Counsellor and Head, Advocacy Program, Canadian High Commission, New Delhi praised the status of the Centre for promoting Canadian Studies by holding such important events.

This international event attracted active participation of eminent scholars from Canada and from almost all parts of India. The important key issues discussed and deliberated upon in various academic sessions included: connections among Canadian and Indian women across diverse communities, understanding of the rights and responsibilities of women's citizenship, creating constitutional mechanisms for gender mainstreaming and the creation and dissemination of diverse Canadian and Indian cultural works, stories and symbols, including oral and indigenous resources.

The conference had focused on a few clearly defined objectives. It provided an interdisciplinary forum for scholars in the Humanities and Social Sciences to bring their own subject expertise from literature, languages, history, political science, economics and gender studies to address the issues. It helped to see Canada and India through the prism of a shared vision and to elicit comparisons that will produce a knowledge base for understanding diversity. The papers presented at the conference addressed contemporary challenges, paradoxes and resolutions at the end.

I am pleased to see the splendid outcome of the conference which is now appearing in the publication of the seminal twenty papers presented in various thematic sessions. The editorial committee that includes Professor Malashri Lal, Professor Chandra Mohan, Associate Professor Devika Khanna Narula and Associate Professor Amrit Kaur Basra deserve our thanks for putting together the selected papers of the conference and ably editing the papers to a publishable level in the volume. I would also like to thank all the colleagues from India and Canada who contributed their valued papers, particularly Professor Sneja Gunew, FRSC, University of British Columbia, Vancouver for delivering the keynote address.

The Centre is highly grateful to the Department of Foreign Affairs and International Trade (DFAIT), Canada for providing financial grant for organizing this conference. The Canadian High Commission, New Delhi, has always played a linchpin role for the development of Canadian Studies in the country. We would like to thank Professor Simon Cridland, Counsellor and Head, Advocacy Program and Professor Bernard Francis from Canadian High Commission, New Delhi for the valuable support provided to the Centre. I must express grateful thanks to Mr Pranit Rawat of Rawat Publications, Jaipur for publishing this volume on time.

Enakshi K. Sharma
Director, Centre for Canadian Studies,
University of Delhi, South Campus, New Delhi

Contributors

Jameela Begum A. is Chairperson, Curriculum Committee, ASAP, Government of Kerala. She was Dean, Faculty of Arts, Head of the Department of English, and Director of the Centre for Canadian Studies, University of Kerala. Prof. Begum was the President of the Indian Association for Canadian Studies and Secretary of the International Council for Canadian Studies. She was a Fellow of Shastri Indo-Canadian Institute at York University, Canada, twice and represented the University of Kerala at the Asia Pacific Conference at Meiji University and University of Wollongong, Australia. She has published extensively in scholarly journals and authored a monograph on *Cyril Dabydeen* in addition to over a dozen articles on Canadian, Diaspora and Third World literatures. Her edited publications include, *Canadian Voices: An Anthology of Poems* (1996), *Literary Theory: Re(reading) Culture and Aesthetics* (1997), *South Asian Canadiana* (1996), *Canadian Diaspora: Asia Pacific Immigration* (2001).

Meenu Anand is an Assistant Professor with the Department of Social Work, University of Delhi. A former faculty with Women's Studies & Development Centre (WSDC), University of Delhi, Dr. Anand has been actively involved in working on issues related to gender and education for almost two decades. She has led several national and international projects focussing on multifaceted developmental issues and has been actively conducting capacity building and gender sensitization workshops for various stakeholders. Dr. Anand has numerous publications in both national and international journals that seek to highlight issues related to gender and development within interdisciplinary frameworks. Her book *Gender and School Education: Challenges and Strategies* seeks to unveil and bring to light, the construction of gender in a school setting based on a theoretical framework of a multilayered sociological perspective.

Smita Banerjee is Associate Professor of English at Delhi College of Arts and Commerce, Delhi University. Her areas of interests include postcolonial and feminist studies. Her present work looks at issues of cinematic modernity and stardom in the Indian context. She has published articles on the condition of Bangla film industry in the 1950s, in the *Book Review* and on Suchitra Sen, the female superstar of the 50s–60s in *Seminar*. Her recent presentations include 'Scandalous Love: Eroticism in/and Popular Bangla Love Films of the 1950s'; 'Writing the Star: Stardom and the Bangla Little Magazine Discourse'; 'Writing the Stars: Issues of Gender and the Archive in Popular Bangla Cinema'; 'Suchitra Sen: Biography of a Female Star'; and 'Audio Visual Translation and Film Studies in India: Issues in Pedagogy'.

Amrit Kaur Basra is Associate Professor of History at Delhi College of Arts and Commerce, University of Delhi . She is also Deputy Dean (Foreign Students); Fellow, History and Academic Secretary, Institute of Lifelong Learning. Her areas of research are Sikhism and Interfaith; Communalism and Communal Riots in Colonial Punjab; Processes of Identity Formations in Colonial Punjab; Gender and Violence; History of Canada and the Historiography; and Print Culture and Built Heritage. She has published 35 articles in books and journals of repute. She has given presentation in 45 national and international conferences including on Sikhism. She is associated with Interfaith Movement since 2007 and was part of peace delegation that visited Pakistan in 2007. She has been recipient of many awards including R&D Doctoral Research Programme, 2012–2013, University of Delhi, Ambassador for Peace, Universal Peace Federation, 2009, Faculty Enrichment Fellowship, 1997-1998 by Canadian Government and minor research projects by UGC, Delhi.

Santosh Bharti is an Assistant Professor in the Department of English, Delhi College of Arts and Commerce, Delhi University. She has done M.A. in English from Jawaharlal Nehru University (JNU), M.Phil. and Ph.D. in Canadian Studies from Centre of Canadian, US and Latin

American Studies, School of International Studies, JNU. She is a recipient of Shastri Indo–Canadian Doctoral Fellowship in 2010. Her research areas are Canadian indigenous literature, postcolonial studies and American literature.

Mohar Daschaudhuri, Assistant Professor of French at the University of Calcutta, has been working on French feminist writers in Quebec and France. She was appointed as Visiting Scholar at the Department of French, University of Sheffield, UK (2013–2014). She worked at the School of Advanced Studies, University of London in a year long inter-disciplinary project on 'Motherhood in Post 1968 European Women's Writing', where she worked specifically on contemporary French and Indian women writers. She has published critical articles in national and international journals such as *Synergies Inde* (3, 2008), *Reflexions* (1, 2014) and contributed chapters in books. She is currently translating French Academy writer, Marguerite Yourcenar's *Oriental Tales* into Bengali.

Sneja Gunew has taught in England, Australia and Canada. She has published widely on multicultural, postcolonial and feminist critical theory and is Professor of English and Women's and Gender Studies at the University of British Columbia, Canada. She has edited and co-edited four anthologies of Australian women's and multicultural writings and in Australia compiled (with others) *A Bibliography of Australian Multicultural Writers* (the first such compilation in Australia) and co-edited *Striking Chords: Multicultural Literary Interpretations* (1992), the first collection of critical essays to deal with ethnic minority writings in the Australian context. Her books include *Framing Marginality: Multicultural Literary Studies* (1994) and *Haunted Nations: The Colonial Dimensions of Multiculturalisms* (2004). Based in Canada since 1993, her current work is on comparative multiculturalisms and diasporic literatures and their intersections with national and global cultural formations.

Garima Gupta is Assistant Professor in the Department of English, University of Jammu. She has participated in numerous national/international conferences, both in India and abroad and has published extensively in journals and anthologies. She is also working with Association for Social Health of India, regional NGO, for rehabilitating women and children displaced due to terrorism and other forms of violence and is recipient of Indira Gandhi Women Achiever's Award, India International Friendship Society, 2010. She is an active translator of Dogri short stories and is associated with the

National Translation Mission, Sahitya Akademi, New Delhi and J&K Academy of Art, Culture and Languages. Her focus areas are Indian literatures, translation, gender studies, communication skills and folklore. She is presently working on a major project of the UGC focussing on a comparative study of Dogri and Kashmiri folktales.

Vinita Gupta Chaturvedi is an Associate Professor in the Department of English at Delhi College of Arts and Commerce, University of Delhi. Her area of specialisation is Nineteenth Century British Fiction. She was awarded her Ph.D. from the University of Lucknow for her work on George Eliot. She has presented papers titled 'Humanising Science and Commerce' and 'Woman's Body: The Gender Question in Fiction and Cinema' at two national conferences in the University of Delhi. In the year 2012–2013, she was a part of the Innovations Project Team which received a research grant from the University of Delhi which submitted a report on the topic 'Symphonies of Life in Nature and Environment: The Folksongs of Punjab, Jammu & Kashmir'.

Jasbir Jain, presently Director, Institute for Research on Interdisciplinary Studies (IRIS), has worked in a wide range of areas. Former Sahitya Akademi Writer in Residence (University of Rajasthan), she has been an Emeritus Fellow and a KK Birla Fellow in Comparative Literature. She has been a recipient of the 2008 SALA Award for distinguished scholarship, IACS's lifetime achievement award, 2003, Karamshree Award 2013 (Rajasthan Lekhika Sangh). Jain has written extensively on cultural and literary issues with a special focus on narratology, gender and Indian literatures. Amongst her most recent publications are *Beyond Postcolonialism: The Dreams and Realities of a Nation, Indigenous Roots of Feminism: Culture, Subjectivity and Agency, Theorizing Resistance* and *The Diaspora Writes Home*.

Shweta Kushal is a faculty member in the area of Communication at the Indian Institute of Management, Indore and prior to this was Assistant Professor, University of Delhi. She has her doctorate in English Literature, Department of Humanities and Social Sciences, Indian Institute of Technology, Madras. Her Ph.D. thesis is a gynocentric study of Punjabi diaspora women's narratives and explores issues of belonging, gender and identity. She works on intercultural spaces that migrants inhabit and the manner in which gender affects the experience of these spaces. Her work has been published in refereed international and national journals as well as in the form of book chapters. Her research interests include communication, cultural studies, media studies and gender studies.

Malashri Lal is Dean of Colleges and Professor of English at the University of Delhi and has held senior administrative positions in the same university. Her academic specialization is in Women and Gender Studies about which she has eleven books. Among her acclaimed co-edited volumes are *In Search of Sita: Revisiting Mythology* (2009) and *Chamba-Achamba: Women's Oral Narratives* (Sahitya Akademi 2012). Her latest international publication is *Tagore and the Feminine: A Journey through Translations* (Sage 2015). As a recipient of several fellowships from the Fulbright, the Rockefeller Foundation, the Shastri-Indo Canadian Institute and the British Council, she has conducted research in prestigious institutions such as Harvard University, USA, and Bellagio, Italy. She has served on international book award committees including the Commonwealth Writers Prize, The Hindu Fiction Prize and the DSC Prize for South Asian Literature.

Hemjyoti Medhi is Assistant Professor, Department of English and Foreign Languages, Tezpur University, Assam. She is the recipient of the 'Preserving Social Memory' Grant of the Sephis Programme, International Institute of Social History, Amsterdam (2009–2011). Her doctoral thesis is on 'The 'Women's Question' in Colonial Assam: A Case Study of Chandraprabha Saikiani and the Assam Mahila Samiti'. Her publications include 'Missionary Writing and Self-fashioning of Assamese Cultural Identity in Colonial India: Revisiting the Past, Understanding the Present' in Robert Fraser and Mary Hammond ed. *Books Without Borders: Volume 2: Perspectives from South Asia.*

Chandra Mohan is currently Advisor, International Higher Education, Central University of Gujarat, Gandhinagar. He is presently the General Secretary of the Comparative Literature Association of India and formerly was Vice President, International Comparative Literature Association, President, Indian Association for Canadian Studies and Advisor, University of Jammu. He has taught English and Comparative Literature at the University of Delhi and several international universities. He is recipient of the senior Fulbright Fellowship and Canadian Research Fellowships. His publications include: *Comparing Literature: Canada and India* (1997); *Decolonizing the Master Narratives: Native Writing in Canada* (2005); *Studies in Comparative Literature: Theory, Culture and Space*, (co-ed.) 2007; *Cultures of the Margin in Multilingual Societies: A Comparative Perspective* (2007) and *Women and Development: Self, Society and*

Empowerment (co-ed.) 2013 and *Interdisciplinary Alternatives in Comparative Literature* (co-ed.) 2014.

Sachidananda Mohanty is Professor, and former Head, Department of English, University of Hyderabad. He is the recipient of numerous national and international recognitions including the British Council, the Fulbright, the Salzburg and the Katha Awards. A contributing editor to the literary journal *Muse India* (www.museindia.com), he is an acclaimed scholar and has published extensively on British literature, postcolonial, gender and translation studies. He has to his credit two volumes on D.H. Lawrence, and the following titles: *Understanding Cultural Exchange Today* (1996); *Travel Writing and the Empire* (2003); *Early Women's Writing in Orissa 1898–1950: A Lost Tradition* (2005); *Gender and Cultural Identity in Colonial Orissa* (2008); *Sri Aurobindo: A Contemporary Reader*, (2008), *Sarala Devi (*2011), *The Tale of My Exile* (2011) and *Cosmopolitan Modernity in Early Twentieth Century India* (2015). Professor Mohanty has lectured at some of the leading universities in India and abroad. His articles have appeared in *The Toronto South Asian Review, The Economic and Political Weekly, South Asian Review* and *Seminar* magazine.

Devika Khanna Narula is Associate Professor, Department of English, Delhi College of Arts and Commerce, University of Delhi. Her area of specialization is postcolonial, gender and cultural studies. She has contributed various papers on the South Asian Diaspora in various anthologies. Her publications include the books, *The South Asian Diaspora: Summer Blossoms in Winter Gardens* (2005), a critical study, *Sounds of Silence* (2005), a collection of self-composed poems, and numerous articles as book-chapters. She has also presented papers extensively in national/international seminars/conferences in India and abroad. Dr. Narula has also been the recipient of a UGC Research Grant for a project on Women Immigrants, the ICSSR Doctoral Scholarship for pursuing research at the University of Toronto, Canada, and co-ordinated a DU Innovation Project on 'Symphonies of Life in Nature and Environment: The Folksongs of Punjab, Jammu & Kashmir'.

Soham Pain is a Ph.D. scholar in the Centre for English Studies, Jawaharlal Nehru University (JNU), New Delhi. He specializes in postcolonial studies, African and Indian writings in English and T. S. Eliot and has a profound research interest in translation studies and Hindu philosophy. Currently, he is a Fulbright-Nehru Doctoral Fellow,

Department of Asian Studies, University of Texas, Austin, USA. His published papers include 'The Doctrine of Karma-Sannyasa and the Theme of Renunciation in R.K. Narayan's Fiction' and 'Poetic Deviation: A Comparative Study of Kuntaka and Shklovsky'.

Enakshi K. Sharma is Professor and Head, Department of Electronic Science and Director, Centre for Canadian Studies, University of Delhi. Her research interests are in the area of optical fiber and waveguide devices and optical control of passive microwave devices. She is a member of IEEE (LEOS and MTTS), Optical Society of America and Optical Society of India. Her work has resulted in more than 100 publications in journals and international and national conferences. She has had international collaborations with Jean Monnet University, France, Karlsruhe University, Germany and Kyushu University, Japan.

Shraddha A. Singh teaches Literature in English at Zakir Husain Delhi College (Morning), University of Delhi. She visited Concordia University, Montreal, Canada, 2008 on the Commonwealth Fellowship. In 2009, she presented her research findings at the World Seminar on Canada, Ottawa, where she received certification as one of the 16 upcoming Canadianist scholars worldwide. She has presented papers at several national/international seminars/conferences and has worked on several international projects funded by the International Council for Canadian Studies, Ottawa and Shastri Indo–Canadian Institute, New Delhi. Her key areas of interest are western philosophy, literary theory, literature and public policy, and gender, especially contemporary women writers across the globe. She has published self-composed poetry in English in national dailies/magazines and one of her poems is part of Norway's school curriculum.

Nilima Srivastava is a trained social worker. She was awarded Ph.D. in 1993 from the University of Lucknow. At present, she is Associate Professor, School of Gender and Development Studies, Indira Gandhi National Open University, New Delhi. Her earlier engagements have been with Department of Social Work as well as the Women's Studies and Development Centre, University of Delhi where she headed a research project on the Girl Child in collaboration with five other institutions in north India. Her areas of specialization are women and work and child welfare. She has been a visiting scholar to Institute of Gender, Race, Sexuality and Social Justice, UBC, Canada. Her publications include two books and several papers in national and international journals and publications. She is widely invited to take sessions on gender issues and conducts training programmes on gender sensitization.

Prem Kumari Srivastava, with a research and teaching experience of more than 26 years at Indian Institute of Technology, Delhi and University of Delhi, is currently an Associate Professor of English at Cluster Innovation Centre, University of Delhi. Recipient of many fellowships and awards, her published research in Cultural Studies, American Studies, Religion of Saints and English Language; and poems in books and eminent journals (national and international) display an overarching focus on gender, the popular and the indigenous. Having edited many issues of *Fortell*, she is on its editorial board since 2009, and on the editorial board of Literaria since 2011. Her publications are *Leslie Fiedler: Critic, Provocateur, Pop Culture Guru* (2014) and a co-authored and co-edited book *Foundation Course: Language, Literature and Creativity* (2013).

Sushma Yadav is Pro-Vice-Chancellor, IGNOU, New Delhi. She has been Professor of Public Policy and Governance as well as the Chair Professor of Dr. Ambedkar Chair in Social Justice, Indian Institute of Public Administration (IIPA). She is recipient of Rai Bahadur Gori Shankar Memorial Medal, Maharshi Karve Memorial prize, ICSSR Doctoral Fellowship and the Inter University Associateship at IIAS, Shimla. She was Member, AC, University of Delhi, 1996–2000, Member, IIPA's five member delegation to a workshop on 'China India Forum' sponsored by the China Executive Leadership Academy, Pudong, Shanghai and is presently Member, AC, Central University, Gujarat and HP University, Shimla. She has presented papers in national/international seminars/conferences and delivered memorial/special lectures. Her publications include: *Centre-State Relations* (1986); *Secularism and Indian Tradition* (1988); *Political Culture in Post-Independent India* (1989); *Issues in Indian Politics* (1994); *Culture and Politics* (1998); *Indian State: Origin and Development* (2000); *Patterns of Gender Violence* (2002); *Gender Issues in India* (2003); *Jal: Kal Aaj Aur Kal* (2005); *Gandhian Alternative: Social and Political Structure* (2005); and *Social Justice: Ambedkar's Vision* (2006).

Introduction

Malashri Lal

Almost fifteen years into the twenty-first century, it is important to look back to the dreams with which the millennium began, especially for women, and chart the journey taken towards empowerment. The book *Gender and Diversity: India, Canada and Beyond* is a reflection on such a journey.

The century dawned under the arch of several issues concerning globalization and diversity. The UN 'Millennium Development Goals' called attention to the most marginalized sections in different countries. In Canada, the conditions among the First Nations' people came to be examined closely. In India, the government launched poverty alleviation plans and major initiatives in education for disadvantaged segments of society. The statistics showed women to be the most economically deprived segment in Canada as well as in India.

A decade into the millennium, academic and field assessments were undertaken by various groups to reckon whether the policies on women's empowerment were likely to ensure equity, equality, justice and inclusive practices. A focus group at the Centre for Canadian Studies at the University of Delhi decided to investigate and collate current studies about shared concerns in both countries relating to gender equity in a rapidly changing scenario. The broad rubric was 'Gender, Diversity and Cultural Pluralism: Canada and India' which later resulted in this book.

The main objectives of the study were five fold:

1. To see gender and diversity issues in Canada and India through the prism of a shared vision and to elicit comparisons that will produce a knowledge base for understanding contemporary conditions.
2. To study and understand government policies in the two countries in relation to constitutional provisions, debates about the same and the possibility of change that is desirable in the context of gender equity and management of diversity.
3. To discuss the data available on women's participation in governance and citizenship roles such as parliamentary presence and in local administration, and address the concerns of balancing self-determination for marginal communities with the overall mechanism for rights and legal frameworks.
4. To share examples from literature, culture and media, including the oral traditions in indigenous communities in Canada and India that reflect the ongoing contentions about gender and cultural pluralism.
5. To adopt a multilingual approach to cover the linguistic debates which are crucial in both countries. Outlying areas such as the North East in India and the extreme western regions in British Columbia, Canada would need to be especially considered.

The study group presented its initial research at a conference in New Delhi in January 2012, attended by participants from Canada and also from diverse regions of India. The mingling of perspectives from various stakeholders – activists and academics, women and men scholars, students and teachers from several disciplines – brought valuable debates to the table. Over the next three years, this study group emerged as a vital network for pursuing the significant areas of comparative gender discourse that the conference had highlighted. A book was conceptualized as the suitable repository of the informed analysis flowing from the discussions.

Finally in 2015, the book, *Gender and Diversity: India, Canada and Beyond,* is in the hands of the public, written in a way that will speak to gender specialists as well as those in comparative cultural studies, international relations, social anthropology and other disciplines with comparative leanings. As one of the scholars, Shraddha A. Singh, has summarized, 'Gender operates at multiple levels. The sites of conflict and resolution are plural and based on contexts pertaining to the individual, the environment, culture and institutions. Studying gender and culture in the context of India and Canada has brought me to an understanding that significant distinctions and often many new ways of thinking emerge when comparative frameworks are employed.'

Why is the timely appearance of this volume to be noted? The United Nations Human Development Report 2014 addressed issues of vulnerability and inequality, with a special mention of how gender equality and development are inextricably linked to each other. India and Canada, though geographically distant, share common ground in terms of the diversity and diasporic population that is common to both. There are lessons to be learnt from each other when research and policy formation are discussed. The current anthology is an endeavour by Indian and Canadian Studies academics to highlight the shifting trends in reading texts and contexts with a focus on gender and culture. The book is divided into four parts, each dealing with a special thrust area. When one delves into comparative frameworks of analysis, often the spotlight is on similarities and differences.

The first section 'Cultural Pluralism' explores this theme in the context of Diaspora, Indigenous Cultures, Public Policy and Historiography, and presents it as a contested territory. The article 'Post-multiculturalism, Diaspora, Immanent Cosmopolitanism: A Future Anterior' by Sneja Gunew sets the tone for the book and makes a bridge between conflicting discourses on multiculturalism, the catchword for the twenty-first century. She says, 'Dealing with difference both inside and outside nation-states remains one of the leading challenges of our times. In the face of emphatic statements by world leaders that "multiculturalism has failed" my paper will examine the ways in which multiculturalism has been transformed within frameworks of globalization with a particular emphasis on women within cultural criticism'. This would be of interest to fellow academicians because the areas that are covered by Gunew and other writers in this section discuss contemporary issues such as post-multiculturalism and plurality and look at practical ways of employing research while discussing policy making and management. Jasbir Jain in her article 'Negotiating Differences: Cultural Spaces, Pluralism and Diversity' confronts the problem of definitions and the assumptions of 'managing' culture. Located within this theoretical framework, connected with multiple and often differing meanings of multiculturalism, plurality and diversity, Jain brings out the discriminations, even in the reform agenda, that move beyond gender to race, colour and histories that inherit the prevailing biases. Even the agendas for development have a 'look-down-upon-the other' attitude, she says, thereby steering her argument towards the real problem that is between the 'need to understand' and the 'need to change'. The paper focuses on the interpenetration of cultural norms of different communities and opens up the issues connected with non-representation of women in public spaces associated with power.

Chandra Mohan in his article 'Shifting Paradigms of Alterity in the Indigenous Culture and Literature: Canadian, Indian and Australian Contexts' focuses on the concept of 'otherness'. He reflects on the ways in which indigenous communities over time and space have accepted their position as the 'rejected' and due to this, unfortunately, they have strengthened their identities as 'others' in a world shaped by the politics of power. The paper brings out three paradigms connected with the colonial, postcolonial and the present world to show that during the colonial times, the 'master' constructed the identity of the indigenous communities. Chandra Mohan points out that in the present globalized world, commercialization of cultures of indigenous people has led to the 'canonization of native culture' constructed as 'otherness'. Thus 'alterity' remains an experiential reality.

In 'Culture, Diversity and Pluralism in India and Canada: A Public Policy Perspective', Sushma Yadav resurrects contentious arguments on cultural pluralism and its outreach to the beneficiaries. She states, 'The criticism comes both from the right, where many argue that it is insufficient to guarantee social cohesion, and also from the left where it is often considered as a guide to mask social inequalities and struggles'. Her article provides an empirical study of Canada and India in the context of the evolution of public policy. It underlines the fact that India is a nation of multiple ethnic groups and needs to have clearly demarcated public policies to ensure participation of all social groups and communities. The use of multiculturalism as a policy in Canada differs from that of the policies shaped by the Constitution of India, grounded in domain-specific contexts. Amrit Kaur Basra in her article 'Gender, History and Historiography in India and Canada: Some Reflections', maps the process of history writing in Canada and India since colonial times and reflects on how emergent sociological constructs carried male bias and presented women merely as a point of reference. She goes on to show that in both Canada and India, it was the thrust of feminist writing that de-constructed pre-existing generalizations and created an awareness of the role of women in shaping historical destinies.

The second section 'Gender Perspectives' turns its lens towards different contexts of gender, where not only women's issues but also the lesbian, gay, bisexual, transgender and queer (LGBTQ) community finds a voice. Since gender issues cannot be seen in isolation, some of the articles attend to culture, caste and history, making available promising perspectives for thought and further research. The woman's body takes on significance as a symbol and a metaphor in a male-dominated community. Authors evolve ways of contending with such commodification. In her article 'Narratology as a Tool in Gender Discourse', Devika Khanna Narula comments, 'Narratology explores possibilities and ways of resisting feminine oppression, and in this context "silence", "voice" and other strategies of protest become significant tropes used as a resonating device.' The article explores the ways in which the woman subverts the masculine attempts to possess her as a commodity and she manipulates the emotions of desire. Through statistical data pertaining to policies on LGBTQ, Garima Gupta's article 'LGBTQ Community: Canada and India' shows how conditions have changed over a period of time. According to her, in Canada, discrimination and victimization have been minimized through law, but in India the situation is still adverse due to prevailing social norms. The article reveals that in India the LGBTQ community does not possess a right to their own body. Vinita Gupta Chaturvedi's article extends the argument further in the essay 'Woman's Body: The Gender Question in Fiction and the Media' revealing that women too have no right over their body, especially in violent times. She focuses on the horror and brutality of communal passions inflicted upon women who become symbolic of the 'other' on whom violence is to be committed.

Mohar Daschaudhuri in her article 'Feminist Mythology and "Cultural Capital" in Nabaneeta Dev Sen and Louky Bersianik' explores the way in which mythology can be considered a 'cultural capital', propagating a male-centric view of human values, of nature and culture. She compares contemporary Bengali and French writing where both women writers re-interpret mythological symbols, and explores how they may read differently, displacing the binary dichotomies of good/evil as well as creating alternative structures of language. In the article 'Gender and Caste Politics in Shauna Singh Baldwin's *We Are So Different Now*' Soham Pain unravels the nuances of cultural fragmentation. He exposes the underlying reality that the patriarchal social system has simply altered its strategies of gender politics, but there has been no substantive change in the social outlook.

Continuing with the theme of violence on the gendered body, Shweta Kushal in her article 'Mnemonic Body of the Female Subject: "Personal" in History in *What the Body Remembers*' prioritises memory and the experiential realm over history and pedagogic rhetoric. She further reveals that this reality of the partition is 'anchored in difference and cannot be homogenized into the mainstream historical narrative'.

Third section 'Life-Story/ Her Story' deals specifically with autobiographies and biographies, some fictionalized, in India and Canada. It's a question often asked as to whether women tell stories differently. Do these narratives reflect a larger context? To ponder on these questions, the articles in this section analyse cross-cultural narratives, ideas of sisterhood, the role of memory, the politicization of the body and the effects and limitations of power in specific contexts. Jameela Begum's essay 'Translating Life Writing Across Cultures: Narratives of Select Indian and Canadian Women Writers' begins the section with the cautionary note, 'Constructing a text of the self and reliving and distancing oneself from one's stories, creates a dialogic of life-writing that explodes conventional narrative structures and translates traumatic experiences.' So what is the nature of authenticity in women's writing? In his article 'Crossing the Boundaries: Feminist Archives and the Redemptive Power of Sisterhood' Sachidananda Mohanty calls for archival research and relates his work on Odisha writer Sarala Devi to the works of Margaret Atwood. He indicates that the experiences of women reflect a similarity across temporal and spatial boundaries and hence create solidarity of sisterhood.

Smita Banerjee's article 'Narrating History/Herstory: Memory Work in Anita Rau Badami's *Can You Hear the Nightbird Call?*' maps the literary retellings of histories of peoples and events, situated and separated across time and space, moving from the Partition days in Punjab to contemporary times in Canada. Using insights from the postcolonial enterprise of narrativising history, Banerjee unpacks the contours of Badami's work on engendered traumatic events in the imaginary of the Indo-Canadian diaspora.

Shraddha A. Singh's article 'Body as Text and Context in the Works of Atwood and Goswami' takes this theme further into eco-feminism as she argues that for Atwood and Goswami the exploitation of nature is connected to the oppression of women, since it affects their ability and desire to become functional political citizens. Hence, not adhering to the socio-cultural stereotypes becomes for women a survivalist act.

Santosh Bharti in her article 'Gender and Identity: Indigenous Women as Symbols of Power' examines the paradox of Canada's indigenous women who face violence, discrimination, racism and subjugation through patriarchal policies that have dispossessed them of their inherited rights. However, says the writer, in spite of all difficulties, the indigenous women are seen as symbols of equitable nationhood in Canada today.

The last section 'Practical Applications' brings together some of the research evolving through field studies in a cross-cultural milieu, aggregating literature, culture and policy formation in the context of gender. It looks at cinema, education, the workplace and non-government organizations to understand the challenges to women's selfhood in the global arena of multiplicity. Prem Kumari Srivastava's 'Knowledge Keepers – Canadian Cinema About the Indigenous: Special Focus on *Atanarjuat* and *Unnatural and Accidental*' offers the rare access to indigenous cinema in Canada and reports interviews with social activists such as Jeanette Armstrong. She makes her point that such material significantly captures the history and knowledge of the Canadian native community and in this process, the people become the 'keepers' of specialized knowledge.

The role of women's organizations in addressing problems and trying to mitigate them is the focal point in the article 'Diversity and Questions of Alliance: A Case Study of the Assam Mahila Samiti, India and the Mahila Shanti Sena, Canada' by Hemjyoti Medhi. By studying women's associations in Assam and Women's Peace Brigade International registered in Canada, she presents their factual histories and policies and how they have tried to critique identity politics. Women labour in India is the subject of Nilima Srivastava's article 'Women and Work in India and Canada: A Kaleidoscopic View'. She discusses the anomaly as to how the increase in women's employment nevertheless channels into obstructions at the work place that do not allow women to realize their full potential. Meenu Anand's article titled 'School Education and the Challenge of Diversity: India and Canada' is based on empirical research. It reflects the complexities of processes that lead to reinforcement of gender identity in classrooms in Canada and India. In both places, educators are striving hard to provide corrective perspectives through dissemination of education in innovative ways and towards equality.

Comprising of twenty thoughtful articles, *Gender and Diversity: India, Canada and Beyond* is a valuable addition to the growing corpus of material on internationalism and cultural diversity. Migration, diversity and transnationalism being realities in the twenty-first century, issues such as history, rootedness, belonging, orality, identity formation, life expressions, family reorientations, and human rights are not merely academic but constituents of everyday negotiation. Yet, the gender angle has been insufficiently addressed in the books in print although media exposure and occasional articles abound. This book stands poised at a critical edge, as it would be of pertinent significance for a comparative stance in gender studies. Easy definitions of multiculturalism and diversity are squarely confronted. Further, pointed and well-illustrated comparisons are made between Canada and India, with original research and fieldwork relied upon to draw conclusions. Women are 'knowledge keepers' as Prem Kumari Srivastava calls them. Their intellectual resources cannot be measured in traditional terms, so we need a new vocabulary and a bold new emphasis to open gateways to these hidden treasures. This book paves the way and hopes, others will tread the path and open it some more.

14 December 2014
New Delhi

I

Cultural Pluralism

1

Post-multiculturalism, Diaspora, Immanent Cosmopolitanism

A Future Anterior

Sneja Gunew

The paper is framed by Vijay Mishra's ominous question in his book *What was Multiculturalism*? (2012): 'What do we do with them now?' (18, 29) and resonates with the recent emphatic assertion by various world leaders that multiculturalism has failed. While we could try and unpack what that means, another direction could be to ask what might post-multiculturalism look like?[1] And here I am using the 'post' in Jean-François Lyotard's sense – going back to ask what was left out in the various constructions of multiculturalism in its double usage: first, as a way for states to manage difference and second, the attempts by various groups and individuals who felt excluded from national formations to argue for their own supplementary inclusions. The logic proposed by Lyotard (1986) was that the condition of Postmodernism consists in part of going back to elements not taken up by Modernism so that the 'post' of postmodernism becomes not simply a future orientation so much as the future anterior (the future in the past) structured by anamnesis, a recollection or going back that discovers other possibilities for alternatives to the period and movement we have come to call Modernism:

> Tu comprends qu'ainsi compris, le 'post' de 'postmoderne' ne signifie pas un mouvement de come back, de flash back, de feed back,

> c'est-à-dire de répétition, mais un process en 'ana-', un process d'analyse, d'anamnèse, d'anagogie, et d'anamorphose, qui élabore un 'oubli initial.' (126)
>
> (My translation.: You understand that when understood like that, the 'post' of the postmodern does not mean a movement as in come-back, flash-back, feed-back, that is to say a repetition, but a process of 'ana', a process of analysis, anamnesis, anagogy, anamorphosis, which elaborates on an 'initial forgetting').

In other words, we might find in this precondition to Modernism not so much the grand narratives of nationalism or internationalism, or even of West and non-West, as the *petits récits* of those differences within: ethnicity, indigeneity, and gender, all of which had of course always been lurking there. I am suggesting that inside these vernaculars we need to expose the cosmopolitan dimensions that connect us to a world that should not remain fully mediated by the nation-state. Another way of putting it is to ask what are the detailed and affective components, viscerally imagined, of being a citizen of/in the world?

I will argue in this short paper that what was left out of the multiculturalism we know was the cosmopolitan element, something that draws us into the world via the perspectives of those 'minority ethnics.'[2] And rather than identifying which writers or artists could be designated as 'cosmopolitan' we might think about cosmopolitanism as a method, a form of reading and analysis, that produces new forms of knowledge.

In the first instance neo-cosmopolitanism is a global political theory associated with theorists such as Ulrich Beck and others and is primarily characterized by attempts to think beyond the nation-state. As Ulrich Beck and Edgar Grande (2010) put it in a recent essay:

> It has become a commonplace that national institutions alone are unable to cope with the challenges of regulating global capitalism and responding to new global risks. ... It is no less obvious that there is no global state or international organization capable of regulating global capital and risk. ... Instead, we can observe a complex reconstitution of political authority, with which to organize the mechanisms of global economic regulation, risk management and control in ways characterized by new forms of political interdependence. (410)

In their introduction to *The Cosmopolitan Reader* (2010), Garrett Brown and David Held argue that there are three 'moral and normative commitments' that are foundational components of cosmopolitanism:

> First, cosmopolitans believe that the primary units of moral concern are individual human beings and not state or other forms of communitarian or political association. ... Second, cosmopolitans maintain that this moral concern for individuals should be equally applied. ... Third, as the etymology of the word suggests, cosmopolitanism is universal in its scope, maintaining that all humans are equal in their moral standing ... *as if we are* all citizens of the world. (1–2)

In other words, cosmopolitanism represents an attempt to give a new analytical frame to the many ways in which we conceive global relations and, significantly, situates universal human rights at the centre. However, as Seyla Benhabib and others have argued, the 'universal' in that conception continues to be permeated by culturally embedded perspectives. Cosmopolitanism as method would demonstrate this reality.

The idea of *vernacular* cosmopolitanism emanates more broadly from cultural theory and grapples with illustrating the ways in which the supposed universalism of cosmopolitanism is nonetheless rooted within specific cultural frames; this last feature associates it with older analyses of multiculturalism. Paul Gilroy provides an example of such an approach in his book *Postcolonial Melancholia* (2004):

> There is another quite different idea of cosmopolitanism to be explored here. Its value to the politics of multiculturalism lies in its refusal of state-centeredness and in its attractive vernacular style. In a sharp contrast with the recipes for good governance that have been pronounced from up above, this variant might be described as 'vulgar' or 'demotic' cosmopolitanism. (67)

This turn in theory has led recent postcolonial theorists, for example, or the increasing number of 'inter-Asia' theorists (Chen and Chua, 2007), to argue that cosmopolitan theory's roots in the eighteenth century (the age of western imperial expansions as well as the work of Immanuel Kant) means its supposed universalism is inevitably compromised by Eurocentrism and, indeed, by European colonialism (Mawani, 2010–11).

What Does the Concept 'Vernacular Cosmopolitanism' Attempt to Capture?

Vernacular cosmopolitanism represents what has also been termed a cosmopolitanism from below or a subaltern cosmopolitanism that makes claims for the recognition of the cosmopolitan nature (interactions with globalization) that are associated with groups that have been marginalized by nationalist enterprises – immigrants, refugees, asylum seekers, itinerant labour groups (in German, 'guest workers', *Gastarbeiter*) seeking work across the world and all the more vulnerable for that (Nyers, 2003). Within cultural theory specifically, cosmopolitanism represents an impetus to use the literary and cultural productions of artists from those subaltern groups or backgrounds as a way to question the supposed discreteness and homogeneity of national cultures as well as the universality of globalization. In Homi Bhabha's (1996) wording:

> The postcolonial endorses a vernacular cosmopolitanism that has to translate between cultures and across them in order to survive, not in order to assert the sovereignty of a civilized class, or the spiritual autonomy of a revered ideal. Vernacular cosmopolitans are the heirs of Walter Benjamin's view of modernity, that every act of civilization is also an act of barbarism. (24)

One model is to see subaltern artists as occupying a Derridean supplementary space that inherently questions the supposed plenitude of a national culture. In the framework of globalization, one site where one may study this revisioning is the concept of 'world literature' as illustrated by Pascale Casanova's study *The World Republic of Letters* (2004). Casanova suggests that there are two impulses in literature:

> The internal configuration of each national space precisely mirrors the structure of the international literary world as whole. Just as the global space is organized with reference to a literary and cosmopolitan pole, on the one side, and a political and national pole on the other, each of its constituent spaces is structured by the rivalry of what I will call 'national' writers (who embody a national or popular definition of literature) and 'international' writers (who uphold an autonomous conception of literature). (108)[3]

In relation to this schematic I would propose that cosmopolitan writers are both/and, that is, they redefine the nation by incorporating self-referential diasporic links to global relations.

How Does Cosmopolitanism Intersect with Multiculturalism?

Multiculturalism is both an area of policy that deals with the management of difference and a philosophy that attempts to explain the ways in which a national culture should either be open to difference, or, put up boundaries and restrictions to the proliferation of differing customs, beliefs, etc. This has become a particularly thorny issue lately in relation to religion since it appears to pit state laws against divine laws and that is difficult territory. As religions once again become a growth area, tackling these apparent incommensurabilities is a matter of some urgency.[4]

Here is a quick summary of the issues associated with that impossible term 'multiculturalism'. Multiculturalism refers to the differing ways in which nation-states consolidate their putative homogeneity by simultaneously acknowledging and managing various kinds of differences that include ethnicity, race, religion, languages, cultures, etc. In other words the very act of citing the differences implies that there is a homogenous core to the nation against which these differences are measured. Multiculturalism is also a term invoked by particular groups in order to argue for retaining their distinctive differences, however they are articulated. Some have argued that one should distinguish between the descriptive term 'multi-cultures' that denote the heterogeneity and hybridity of many nations and reserve the term 'multiculturalism' for naming the strategies of governance employed by states to manage such heterogeneity (Hall, 2000). As debates on globalization have gathered momentum, multiculturalism has been used as a way of indicating both the local discrepant meanings of the term at the same time that it has been linked to notions of global diasporas. Diasporas appear to threaten the sovereignty of nation-states and are much discussed in the globalization debates. It is also noticeable that in the face of persistent economic inequalities, resistance movements within nation-states are often symbolically expressed in terms of ethnic or multicultural differences thus giving rise to the charge that identifying differences contributes to fragmentation rather than merely describing or acknowledging its reality (Vertovec and Wessendorf, 2010). Hence we encounter the recent statements by world leaders.

Some of the confusions generated by multicultural discussions and studies have to do with the fact that there are many versions designated multicultural. For example, it might be helpful to distinguish between multiculturalism as a political theory and as a philosophy as well as trying to unpack the term 'culture' itself. As a political theory with policy dimensions, multiculturalism has often been described as marking a shift from previous stages where differences remained unrecognized and were simply subsumed into dominant groups and institutions. When linked with migration the idea was to assimilate into the dominant group's version of nationalism or narratives of the nation. Other terms such as 'integration' or 'social cohesion' also effectively meant assimilation. The multicultural era marked the emergence of a period where groups were permitted to retain varying degrees of differences so long as they maintained allegiance to core institutions and values. But from the beginning there was uncertainty about how these underlying allegiances were meant to be measured. Critics of multiculturalism saw the emphasis on culture as demonstrating an homogenizing impetus and that the focus on culture was a way of occluding persistent underlying racism – in other words the logic was that it wasn't your race to which I objected but to your cultural differences or *mores* (Balibar, 1988).

Multiculturalism as philosophy is linked with preserving rights for both individuals and distinctive groups, although there are often tensions between the two. Reference is often made to the work of Kant and his notion of universal hospitality but Jacques Derrida reminds us that all hospitality also carries an inherent notion of hostility leading him to coin the term *hostipitality*. While arguments for the recognition of distinct cultures (Taylor, 1994) and even of nations within nations (Kymlicka, 1995) proliferate there have also been increasing questions regarding the limits of accommodation, particularly when such cultural differences are entwined with religions other than the state religion. Sometimes such debates are characterized as being between the public and private domains, that is, one's religion belongs to the latter and should be outside the purview of state control.[5]

It is also important to distinguish the historical periods when particular geopolitical entities engaged with multiculturalism. Generally speaking, the settler colonies such as Canada and Australia are credited with producing multicultural policy frameworks because they had to deal with the implications of calculated postwar immigration that recruited groups from beyond the British Empire. Thus, for a time, both Canada and Australia defined themselves as inherently multicultural nations who insisted that the absorption of immigrants did not threaten the historical foundations of the settler colonies as demonstrated by the fact that both countries retain the Queen of England as head of state.

Such multiculturalism is at odds with what has happened in Europe (Modood and Werbner, 1997) and the UK (Hall, 2000) where it often refers to non-white groups entering predominantly white nations. This had to do with historic colonialism in the UK (the empire 'returning') and with postwar labour shortages in Europe where guest workers, (e.g. Turks in Germany; Africans in Spain) were permitted residence for brief periods and were expected to return to their home countries rather than seeking citizenship. Multiculturalism also names different practices in the US where in the past it was reserved for managing educational diversity in the wake of Hispanic and 'Asian' migrations and the continuing attempts to deal with the aftermath of slavery and African-American differences (Willett, 1998).

Questions concerning how and by whom groups or 'communities' were constituted also led feminists, for instance, to question the roles and rights of women within such structures (Oikin, 1999) and whether a de-emphasizing of culture and a shift to maintaining individual rights might not in fact advantage women who are often ill-served by being embedded in communities where they rarely have a significant voice (Phillips, 2007).

Some of the rather neat frameworks implied above have been confounded over time, largely because it is not possible to credibly maintain (even briefly) the discrete categories where groups are homogeneously defined in terms of their 'culture' and leave their differences behind when they enter the new homeland and engage with a nation's major institutions. While some critics abandoned the term 'multiculturalism' as being nothing but a 'floating signifier', some followed the Chicago Cultural Studies Group in arguing for a 'critical multiculturalism' that would function to analyse the continuing power dynamics within invocations of multiculturalism. Another way of interpreting such dynamics is to look at the relationship between terms within multiculturalism such as ethnicity and race. The former was often mistakenly seen as a benign alternative to the latter but increasingly multiculturalism has primarily devolved into acknowledging the paramount need for consolidating anti-racist practices (Gilroy, 2006). Indeed, Stuart Hall trenchantly critiques the supposed biological foundation of race and cultural differences that define 'ethnicity', seeing them both as discursive 'chains of equivalence' that are read off each other.

As a result of looking at histories of colonialism and migrations over the last century (or so) anti-racist approaches have gained purchase and resulted in the development of whiteness studies as a robust field of research (Goldberg, 1994). In relevant settler colonies there has also been an increasing presence of indigenous studies where the specific demands of indigenous groups have argued, for example, that multiculturalism functions as a deliberate distraction from indigenous demands for separate nationhood and attendant land claims (Povinelli, 2002). Should indigenous groups, for example, be designated as distinctive groups permitted to retain their own separate nationhood to allow them self-determination and separate areas where they could restore their own cultures almost eradicated by colonialism? (Kymlicka, 1995)

Most recently, religious differences or, as some have argued, the politicization of religion, have loomed large as presenting incommensurable differences, notably around Muslim identities (Parekh, 2006; Modood, 2007) but also, for example, the Tibetans in China. Old fault lines within nations-states have, for example, coalesced around a convenient Islamophobia that has been strengthened by the recent 'war on terror' including what Allen Feldman (2004) has called the 'securocratic wars of public safety'.

Debates concerning the tensions between group rights and individual rights proliferate, for example, in relation to gender (Oikin, 1999; Phillips, 2007; Shohat, 1998). This debate also occurs at the global level in relation to asylum seekers and refugees where the very people whose rights are being debated within nations are generally excluded from voicing their concerns (Benhabib, 2006). With respect to the demands of citizenship, theorists such as Aihwa Ong have coined the term 'flexible citizens' where allegiances to the family are stronger than nebulous notions of nation in relation to Asian diasporas. When multiculturalism is invoked by groups arguing for distinctive rights it often becomes a launching place for anti-western critiques (Modood, 2007; Parekh, 2006). On the other hand, multiculturalism is belabored as scapegoat whenever supposedly intransigent non-Western differences and intolerances are identified (Vertovec and Wessendorf, 2010).

There is an inherent tension in bringing together multiculturalism and cosmopolitanism because multiculturalism is closely linked to governance within the nation-state – ways in which one can recognize (critics such as Ghassan Hage would say cage or domesticate) the diversity that always exists in all nations while at the same time ensuring that it does not challenge the imaginary integrity of the nation. Some of these fears are behind the recent pronouncements by world leaders that multiculturalism has failed. What they generally mean by this is that diverse groups have been given too much freedom to retain their own beliefs and rituals and that these are often perceived as being at odds with national beliefs and legal structures. As I've mentioned, the conflict is often cast as between private and the public domains and where those boundaries should be drawn.

At the same time nations clearly wish to signal their modernity and that they participate self-consciously in robust global relations. However, within this drive, the role of minorities is an ambiguous one. And this is where we encounter such terms as rootless cosmopolitanism or cosmopatriotism, in other words that the national and political allegiance and loyalty of groups with diasporic connections is frequently challenged. Yes, they are concrete manifestations of global interactions and intersections, but to what degree do they have the interests of the nations in which they now dwell at heart? One of the manifestations of the new cosmopolitanism is the rise of a new kind of urban novel: Dionne Brand's *What We All Long For*, Teju Cole's *Open City* and Miguel Syjuco's *Ilustrado* are a few examples. What they have in common is a representation of the city as a crucible for global relations. One thinks as well of films such as those by González Iñárritu (*21 Grams*, *Babel* and *Biutiful*) which illustrate in everyday ways the abstract impetus behind Beck's assertions concerning the interdependence of the global.[6]

But what do I mean by this immanent cosmopolitanism in my title? It is both inside and outside the nation and represents the potential for weaving into the nation a different model of globalization or Beck's global interdependence. Such perspectives are signalled by Gilroy's definition of cosmopolitanism as cultivating an estrangement from one's own culture.[7] We also need to distinguish what we mean by 'globe' and 'world' terms that tend to be melded together in references to globalization. As Pheng Cheah (2008) reminds us:

> The world is a form of relating or being-with. The globe, on the other hand, the totality produced by processes of globalization, is a bounded object or entity in Mercatorian space. When we say 'map of the world,' we really mean 'map of the globe.' It is assumed that the spatial diffusion and extensiveness achieved through global media and markets give rise to a sense of belonging to a shared world, when one might argue that such developments lead instead to greater polarization and division of nations and regions. The globe is not the world. (30)

What do I mean by finding the cosmopolitan in the vernacular that comes to us from the spaces we used to call multicultural? Much of my analysis involves trying to conceptualize both the one and the many, something Bhabha analysed in his distinction between the pedagogical and the performative (adding to does not mean adding up). It is a tension that I find in the work of the Canadian writer Anita Rau Badami to whose recent novels I shall now turn.

Badami

Anita Rau Badami was born in India in 1961 and emigrated to Canada in 1991. She has published four novels, *Tamarind Mem* (1996), *The Hero's Walk* (2001), *Can You Hear the Nightbird Call?* (2006) and *Tell It to the Trees* (2011). Badami is often viewed as a quintessentially diasporic writer. Diasporic subjects function to represent deviations from the supposedly 'pure' and 'rooted' characteristics of national citizens. They supposedly indicate the instabilities of hybridity, métissage, creolization and contamination, elements that have also defined the condition of (post) modernity more generally. For example, in Badami's third novel, *Can You Hear the Nightbird Call*? the semi-divine King Trishanku hanging between heaven and earth is a compelling illustration of a tragic, or at least traumatic, state of un-belonging (76–77).

In general etymological terms, diaspora is connected with notions of seeding and dissemination. When specific writers take up this generalized image, the implications are multiple and complex. Consider the following passage in Badami's *Can You Hear the Nightbird Call*?: 'Without history you were nothing, a nobody, one of those fluffy seed-heads floating in the summer breeze, unaware of your origins, careless of your destination. Meaningless, mythless, shapeless' (206). The dual movement in this image raises a number of issues. In the first instance, it is a subtle reminder that Badami's text engages throughout with the clichés of Canadian state multiculturalism and at the same time shows the ways in which diasporic subjects sometimes respond.[8] In some ways, one could argue that Badami's work knowingly illustrates the perils of diasporic imaginative investments in homeland, hostland and those diasporic subjects caught between them. In this instance the image evoked focuses on the centrifugal question of what holds people together in an imagined diaspora? The image is also a reminder that diaspora is fantasized as much by the homeland as hostland and often spawns those anxieties that quickly turn diasporic individuals and groups into targets. The nation is provoked by the perception that diasporic groups are bound together by alternative relations to those associated with a 'local' nationalism.[9] Gender is central to these concerns and raises the issue of whether women and men are perceived to carry differing responsibilities in maintaining cultural links. Women are often construed as the bearers of tradition, more emphatically so when in transition.[10] Psychoanalysis and its structures of mourning and melancholia offer further frameworks of meaning,[11] as does the burgeoning field of affect theory.[12] Certainly psychoanalytically inspired studies suggest that the children of diasporic peoples often inherit disabling guilt and longings from their parents.[13] Suffice to say that while the diasporic subject exists (like all subjects) in a permanent state of misrecognition in the mirror of the social, it simultaneously functions as an enduring symbol for the nation-state because this misrecognition is, in a sense, inescapable. It is another way of formulating the instability that exists at the core of national cultures or any cultures aspiring to homogeneity.

Politics of Location: Here as Much as There

Badami to some degree represent a mixture of both the old and new diasporas identified by Mishra (2007: 2–4). In *Can You Hear the Nightbird Call*? Badami creates a study of a diasporic community in Vancouver that weaves together the ways in which these networks intertwine locally, nationally, and transnationally. Using specific historical events Badami explores their local impact on individuals in India and Canada. Badami's text begins in India in the late 1920s and focuses mostly on the two turbulent decades of the late sixties to the eighties, concentrating on events in the Punjab and thereby giving historical and affective insights into the considerable Canadian Sikh community. What needs to be stressed is that Badami's novel is profoundly Canadian, with constant references to familiar Canadian cultural markers, but by imbricating this 'here' with a less familiar 'there' she interpellates Canadianness in fundamentally new ways and it is this process that I am identifying as the beginnings of cosmopolitanism as method.

In her new novel *Tell It to the Trees*, located firmly in a small town in British Columbia, Badami deals with the problems of rural (and ethnic) isolation and domestic violence. The results are unexpected. If one considers the trailer for the book that is available on Badami's website (http://anitaraubadami.ca/) we encounter a voice-over purportedly spoken by the teenager Varsha as well as close-ups of a soulful face that is phenotypically 'South Asian'. The voice is accented and reads passages from the novel describing the physical abuse the father inflicts upon her. Canadian scenes of the snowbound rural landscape culminate in the view of a woman in a sari filmed from behind. The trailer defies the logic of the book itself since Varsha was born and grew up in Canada and so should not have an accent; nor does she wear a sari. The expectations the trailer sets up are that the novel deals with ethnic isolation and the particular perils faced by immigrant women who may not have access to outside help in the form of friends and communities as well as state support. The media constantly portrays violence against South Asian women as being supposedly embedded in and an outcome of their particular cultural circumstances (honour killings, etc.) rather than situating the violence within the broader picture of Canadian contexts for violence against women and children (Pickton case).[14] The trailer appears to reinforce the usual stereotypes held about South Asian women within North America whereas Badami's text actually counters such representations. The novel emphasises the ways in which domestic violence shapes the children. Varsha, the adolescent daughter, is the ambiguous centre of the novel whose problems are not self-evident when she is first introduced to the reader:

> I am thirteen years old, almost fourteen. I love reading. I love my family. I prefer to have no friends. I plan to go to university. When I grow up I will be a lawyer. Maybe a writer. A scientist even. I can be anything I set my mind to. I am super smart. (9)

As we learn progressively, her malevolence has been sculpted by violence in monstrous ways. Once again Badami plays against stereotypes. The text begins with a murder and, until the final section, the assumption is that the perpetrator is the abusive family patriarch. However Badami is as concerned with portraying, once again in her work, the friendships between women as well as their betrayals. Readers are introduced to the matriarch who may or may not have begun the cycle of violence in her possible manslaughter of her own husband (tales which imprinted themselves on Varsha and her half-brother Hermant with devastating results). In this instance Badami's cosmopolitanism consists of demonstrating the Canadianness of her characters rather than reinforcing their exotic ethnicity. In spite of the misleading nature of the trailer the text deals with a robust and even likeable North American teenage character whose energy is simply misdirected due to the consequences of violence and the reinforcements of the family fortress – a feature that is often at the centre of women and child abuse in all cultures.

The illusion that one may claim universalities and internationalisms, access to this conceptual economy is currency available to some and not others. Vernacular cosmopolitanism is a way to defamiliarize the old elitist cosmopolitan 'citizen of the world' as well as allowing us to rethink the place of 'multiculturalism' within our versions of the nation-state. The cosmopolitan vernacular has the ability to combine the global with the minutiae of the local via diasporic networks and knowledge systems. All help construct the estrangement from one's own culture identified by Gilroy as one of the necessary symptoms or attributes of cosmopolitanism. Such perspectives are not majoritarian, not the god's eye view of the old cosmopolitanism (as exemplified in Pico Iyer's 'global soul'), but instead comprise the stammering pedagogies, the minoritarian interjections that disrupt the business as usual of certain forms of globalization.

All of these debates have at their core attempts to imagine fully the contradictory tensions that inhabit considerations of the one and the many, Bhabha's adding to does not mean adding up. Cosmopolitanism in its most useful form enables this tension to exist constructively and, not surprisingly, writers and artists have presented us with ways of imaging and imagining this dynamic. The new cosmopolitan cultural texts that elaborate and animate statistical data reach out to us from those cages that too often comprise multiculturalism. Mishra's question might be reframed from another perspective, another 'we' that is not the state but these new embodiments of cosmopolitanism: 'What can we do here, now?' Badami's work represents one kind of response.

Notes

1. Interestingly, the three leaders concerned, England, France and Germany are relatively recent promoters of state multiculturalism.
2. Another model that suggests itself is provided by Kuan-Hsing Chen in his *Asia as Method: Towards De-Imperialization* (2010). Chen analyses postcolonialism, globalization and what he terms the rise of Asian studies within Asia. He also distinguishes carefully between decolonization and de-imperialization and situates 'Asia as method' as posing a new global history (14–15). 'Knowledge production is one of the major sites in which imperialism operates and exercises its power' (211).

3. See Debjani Ganguly's (2008) critique of her approach.
4. See Ahluwalia (2010) for an interesting discussion on the role of religion in recent national and diasporic configurations dealing with the Sikh pogroms in India in 1984.
5. That religion remains a disavowed reference point in these discussions was superbly demonstrated by Brian Klug's analysis of David Cameron's speech in the 'Cultural ReOrientations and Comparative Colonialities' conference of the CSAA Annual conference 2011, 22–24 November, Adelaide, South Australia.

   One could also argue that sexuality is akin to religion in that it includes core element of belief as in same-sex relations.
6. See Berthold Schoene's critique (2009: 14–15).
7. Gilroy's example is George Orwell.
8. For example, there is a popular and much-screened television series (beloved by teachers) titled *A Scattering of Seeds* (52 episodes) which draws attention to the 'success stories' of Canadian multiculturalism. http://www.whitepinepictures.com/seeds/index.html, accessed on 31 January 2008.
9. Mishra (2007: 14–15) discusses this hostility to manifestations of other allegiances in terms of a Hegelian and Zizekian 'Nation Thing' in which the nation is paradoxically both fantasized and material, whereas Hage (2003: 36–43) compares it to the imaginary unconditional love a mother has for her child: both models are of course fantasy structures.
10. See Kandiyoti (1994) and Yuval-Davis (1997) for further discussion of these complex issues.
11. Vijay Mishra (2007: 7–10) explores diaspora in these terms.
12. Affect theory could be described as an attempt to analyse and theorize the complex field of emotions and the ways in which they shuttle between private and public realms, between biology and abstract philosophical categories. For an outline of how we might begin to 'decolonize' affect theory, see Gunew (2009).
13. Both Rashkin (1992) and Cheng (2001) discuss generational guilt.
14. Robert Pickton is a serial killer who was convicted of horrific murders in 2007 in British Columbia.

References

Ahluwalia, Pal, 'The Politics of Intimacy: (Re)Thinking 1984', *Sikh Formations* 6.2 (2010): 105–117.

Badami, Anita Rau, *Can You Hear the Nightbird Call?*, Toronto: Vintage, 2006.

——, *Tell It to the Trees*, Toronto: Knopf, 2011.

Balibar, Etienne, 'Is There a Neo-Racism?', in Etienne Balibar and Immanuel Wallerstein (eds), *Race, Nation, Class: Ambiguous Identities*, London: Verso, 1988, pp. 17–28.

——, *We, the People of Europe: Reflections on Transnational Citizenship*, Translated by J. Swenson, Princeton, NJ: Princeton University Press, 2004.

Beck, Ulrich and Edgar Grande, 'Varieties of Second Modernity: The Cosmopolitan Turn in Social and Political Theory and Research', *The British Journal of Sociology* 61.3 (2010): 409–442.

Benhabib, Seyla, *Another Cosmopolitanism*, New York: Oxford University Press, 2006.

Bhabha, Homi, 'Unsatisfied: Notes on Vernacular Cosmopolitanism', in L. García-Moreno and P.C. Pfeiffer (eds), *Text and Narration: Cross-Disciplinary Essays on Cultural and National Identities*, Columbia, SC: Camden House, 1996.

Bhabha, Homi and John Comaroff, 'Speaking of Postcoloniality in the Continuous Present: A Conversation', in David T. Goldberg and Ato Quayson (eds), *Relocating Postcolonialism*, Oxford: Blackwell, 2002, pp. 15–46.

Brown, Garrett W. and David Held (eds), *The Cosmopolitan Reader*, Cambridge: Polity, 2010.

Casanova, Pascale, *The World Republic of Letters*, Translated by M.B. DeBevoise, Cambridge, MA: Harvard University Press, 2004.

Chakrabarty, Dipesh, *Provincializing Europe: Postcolonial Thought and Historical Difference*, Princeton, NJ: Princeton University Press, 2000.

Cheah, Pheng, 'World Literature as World-Making Activity', *Daedalus* 137.3 Summer (2008): 26–38.

Chen, Kuan-Hsing, *Asia as Method: Towards De-Imperialization*, Durham: Duke University Press, 2010.

Chen, Kuan-Hsing and Beng Huat Chua (eds), *The Inter-Asia Cultural Studies Reader*, New York: Routledge, 2007.

Cheng, Anlin C., *The Melancholy of Race: Psychoanalysis, Assimilation, and Hidden Grief*, New York: Oxford University Press, 2001.

Chicago Cultural Studies Group, 'Critical Multiculturalism', in David T. Goldberg (ed.), *Multiculturalism: A Critical Reader*, Oxford: Blackwell, 1994, pp. 114–139.

Derrida, Jacques, *Cosmopolitanism and Forgiveness*, Translated by Mark Dooley, New York: Routledge, 2002.

Feldman, Alan, 'Securocratic Wars of Public Safety', *Interventions* 6.3 (2004): 330–350.

Ganguly, Debjani, 'Global Literary Refractions: Reading Pascale Casanova's *The World Republic of Letters* in the Post-Cold War Era', *English Academy Review* 25.1 (2008): 4–19.

Gilroy, Paul, *After Empire: Melancholia or Convivial Culture?*, New York: Routledge, 2006.

——, *Postcolonial Melancholia*, New York: Columbia University Press, 2004.

Goldberg, David T. (ed.), *Multiculturalism: A Critical Reader*, Oxford: Blackwell, 1994.

Gunew, Sneja, 'Subaltern Empathy: Beyond European Categories of Affect Theory', *Concentric: Literary and Cultural Studies* 35.1 (2009): 11–30.

Hage, Ghassan, *Against Paranoid Nationalism: Searching for Hope in a Shrinking Society*, Annandale, NSW: Pluto, 2003.

Hall, Stuart, 'Conclusion: The Multi-cultural Question', in Barnor Hesse (ed.), *Un/settled Multiculturalisms: Diasporas, Entanglements, Transruptions*, London: Zed, 2000, pp. 209–241.

Iyer, Pico, *The Global Soul: Jet Lag, Shopping Malls and the Search for Home*, New York: Vintage, 2000.

Kandiyoti, Deniz, 'Identity and Its Discontents: Women and the Nation', in Patrick Williams and Laura Chrisman (eds), *Colonial Discourse and Post-Colonial Theory: A Reader*, New York: Columbia University Press, 1994, pp. 376–391.

Kymlicka, William, *Multicultural Citizenship: A Liberal Theory of Minority Rights*, Oxford: Oxford University Press, 1995.

Lyotard, François, *Le Postmoderne éxpliqué aux enfants: Correspondance 1982–1985*, Paris: Galilée, 1986.

Mawani, Renisa. 'Indigeneity, Asian Migration, and (Post)colonial Time', 'Sustainable Asia', Workshops held in Vancouver, Wollongong, Singapore 2010–11, Unpublished paper.

Mishra, Vijay, *The Literature of the Indian Diaspora: Theorizing the Diasporic Imaginary*, London: Routledge, 2007.

——, *What was Multiculturalism?*, Melbourne: Melbourne University Press, 2012.

Modood, Tariq, *Multiculturalism*, Cambridge: Polity, 2007.

Modood, Tariq and Pnina Werbner (eds), *The Politics of Multiculturalism in the New Europe: Racism, Identity and Community*, London: Zed, 1997.

Nyers, Peter, 'Abject Cosmopolitanism: The Politics of Protection in the Anti-deportation Movement', *Third World Quarterly* 24.6 (2003): 1069–1093.

Oikin, Susan M., *Is Multiculturalism Bad for Women?*, Edited by J. Cohen, M. Howard and Martha Nussbaum, Princeton, NJ: Princeton University Press, 1999.

Ong, Aihwa, *Flexible Citizenship: The Cultural Logic of Transnationality*, Durham: Duke University Press, 1999.

Parekh, Bhikhu, *Rethinking Multiculturalism: Cultural Diversity and Political Theory*, 2nd edition, Houndsmill, UK: Palgrave Macmillan, 2006.

Phillips, Ann, *Multiculturalism without Culture*, Princeton, NJ: Princeton University Press, 2007.

Povinelli, Elizabeth A., *The Cunning of Recognition: Indigenous Alterities and the Making of Australian Multiculturalism*, Durham: Duke University Press, 2002.

Rashkin, Esther, *Family Secrets and the Psychoanalysis of Narrative*, Princeton, NJ: Princeton University Press, 1992.

Schoene, Berthold, *The Cosmopolitan Novel*, Edinburgh: Edinburgh University Press, 2009.

Scott, Joan W., *The Politics of the Veil*, Princeton, NJ: Princeton University Press, 2007.

Shohat, Ella (ed.), *Talking Visions: Multicultural Feminism in a Transcultural Age*, New York: New Museum of Contemporary Art, 1998.

Taylor, Charles, 'The Politics of Recognition', in Amy Gutman (ed.), *Multiculturalism: Examining the Politics of Recognition*, Princeton, NJ: Princeton University Press, 1994.

Vertovec, Steven and Susanne Wessendorf (eds), *The Multiculturalism Backlash: European Discourses, Policies and Practices*, London: Routledge, 2010.

Willett, Charles (ed.), *Theorizing Multiculturalism: A Guide to Current Debate*, Malden, MA: Blackwell, 1998.

Yuval-Davis, Nira, *Gender and Nation*, London: Sage, 1997.

2

Negotiating Differences

Cultural Spaces, Pluralism and Diversity

Jasbir Jain

The development agenda never works in a linear manner. There are always several intervening forces such as human material, political strategy, social and religious divisions and societal hierarchies which are not always gender based but are often entangled in race, culture and economic power. Can the balance be maintained by shifts in terminologies? I intend to focus on three main issues – the terms we use, that is the meaning and implication of words; cultural interaction, responses and conflicts and finally the contesting values that are reflected in gender and cultural interaction.

The concept of 'culture' is multilayered, complex and heavily loaded with inputs which stretch far and wide and include religion, rituals and relationships. Somewhere along the line there has been a shift from 'multiculturalism' to 'diversity' and 'plurality' and more recently to 'cultures of plurality'. All of us may not interpret these words in a similar manner. But one may well ask: why this shift in public and political discourse? Multiculturalism has had its own share of criticism from amongst the immigrant populations. Neil Bissoondath (1994) and Himani Bannerji (2000) are two critics who have questioned this concept on different grounds. While Bissoondath's concern was with the nature of belonging to the country of adoption, Bannerji critiqued it on the grounds of its racist bias. Do the new terms provide anything different and does meaning, implication and implementation shift with the shift in the terms used in popular discourse? Is the relationship to be limited to 'tolerance' or is it a matter of non-interference, a 'live and let live' policy, or of imposition and civilizing the 'other' or of grants and representation? Gayatri Spivak and Sneja Gunew (1993) in a dialogue, carried out sometime perhaps in the early nineties, debated the issues of 'authenticity', cultural franchise, and representation in the context of multiculturalism. Some of the issues they discussed were whether government policies were only half-hearted accommodative measures which mock the 'whole notion of equality' leaving the immigrants hanging between the dominant culture of the host country and the distanced home culture or were they sincere in their proposals. It was in this context that the question of authenticity becomes relevant. Similar arguments could be shifted to India where economic progress does not necessarily imply equality, bridge difference or indicate a harmonious cultural interaction. Separate but equal doesn't work, especially not during times of crisis, as the Kanishka tragedy and its subsequent history have proven. It is because of these divisions between the insider and the outsider, between the native and the non-native that the question is asked: who belongs where and how?

Returning to the Spivak-Gunew dialogue, which incidentally is about multiculturalism and not pluralism, one of the issues which crops up is of the separation between the public and the private spheres the traditional 'home and the world' division which directly affects gender, the institution of marriage, dating, sexuality and acceptance. Simon During (1993) in his introduction to the dialogue 'Questions of Multiculturalism', points out that questions of different histories are also relevant as is the realization that subjectivities of the others are 'constructed across many registers, which do not necessarily work in harmony' (193).

Cultures are constructed by languages, traditions, histories and religious, aesthetic and moral structures. It is just not possible to merge or submerge all or alter and reject all: how does then one confront the issue of cultural plurality? Is it side by side, or of sharing and understanding, or of give and take? The community ghettoization bring with them a semblance of colonialism. Gunew suggests constant political campaigning and a continued alertness to cultural politics while Spivak voices the fear which lies behind the equation of belonging to a different culture and being placed under suspicion as a native informant.

Clark Blaise and Bharati Mukherjee in their work *The Sorrow and the Terror* (1987) on the Kanishka air crash have researched this aspect in wrote and observed that a gap between the immigrants and others was visible and there was a need for a sense of national belonging, of being a nation. If only the Indians were concerned and herded together to mourn their dead, then in what way did they relate to Canada? These are also the issues which Uma Parameswaran takes up in several of her writings. In fact, one can see in her work, a constant transference and grafting of landscape and nature to Canada such as 'Ganga in the Assiniboine' and *Mangoes on a Maple Tree.* The immigrant asks for an acceptance and a reciprocal relationship. One of her plays 'Dear Deedi, My Sister' (1998) by juxtaposing the two languages in the very title is indicative of the division. It is a play about the alienation experienced by the new Canadians, either from others or from their own cultures and heritage. It is a beautiful play with several monologues placed in a sequence, with temple bells ringing in the background, and the speakers occupied in various activities. There is Sapna, the main voice, writing a letter home, nostalgically remembering the smells and sounds of home (63); and Mariella a young Nicaraguan woman indulges in similar memories while the Kenyan young woman Wamahu is conscious of her loneliness and alienation. Another Indian, Nayana, from Gujarat, shares her experiences of newness with a fellow Indian. Unused to the strange smells, she pretends not to notice the difference but she admits it is hard for her to speak English (66). Women have, over the years, migrated from their homelands for different purposes and at different ages. Aziza, from Pakistan is in these alien surroundings on account of her son. She is unused to the closed windows and the locked doors; she 'cannot breathe this stale air/with yesterday's cooking smell/going round and round'. She wants her son to open the windows. The play also has several male characters as well, of all ages: Choi Chan, a middle-aged man from Hong Kong who like Wamahu is lonely; Sekoni, a Nigerian who feels invisible and out of place and a young Phillippino boy called Ilago. He is the one puzzled by difference and longs to be like the whites. Fascinated by the consumer culture, he is obsessed by the dreams of being 'less brown' and wants a change of name, a move in the direction of being like them:

Ma, you think you could change my name
To Jim, or David, or something?
...
When the snow comes, Ma,
I'll get less brown, won't I?
It would be nice to be white

more like everyone else
you know? (65)

Does equality mean giving up the very essentials of one's existence? And is the choice only between erasure and alienation? Such cultural relationships form a complex pattern not only for the Asian and African immigrants but also for the First Nations and the neglected regions of the North, the Canadians who have been suppressed and pushed into reservations and no extent of alternative action (which is often a tokenism) can help heal these memories or erase those histories.

Wendy Lill's play *The Occupation of Heather Rose* (1986) explores this Indian past of the Canadian white. How does the dominant culture interact with the 'Other' and what kind of 'superiority' invests it? These are some of the questions she takes up through four interrelated strands: Indians, whites, the harsh conditions of the Canadian North and inherited prejudices. The Introduction to the play traces the origins of the play. In an interview with Judith Rudakoff, Wendy Lill refers to her experience as Canadian Mental Health Association consultant, when her job was to assess the workability of development projects and whether they should 'set up an operation there'. From the experience there she realized how, over and above the cultures, it is attitudes that are different (429). The whole scene is overcrowded with associations and the organizers are possessed by a self-image of importance. The play is also about a growing impatience with the racist, imperialist assumptions that underlie interference in others' cultures. Working with the assumptions of racial superiority, patronage and the attitude of condescension, it exposes the foregone failure primarily because of the air of superiority and the sense of having been placed in the situation of a giver; never friendship, never equality, and never reciprocal learning. Referring to one of the epigraphs, the Introduction points towards *The Heart of Darkness* as one of Lill's major intertextual supports (430). *The Occupation of Heather Rose* is a monologue, like the monologues of 'Dear Deedi', a strategy which rules out dialogues and even when they are there, they are part of a 'pretend' game with Heather enacting the dialogues with the other characters. Heather Rose lands up in the Indian Reservations with her head filled up with romantic notions of bringing about a remarkable change in the Indians' living conditions. She carries with her the white woman's burden to the Reservation which is otherwise visited by the authorities only for emergencies. The minority group of whites is isolated, medical supplies are in perpetual shortage, directions sent home for deliveries are mislaid, and the Indians are treated as objects on whom experiments can be carried out on them treating them as human guinea pigs. Heather thinks of herself as 'the Queen' when she looks upon the 'sea of brown faces'. When she takes charge of the nursing station, the task of settling down consists mainly of two: one of putting up her mother and grandmother's, the 'maternal guiding figures' pictures on the wall, the other of clearing up her predecessor's mixed legacy of diary entries and empty alcohol bottles. Everything is strange – names, habits, customs. But she is not at all curious to know instead she has already formed her opinion. She considers their names funny, names that hold laughter one bubble below the surface. She is well meaning and feels an 'overwhelming urge to hug each one of them. To engulf them, as if some of the good things may rub off them to me'. And vice versa (436). But this is a passing impulse. She feels she has learnt all that was to be learnt during the orientation week. Now all that is required is to find solutions for the problems; the side-effects of developmental schemes do not interest her. Her idea is to start 'an exercise club for women to improve their self image ... .' (436), to teach them about nutrition, to de-addict them of alcohol and drug habits. The play is punctuated by Heather's occasional writings on the blackboard, which may be taken as another character, a witness and a recorder both. Imagined conversations, remembered meetings are enacted in short bursts, mixing up friendship with drink, bootlegging and water purification schemes. It's like a see-saw or a spiralling door with no stability and no continuity and symbolically represents the white (wo)man's relationship with the Indians. They are different and hence all meetings points are uneven and transient. There is no love lost between Heather and the Indians. She recalls Lorraine's reference to them as 'broken' people, people she didn't like. They in their turn also look upon the whites as temporary visitors; and do not like them. Finally the enormity of her task and her own inadequacy for it strike her. What business did she have to find fault with them? 'Saying someone has a different culture is just a polite way of saying they're *weird.* Not special not privileged. Not exotic

Not mysterious at all. They're inferior. And therefore need to be helped translation. Altered' (439).

Besides the health services the other intervening agencies are the school and the church. The play is reminiscent of other similar explorations by missionaries/imperial agencies'. Caryl Phillips, the British author of Caribbean origin, in his novel *Crossing the Bar* (1994), also critiques the half-hearted efforts of the white man and the damage they do to human life. Heather is lonely and is on the look out for the absent lover but is constantly engaged in visiting people, peering into their homes, guiding them on food habits, duties she hates to perform and which are much against her own upbringing. Gradually she slides into a vulnerable position. She reacts negatively to their music and her outsider status pulls her down, fantasies fade and she begins to drink heavily. Nothing works. People should stay where they belong. Her own history and identity now matter more than ever to her. All is reduced to the need of surviving. No matter if it is in tears (446). The very word 'occupation' reveals the mentality behind the relationship. Such plays need to be read against a double perspective. If on one side is the discourse of development and of civilizing the savage, on the other is the history of the First Nations. Daniel N. Paul in his work *We Were Not the Savages* (2000) has traced the history of conflict, of treaties and legal measures which have been unfair and imperialistic. The interpretation of the term civilization has always been narrow and limited in its perspective.

Do climatic conditions create cultural differences and bring about inequality? Is it a politics of difference demanding eternal opposition? Brian Barry in *Multiculturalism and Equal Treatment* (2001) admits that it is confusing when terms like multiculturalism and pluralism are freely used to describe both a state of affairs and a political programme. Pluralism, Barry comments, has been used both as a descriptive and a prescriptive term. He reserves the term multiculturalism for the political programme of the 'politics of difference', and pluralism for a programme that aims to 'institutionalize cultural difference by segmenting society'. He further insists that this would be in line with a distinguished tradition of sociological analysis which recognizes that culturally differentiated sections will differ in their internal organization, and their system of belief and value (23). This kind of pluralism is bound to encroach upon even those areas where difference functions positively. By commending a separatists, segmental policy, the state is likely to adopt an authoritarian role dismissing such terms as 'neutral' or 'secular'; and instead of learning to live together or going across, intermarrying, adopting lifestyles and cultures which are inclusive, both exclusion and opposition will persist. State institutionalization of difference could become coercive. Barry points out that a policy of pluralization could be carried even further and made not merely facilitative but compulsory thus doing away with freedom and choice. But would it provide equality? A rather dismal situation, which may lead one to ask like the economist Amartya Sen, 'Equality of What?' On the other hand, Barry's purpose seems to be to draw attention to differences of dress like the Muslim hizaab, the Sikh turban and the different practices of worship – such as the time of saying the prayers for Muslims. Pluralist approach would protect privacy and religious rights but in such a form, it is also likely to promote conservatism and fundamentalism, damaging more than anything else to women and to all ideas of freedom, growth and education, taking cultures beyond a residential ghettoization to emotional and intellectual ones. It would most likely also lead to narrow loyalties. The question such an extreme view asks is: do cultures evolve? Can religions practices outgrow some inherited models? Or alternatively does it not imply a choice between freedom and equality? Can alternative structures live in harmony? And do cultures contribute to each other? These issues open up several areas of debate which have both ethical and artistic value. Cultures do grow and evolve, that's the only way they can avoid being fixed and static, moreover circumstantial shifts and economic conditions lead to change. In architecture one finds that churches, temples and gurudwaras very often do not adhere to the traditional architectural expectations. Alain Locke in his cultural philosophy expresses the idea that the artistic contribution of component cultures in a society needs to be recognized. Though his reference is to African Americans and their contribution to music, this view is applicable across aesthetic mediums and geographical spaces. This recognition achieves several things simultaneously – it lifts if from being confined to ethnic or propagandists value, provides a well-deserved place in national culture, is integrationist and bridges gaps and more than all else reduces cultural antagonisms thereby keeping fundamentalist ideologies at bay. In Indian tradition Sufi thought and music have played this role and in America the black presence, as Toni Morrison observed in *Playing in the Dark* (1993), has contributed to the shaping of white culture (6–7). Currently Dalit writing in India, in its evolving aesthetics has moved on to a cultural exchange and shared histories, even though narrated from oppositional locations. The very fact that both *Ramayana* and *Mahabharata* find parallels in early folk, Dalit and tribal narratives and mainstream art of the different religions, provides a classic example of cultural pluralism, which should not be one of segmenting it but of an identifying a shared ground, no matter how minimal. The Dalit narrative Kalyana Rao's *Antarani Vasantam* (2000), (translated into English as *Untouchable Spring*, 2009) presents an alternative version of the story of creation and takes up figures from the Hindu pantheon to create parallel structures such as the 'tandav naach', the dance of destruction, parallels to Arjun, Subhadra, Abhimanyu and other characters, and goes on to reflect biblical tales which the Dalits had absorbed through conversion. In themselves none of them is proof enough of cultural pluralism but when we frame them through experiential aesthetics, oral and folk performances, the contribution of this culture has to be acknowledged. And one of the reasons is the common origin of art forms, many of which acquired the garb of respectability much later when they were appropriated by the upper classes. Dalit autobiographies, however, work through exclusion and recount narratives of marginality, beginning from the school classroom to hiring a house or being hired for a job. They are trapped within caste boundaries and the taboos prescribed by elitist classes.

I intend to work with two texts to illustrate my point that cultures rub off on each other. The first of these is Uma Parameswaran's play *Rootless but Green are the Boulevard Trees* (1998), a story of two Indian families, and of two generations. The parents are immigrants and their children have adopted western dress, and are conscious of a gradual change in their value systems. The three-act play is about choices which include freedom, visibility, identity, moral values, and family ties. Areas of privacy and control are differently defined than if they would have been in India. Parents don't feel free to intervene in the lives of their children and advice is not offered unless asked for. In this mixed population of men and women there are two women who are called upon to decide. One is Jyoti, the Bhave daughter, who has been dating Andre and who has not responded to Sridhar's emotional interest in her and the other is her aunt Veejala, who is a successful scientist and wife of an equally successful husband, but no longer wants to be part of this rat race which is entangled in racist discrimination.

As the play progresses decisions and likely trends are reversed. Jyoti, through talking to her mother and aunt is exposed to other perspectives on love and happiness and rises above mere physical attraction. She tells Andre that she needs time to sort herself out. Veejala gives her another view of marriage where a relationship is for keeps. Her decision to go it alone is not influenced by another man, but by her own self. Jayant decides not to go on his adventure trip and commits himself to attend to his cousin's school going schedule. Time has come to accept that life is in the present, and that cultures give and take, time has come to chop the evergreen tree and bring it in. 'No one has roots anywhere because that's the way things are in 1979 AD' (127). Whereas the older generation feels 'different' as Sharad, the father, says, 'It upsets me profoundly to find myself in a crowd. All those alien faces staring at or through you. It makes me wonder. Makes me ask myself. What am I doing here? Who are these faceless people among whom my life is oozing away? Each so self contained, so complete, looking at me as though I shouldn't be there. It's a strange eerie feeling, all those discreetly questioning eyes that make me ask endless questions.' The immigrant feels an oddity, both unwanted and unaccepted, not belonging anywhere. But the second generation has moved away from the split dialogues of 'our people and native soil' and the experiences of being outsiders who sought protection in closed structures of the self (82), to professions such as 'this is our land and here we shall stay' (83), views that mean that cultural pluralism present in the outside world can step into individual lives as friendship and adjustment in the cultural value systems.

My final reference is to Nayantara Sahgal's *Lesser Breeds* (2003) which depicts a plural society woven into a web, with some hierarchies persisting and couple of stereotypes sneaking in, but for the rest, the mixing together represents both a period in history and an idealistic coming together of several parallel strands where the political and personal flow side by side. The very character of Nurullah is a vision of a plural society and an accident of history. *Lesser Breeds* begins in the thirties and takes us to the sixties and after – a narrative that encompasses several phases of the country's history. Born of a raped mother, Nurullah, a young teacher, takes up the tutorship of Bhai's young daughter Shan. Bhai, a Kashmiri, is constantly in and out of jail. His home is filled with people from different communities, cultures and races, the Framjees, mother and son, from Bombay, the Muslim Nawabs and their Begums, Joseph from the Christian workshop, the Tiwaris, Eknath and a host of others. Nurullah is commissioned to help Shan find alternative perspectives and learn to look at things differently, to counterbalance the one-sided school education. Nurullah's own love life travels from his early experiences with Mrs Rekha Tiwari to Leda Knox who lives in the US, is a multi-linguist and collects fairy tales – which is her way of knowing the world differently. Spread across war and romance, *Lesser Breeds* moves from imperialism to the new power struggles of the global world, where fairy tales have turned into bomb wars and oil wars. It is in this world that Shan, now minister of commerce has to stand for herself and for her country. The policy she proposes at the conference in New York is the Asia Doctrine, pro-third world and unacceptable to the west. The flight home never arrives. It ends in an air crash, a crash which also ended the dreams of a new world order, Shan's death is the death of an empowered woman, one empowered through a home background of a plural culture, education and travel which equips her with strength, boldness and clarity. Yet, she is frail against the onslaught of a political conspiracy. Shan's death in an age of power and violence holds a message for the feminist agenda, which has shifted ground in the last two decades, especially in strife-torn areas, from feminism to human rights. Asma Jahangir in Pakistan is involved in human rights, Mahasweta Devi does not identify herself as a feminist, but instead critiques the power structures from a humanist perspective. Irom Sharmila has been on fast since 2000 against the AFSPA (Armed Forces Special Protection Act, 1955) in the North East. And in Nagaland peace movements like 'mothers for peace' have been initiated by women. As mothers, not only is their need for peace more intense but they also possess the sensitivity and the position to spread the message of peace. The space of the kitchen rather than the political platform is being used for spreading this message which is important for the survival of all human values. Moving outside gender issues, feminists and women's activism has begun to address political issues frontally as initiators, negotiators and decision makers. Domestic violence is an offshoot of the internalization of aggressive masculinity as are fundamentalism and communalism. Anand Patwardhan's *Father, Son and Holy War* (1995), a documentary about the Babri Masjid, problematizes the self-image of each conflicting community as it is anchored in the idea of masculinity. Women are the worst affected by civil strife, communal riots and war. The scenario in Bangladesh, Sri Lanka and Pakistan is no better. The recent riots in London were race riots even if their basis was economic. Violence is often the natural fall out of difference in political identities and ideologies.

Urvashi Butalia (2001) has pointed out that despite women's initiatives in forming peace groups and working for conflict resolution, they are absent from formal negotiations. She cites the example of the Kashmir Committee led by Ram Jethmalani and the negotiations of the peace accord in Sri Lanka, where women were not represented. Feminist resistance has primarily been against discrimination and constrictive space perhaps, now the time has come for it to assert the right of women to an effective citizenship and nationhood, to a legitimate, independent adulthood and full participation in the making of a social environment, which is open and hospitable to diversity. Undeniably the role of the intellectual has changed both of the writer and the artist. But perhaps a similar change in political environments has not yet taken place. It is here that the hurdles lie. Will it happen or will it not? Histories of evolution and change do not necessarily progress in the same direction. There are lapses, reversals and resistance. Cultures of plurality grow only if they sift and absorb their histories and constantly weigh the internal with the outside world. Is it change of mind, of heart, experience or memory?

References

Bannerji, Himani, *The Dark Side of the Nation: Essays on Multiculturalism, Nationalism and Gender*, Toronto: Canadian Scholars' Press Inc., 2000.

Barry, Brian, *Culture and Equality: An Egalitarian Critique of Multiculturalism*, Cambridge: Polity Press, 2001, pp. 19–41.

Bissoondath, Neil, *Selling Illusions: The Cult of Multiculturalism in Canada*, Toronto: Penguin Books, 1994.

Blaise, Clark and Bharati Mukherjee, *The Sorrow and the Terror*, London: Penguin Books, 1987.

Butalia, Urvashi, 'NGO Interventions in Situations of Conflict', *Indian Journal of Gender Studies (Special Issue: Gender and Security: Perspectives from South Asia)* 11 (2001): 105–116.

During, Simon, Editor's Introduction to 'Questions of Multiculturalism', *The Cultural Studies Reader* (1993): 193.

Lill, Wendy, *The Occupation of Heather Rose: Modern Canadian Plays*, Vol. 1, Edited by Jerry Wasserman, Vancouver: Talon, 1986, pp. 433–446.

Lott, Tommy Lee, 'Nationalism and Pluralism in Alain Locke's Social Philosophy', in Lawrence Foster and Patricia Herzog (eds), *Defending Diversity: Contemporary Philosophical Perspectives on Pluralism and Multiculturalism*, Amherst: University of Massachusetts, 1994, pp. 103–120.

Morrison, Toni, *Playing in the Dark: Whiteness and the Literary Imagination* (1992), London: Picador, 1993.

Parameswaran, Uma, 'Dear Deedi, My Sister', in *Sons Must Die and Other Plays*, New Delhi: Prestige, 1998, pp. 63–73.

——, 'Rootless but Green are the Boulevard Trees', in *Sons Must Die and Other Plays*, New Delhi: Prestige, 1998, pp. 74–128.

Patwardhan, Anand, *Father, Son and Holy War*, Documentary, 1995.

Paul, Daniel N., *We Were Not the Savages*, Halifax: Fernwood Publishing, 2000.

Phillips, Caryl, *Crossing the Bar* (1993), London: Pan Macmillan, 1994.

Rao, G. Kalyana, *Antarani Vasantam* (2000), Translated into English from the original Telugu novel as *Untouchable Spring* by Alladi Uma and R. Sridhar, Hyderabad: Blackswan, 2009.

Sahgal, Nayantara, *Lesser Breeds*, New Delhi: HarperCollins, 2003.

Spivak, Gayatri and Sneja Gunew, 'Questions of Multiculturalism', in Simon During (ed.), *The Cultural Studies Reader*, London and New York: Routledge, 1993, pp. 194–202.

3

Shifting Paradigms of Alterity in the Indigenous Culture and Literature

Canadian, Indian and Australian Contexts

Chandra Mohan

The term 'Alterity' over the last couple of decades has acquired a special significance with regard to its use for the explication of the 'other'. Brian Treanor defines it in his book *Aspects of Alterity,* as 'that aspect of things, and others, that is (absolutely) unfamiliar, alien or obscure. Alterity refers to that to which we have no clear or direct access. Alterity itself cannot be spoken or heard or read. It is something that works and other human constructs cannot express.'[1]

It remains obvious that the 'other' in a colonial or postcolonial context invariably belongs to the people of colour, visible minorities, marginalized section of society such as aboriginal and tribal communities and thus develops a relationship between race, ethnicity and alterity. In the colonial context, it denotes the socio-cultural and economic gap between the oppressor and the oppressed (the 'other'). This has been a centuries old phenomenon. It is found everywhere in the world since the inception of the human existence in all the civilizations in one form or another.

The paper picks up the sensitive question of shifting paradigms of Alterity and examines it in the indigenous culture and literature of the First Nations, Indigene and tribal communities existing in Canada, India, Australia, and in the rest of the countries in the world. The term 'indigenous', for instance, is accepted and as employed by the International Labour Organization (ILO) and United Nations Educational Scientific and Cultural Organization (UNESCO), seeks to represent over a thousand different communities spread over all continents. G.N. Devy has aptly described them in the following words: 'Recognized as 'Aborigines' in Australia, as 'Maori' in New Zealand, as 'First Nations' in Canada, as 'Indigenous' in the United States, as 'Janajatis' in India, or as 'Tribes' in anthropology, as 'Notified Communities' in the administrative parlance of many countries, as 'Indigenous People' in the discourse of Human Rights, and as 'Advasis' in the terminology of Asian activists, these variously described communities are far too numerous and dispersed in geographical locations to admit of any single inclusive description. It would be simplistic to perceive them as divergent victim groups of any shared epochal phenomenon such as colonialism, imperialism, modernity or globalization.'[2] The paper thus engages an interesting exploration that seems to have taken place identically in three well articulated phases.

I

The First Phase: Political Representation

The question of political status examines the indigenous communities' direct confrontation with the advent of colonial power on their own land. It is an acknowledged fact that the colonizers who captured and controlled people in their respective colonies were invariably known as the cruel masters. The aboriginal communities became the most passive sufferers at their hand. They were treated in the crudest form of human behaviour. In the long drawn struggle, between the colonizer and the colonized, the oppressed 'other' was completely dispossessed of his or her self identity, the concerned communities' social and political representation on their own land.

I begin with the historic statement made by the leader of the Indigenous community during colonial period. The leader of the Metis people of North America, Louis Real, shortly before his execution on the charge of treason in 1885 by the then British Rules Government of Canada made a prediction. He said, 'My people will sleep for 100 years, and when they awake, it will be the artists who give them back their spirit.'[3] This statement acts as a double-edged weapon. On the one hand, it denotes the brutal act of the execution by the colonizers on the subjects of the Aboriginals upon whom they ruled illegally. On the other hand, it forecasts the futuristic onslaught of the 'other', i.e. the depressed class that later on attains the position of attacking the oppressor in their own land. No one but a great prophet could have imagined over 100 years ago what a terrible impact the artists and cultural heroes among the Metis, Inuit and First Nations would have in the late 20th century Canada.

It is depressing to see that during the colonial period, the Alterity presented the crude erosion of the identity and representation of the 'other' from the society. The English soldiers drove the First Nation communities in Canada and Aborigines in Australia from their native sovereign domain. To legalize the 'dispersion', the soldiers of the colonizers asked the oppressed people to bid, three times in the name of the Crown of England and give up their land. The concerned communities did not immediately surrender, they were fired by the colonizers instantly. Such a situation keeps the oppressed classes in a dilemma. They could not understand the English nor the English language, as a result, aboriginal people died in the 'catch 22' cross-fire. Thus in this way, 'these representative of the Crown are very quickly able to kill the rightful owners of the land and instead they claim to be the sole proprietor of their land. Ironically the oppressors call this process of usurping the poor persons land as their 'right' in a peculiar way of 'peaceful settlement'.'[4]

The poetic description of this ironical situation goes on like this:

I look at the open fields and see
The space where my people used to be
I see the scars of wounded ground
I cry as I hear the death call sound
of curfew mourning by.[5]

The Indigene were finally exiled in areas emphatically called the 'reserves', where they were kept under the barbaric control of police and camp commandment or under the less barbaric control of the missionaries. Apartheid laws were enacted and co-habited with the whites in loving relationship, were savagely punished, white house slavery and sexual abuse was considered more or less having civilizing effect .... 'In so doing, he lied away Aboriginal life, proprietary right and therefore right of Sovereign to our rightful land and gave every murderer, every rapist, every thief, every sadist, every racist an open pass to kill, torture, enslave and take at will everything that had been protested, nurtured, sanctified and kept spiritually intact from the Dreaming.'[6]

Such actual happenings of helplessness are described with satirical remarks in the following poem:

No one to Guide us:
Feeling down
depressed
wondering why
What is happening
in this society
Police bashings in Roebourne
John Pat dies
There is no Justice
Suicide in Broome
Another in Meeka
All young Aboriginals
Dying for what?
Feeling down
I don't understand
What is happening
Where are the spirits
Of our Ancestors?
Of our people?
To guide us.[7]

An illustration of the socio-cultural and literary text quoted here opens up the space between 'heterological' and 'thetic' moments of alterity.[8] Politics of representation come to the fore in the nexus between the Colonialism and Nativism. The colonizers were so clever that they did not leave a single chance to make use of the merits of the aboriginal literatures for their own benefits.

Each linguistic group in an indigenous community has its own particular set that accords with its own religious and philosophical beliefs which make this body of literature unique and culture specific. The history of the native Indian's officially acknowledged contributions goes back to the 18th century in Canadian Literature. It is interesting to know that as back as in 1745, Dr Samuel Johnson, the eminent English biographer, poet and critic published a 'Greenland Ode', an Eskimo-language poem with an English translation (quoted in Sherbo, 575). 'This ode celebrates the birthday of King Christian of Denmark, and was the first Inuit poem to be available to the English-speaking world. In the two and half century since this poem appeared, more and far better Inuit poetry has been published.' During the British rule in India the general approach of the administration, according to Sitakant Mahapatra, 'was of non-interference with the tribal world. This not only meant not interfering with their traditional life-styles, customs and manners but also a high degree of indifference towards the knowledge, and understanding of these system.'[9]

The massive literatures of the tribal societies are often embedded with a sense of pride with their own cultures. This is true of Indian and Canadian native writings. The themes of native identity and ethno-nationalism are of great potential, as they engage our attention in the literary narrative of the above communities. Their songs such as the festival songs, marriage songs, ever-returning cycle, rites of propitiation, invocation songs, playing with words, the riddles, etc. are the voices of the legendry ancestors sung through the voices of the children and grand children. The new voices echo meanings and bring meanings and bring fresh currents of human knowledge 'in the arid Western world'. One of the innumerable example of cultural self-assertion and native identity is made in 'Me' – a poem by an aboriginal shawna Lynn Danielle Panipekseesick, which goes as follows:

> You can judge me by the colour of my face
> You can judge me because I'm not one of your race
> You can strip me of my beliefs and my pride
> But there's a fire inside me that will never die.
>
> So, I'll tell you once again.
> I am damn proud to be an Indian.[10]

In a similar vein, a part of the Munda Song of the Santali tribe from Odisha, India, presents a concrete reality symbolized by the stones on the village street which are memorial to their ancestors:

> Dreaming of you in bed
> I woke and took to the road;
> Stumbling on the stone
> I remembered my caste, my gotra
> And stood transfixed.[11]

Sitakant Mahapatra very appropriately cites the powerful and inimitable sense of identity which is further reinforced by the remarks of the eminent British poet and critic David Holbrook: 'The songs and the illuminating comments on Oraon and Munda culture belong to a worldwide struggle among men to try to find a sense of their identity, not in mere 'nationalistic', terms but in terms of how, since they live in their symbolism, they can find particular meanings and forms of 'authenticity' in their own lives, in their own place and time'.

Theorizing resistance in terms of Alterity during colonialism generates several alternatives. The resisted (the other) gets interwoven in the texture of the discourse of resistance. The image of resistance reflects and in the psyche of the other gets embodied in language, culture and literature. The struggle of the 'other' against power of resistance becomes the struggle of memory against forgetting. The colonizing forces would like to 'other', i.e. the victim to forget the past, for it is a record of their acts of atrocities.[12]

As such, resistance manifests itself in three forms – its practice, its narration and theorization. It takes cognizance of the illegitimate oppression upon 'the other', as a result the exploitation of native resources lead to resistance against these practices. Resistance thus appears as a compulsive weapon against the tyrannical and colonial forces that exploit the 'other' for their ends.[13]

Such a theoretical position points out two perceptive points: First, an underpinning of this inversion of the 'other' at the hands of the oppressor is the recognition by the subaltern of his dominated position which obtains within the dominant discursive formation of political structure. The political atmosphere becomes so vicious that it does not allow 'the other' representing the aboriginal community to articulate himself as a subject of the colonial power. Secondly, within this hegemonic order the 'other' is constituted as an object of the knowledge of subjects. Speaking from the theoretical postulation the concept of marginality represented by the 'other' (aboriginal) under domination of the colonizers tantamount to destabilizing the institution practices. That started happening within the culture of Native Canadians and Australians. For example, it is visible in the books: *I am Woman* by Lee Maracle and *Slash* by Jeannette Armstrong, both written from within the political activity of their communities as the challenge dominant institutions and their representations of Native concerns, denoted here as the 'other'.

II
Minority Literature vs Mainstream Literature

The second phase points out the paradoxical and ironical situations emerging from the placement of minority literature against the mainstream. The 'other', here is given the status of literature of Lesser Diffusion as against the Mainstream Literature of a country. This is true of postcolonial and multicultural situations. The 'other' here becomes the marginalized object of multiracial and multicultural societies such as Canada, India and Australia.

There are quite a few noticeable fallacies that exist in this sphere. While the country (Canada) officially claims to be bilingualism as its pride achievements in the free and democratic society, at the same time, the original inhabitants of Canada, aboriginals, though regarded as 'First Nation' in Canada are counted in the category of ethnic communities. In this way, they remain 'Other' in Canadian society.

The second fallacy is seen in the usage of the mother-tongue by the indigenous communities denoted as the 'other' and set against the demands of the modernization, especially realizing the ambivalent nature of the situation arising from the need to express through mother tongue rather than through an acquired tongue, i.e. English. The research studies carried out in both cases reveal the fact which the native writers inevitably sense and realize from the outset that English is far from being the narrator's mother tongue or his language of first choice. For the native, wholeness is not available without largely surrendering claims of individuality in favour of claims of community living. That is why the role of language in most native texts always strives towards a condition of community. That itself contributes to the de-colonizing process. An idea of what kind of loss the colonizing process represents here is given to us by Rita Joe's poem 'I lost my talk':

> I lost my talk
> The talk you took away
> When I was a little girl
> At Shubenacadle school.
> You snatched it away
> I speak like you
> I think like you
> I create like you
> The scrambled ballad, about my word.[14]

Almost in an identical situation and in order to illustrate this view of the use of native with regard to the subject of the Dalit writings in India, the following poem by Arun Kamble, titled 'Which Language Should I Speak?' may be befittingly cited:

Chewing trotters in the badlands
My grand pa
The permanent resident of my body
The household of tradition heaped on his back hollers at
me,
'You whore-son, talk like we do.
Talk, I tell you.'
Picking through the Vedas
His top-knot well-oiled with ghee,
My Brahmin teacher tell me,
'You idiot, use the language correctly'
Now I ask you
Which language should I speak?[15]

These illustrations, as rightly pointed out, highlight the issue relating to the distance between the dialect of the natives spoken at home and the refined speech of the middle class which charts the social space and divides the marginalized forms of popular speech and imperatives of the authoritative centres of language. The point may be further explained in the light of Bakhtin's dialogical principle that the word as a sign is an index of the cultural and social conflict. This point further underlines the 'continuous flow of verbal interaction' as the fundamental reality of language.

Another fallacy that emerges in the treatment of the 'other' denoted by the aboriginal aptly posits the aboriginal writings both as a supplement to the master-narratives and also as a subversion of them. This process denotes a post-modern function in the sense that it questions the legitimized versions of these master-narratives, which involve the Canadian Literature canon, Western values, humanistic tradition, privileging of the 'I' position and aesthetic form, etc.

It is interesting to see that in the recent aboriginal writings, the writers attempt to deliberately undermine the master-narratives with a view to developing cultural specificity. This subversion operates ideologically and politically against white (non-native) hegemonic models. Thematically these writings deal with the vivid and authentic description of the native; sometimes they provide a mediation or critique of the appalling condition of the natives. Here, I would prefer to confine myself to examining some native texts and modes adopted by the Native Indians which have enabled them to 'write' themselves into existence.

III
Going Global: Marketing Multiculturalism

The third paradigm is of particular interest. It stems from the current concept of going global and marketing multiculturalism the world over. In the process of institutionalization of multiculturalism, the indigenous or aboriginal culture unfortunately become the 'other'. It assumes the shape of a political and commercial proposition. Here, politicians find their scope of action influenced by the decisions of multicultural organizations and business people must respond to the effects of global markets on local developments and plans.

This situation is entirely different from the previous two paradigms. Here, there is no confrontation with the colonizer or colonial power. Nor there is imposed any legal binding within the orbit of any Act passed by the democratic government by which the subsistence of the aboriginal communities are governed. In this paradigm, the governing forces come from the community itself. The money power and the greed for its possession blind the eyes of the chiefs of the aboriginal communities. It is seen in Canada, Australia, India, USA, or South Africa. Almost all these countries which have come under the impact of globalization and corporate sector are whose chief objective is to spread money culture. The operative part of the commercial deal takes place in the following way:

(a) In the name of globalization, the 'disneyfication' of indigenous cultures is happening. The global reproduction of indigenous culture, music and landscape is being sold by the chiefs of the aboriginal communities to the commercial partners from the culture industry who run commercial entertainment shows on American Television through the Aboriginal Art and Culture Centre, Alice Springs Australia.

(b) The chiefs of the Indigenous communities don't suffer from any guilt feelings by their act of 'othering' the 'self' (their own people). They openly enter into commercial contracts with the entertainment business companies to sell the indigenous products, cultures and precious literary narratives of oral traditions, with a selfish objective to gain commercial benefits and enter into money making enterprises under the ongoing impact of globalization. This phenomenon has been described as Casinonization of Native Culture. In some cases, the business deal gets the official stamp of the financial power of the political forces. This is an interesting but a crude example of 'othering' the 'self'.

In her analytical study of the scenario, Coomi Vevaina, quite aptly points out that the 'thingification' of the First Nations Peoples in Canada, particularly in the wake of globalization, is powerfully articulated by the Okanangan writer Jeannette Armstrong in her collage-like, political and lyrical novel *Whispering in Shadows*. In a poem in her diary, Penny, the protagonist of the novel, underlines the political undertones of this glitzy concept with:

Globalization
Something about breathing
In the dirty
buzz words
and missed manners
a global design
of conjure and conquer
situating the hilarity
as common text
a mastering and the master class.

...

the question of globe plotting
plotizing the globe
marking into plots
as in the house plots
as in evil plots
as in grave plots.[16]

People are conned into believing in the idea of 'free enterprise' or 'the American Dream' which promises that every individual can become rich. Such an action prevents them from realizing 'the fact that there is a rigid class system that keeps the rich powerful and the poor powerless'. The entire global system is set up with diabolical intelligence 'to suck everything from the powerless to serve the rich'. In fact, the system relies on 'the violence of poverty itself as way to insure commerce continues and expands ... . It makes work-depended have-nots out of the local people and cold murderers out of the have's. Corporate rights versus human rights'.[17]

All these illustrations enable us to think that the respect and honour for the 'other' and his culture becomes a source of entertainment for those who hold the reigns of political and economic power. Instead of honouring their local cultures, the oppressed 'other' is invited to adopt what is euphemistically called a 'global culture'. Regrettably, the chiefs of the tribal and indigenous or aboriginal communities are tempted by this witchcraft culture of globalization. Yet, at the same time, it is heartening to note that there are some sane and sagacious voices also heard who forbid the native community to relinquish its identity as a Native and embrace a vague global identity.

I would therefore like to make a point in the summing up statement that in the current scenario of globalization where the commercialization of ethnicity has crossed all limits of alterity, here the 'other' (mainly the chiefs of the aboriginal communities) should obstain from their act of othering the self (their own people) and not openly come out to commercialize culture, precious literary narratives of oral tradition with the special motive to gain commercial benefit and entering into making money through enterprises in connivance with the global corporate world.

Evidently, therefore the alterity is being experienced by the marginalized community as a curse from the forces who have ruled upon them since the inception of their existence in this world. Irrespective of the location of any region, country or environment, these communities have continuously faced this gift of the old and new colonizers and this process ironically continues to exist even in the 21st century.

Notes

1. Brian Treanor, *Aspects of Alterity: Levinas, Marcel and the Contemporary Debate*, New York: Fordham University Press, 2006, p. 196.
2. G.N. Devy, Geoffrey V. Davis and K.K. Chakravarty, *Indigeneity: Culture and Representation*, New Delhi: Orient Blackswan, 2009, p. xi.
3. Stephen Inglis, quoted from the *Indigenous Art and Economic Development in Canada and India*, a bulletin issued by the Centre for Canadian Studies, Dr Harisingh Gour University, Sagar (MP) at its international conference, held at Khajuraho on 25–28 September 2008.
4. Kevin Gilbert (ed.), *Inside Black Australia: An Anthology of Aboriginal Poetry*, Ringwood Victoria, Australia: Penguin Books, 1988, p. xxi.
5. Ibid.
6. Ibid.
7. Ibid.
8. Winfried Siemerling, *Discoveries of the Other: Alterity in the Work of Leonard Cohen, Hubert Aquin, Michael Ondaatje and Nicole Brossard*, Toronto: University of Toronto Press, 1994.

9. Sitakant Mahapatra, *The Endless Weave: Tribal Songs and Tales of Orissa*, New Delhi: Sahitya Akademi, 1991, p. 4.
10. Jeanne Perreault and Sylvia Vance (eds), *Writing the Circle: Native Women of Western Canada*, Edmonton: NeWest Press, 1990, p. 230.
11. Mahapatra, op. cit., p. 8.
12. Avadhesh K. Singh, *Discourse of Resistance in the Colonial Period*, New Delhi: Creative Books, 2005, p. 11.
13. Ibid., p. 12.
14. Daniel David Moses and Terry Glodie (eds), *An Anthology of Canadian Native Literature in English*, Toronto: Oxford University Press, 1992, p. 113.
15. Arun Kambli, 'Which Language Should I Speak?', in Arjun Dangle (ed.), *Poisoned Bread: Translations from Modern Marathi Dalit Literature*, Hyderabad: Orient Longman, 1992, p. 54.
16. Coomi S. Vevaina, 'Never Smile at a Crocodile: The Politics of Globalization in Jeannette Armstrong's Whispering in Shadows', in Hartmut Lutz and Coomi S. Vevaina (eds), *Connections: Non-Native Response to Native Canadian Literature*, Delhi: Prestige Books, p. 161.
17. Ibid., p. 162.

4

Culture, Diversity and Pluralism in India and Canada

A Public Policy Perspective

Sushma Yadav

During last few decades, cultural pluralism and the ways of tackling the plurality and diversity have become a site of intense academic debate and public concern in many societies, whether the presence of a diverse population in these societies is deeply rooted in history or linked to more recent migrations. The criticism comes both from the right, where many argue that it is insufficient to guarantee social cohesion and from the left, where it is often considered as a guide to mask social inequalities and struggles.[1] Many analysts, using data or frameworks from various disciplines, also denounce the essentialist position of countries on identity and ethnic relations and favour a more critical and dynamic analysis of these phenomena. At the policy level in India, the debate on affirmative action or reservation and protection of cultural and linguistic rights of minorities is getting intense as the consensual way of social engineering. Similarly, in Canada some multi-cultural programmes and initiatives implemented in the 1980s and 1990s are now considered inadequate, irrelevant or even counterproductive in dealing with issues linked to ethnicity, in institutional settings as much as in civil society:

> India and Canada share the diversity and plurality of culture. It is believed that India is racially, culturally, linguistically, ethnically and religiously the most diverse place on earth after Africa (which is a

whole continent, not a single country). The fact is that the culture of India has been shaped by its long history, unique geography and diverse demography. India's languages, religions, dance, music, architecture and customs differ from place to place within the country presenting a beautiful mosaic. The Indian social system is usually defined in terms of the social stratification and hierarchies, in which social classes are classified into thousands of endogamous hereditary groups, often termed as *jatis* or castes which also impact the gender diversity. However, the term multiculturalism is not much used in India. Within India, the terms diversity and pluralism are more commonly used.

Culture (Latin: *cultura,*), i.e. 'Cultivation' is a modern concept based on a term first used in classical antiquity by the Roman orator Cicero: '*cultura animi*' (cultivation of the soul), which re-appeared in modern Europe in the 17th century referring to the betterment or refinement of individuals, especially through education.[2] During the 18th and 19th century it came to refer more frequently to the common reference points of a whole set of people, and national aspirations or ideals. Some scientists used the term 'culture' to refer to a universal human capacity. In the 20th century, 'culture' emerged as a central concept in anthropology, encompassing the range of human phenomena that cannot be attributed merely to genetic inheritance.[3]

Culture has been broadly defined as an integrated system of learned behaviour patterns which are characteristic of the members of a society and which are not a result of biological inheritance. By doing so, distinctions are made between the physical artifacts created by a society, its so-called material culture, and everything else, the intangibles such as language, customs, etc. which remain the main referent of the term 'culture'.[4]

The concept of diversity encompasses acceptance and respect for differences. It means understanding that each individual is unique, and recognizing this uniqueness with our individual differences. These can be along the dimensions of race, ethnicity, gender, sexual orientation, socio-economic status, age, physical abilities, religious beliefs, political beliefs, or other ideologies. It is the exploration of these differences in a safe, positive, and nurturing environment for understanding each other and moving beyond simple tolerance to embracing and celebrating the rich dimensions of diversity contained within each individual. Lately, public discourse in Canada has used the term 'cultural diversity' to refer to the apparent growth of non-white population, other than the aboriginal people, in Canadian society. Underlying the popularity of the term 'diversity' is a rising public awareness towards differences of people. The sensitivity towards racial differences has partly to do with a widely held belief that immigration since the late 1960s has altered the cultural mix of Canadians, and that the increase in diversity has caused, among other things, tensions and adjustments in Canadian society.

Canada's demographic composition is ethnically heterogeneous, in the sense that its citizens have come from many countries of origin and cultural backgrounds. One customary way to depict cultural diversity in Canada is describe it in terms of the population size of those not belonging to the two charter groups. Indeed, this was the method adopted by the *Royal Commission on Bilingualism and Biculturalism* in the 1960s, which coined the term the 'Third Force' to refer to Canadians not of British and French origin (Canada, *Royal Commission on Bilingualism and Biculturalism*, 1965: 52). In its final report, the Royal Commission stressed that Canada was a mosaic, or a multicultural society, made up of three basic elements: the British, the French and other Canadians. While recognizing the charter status of the British and the French, the Royal Commission also acknowledged the contributions of other non-charter groups. Increased racial diversity in Canadian society in the 1980s had created a new demographic and political reality that demanded changes in the multiculturalism policy. Judging from the changes in the multiculturalism programme and the statements made by the Minister of State for Multiculturalism in the 1980s, it is clear that a greater emphasis was placed on the multiculturalism policy as a vehicle to promote more racial equality and racial harmony in Canadian society.[5]

It would be incorrect to assume that the demographic basis of racial diversity alone was sufficient to promote an emphasis of the multiculturalism policy towards greater social equality. It must be remembered that the federal government in the early 1980s was very much concerned with the patriation of the constitution from the United Kingdom, and in the process, was trying to seek an agreement from provinces and lobbying groups to enshrine a charter of rights and freedoms in the constitution.[6]

All of diversity, old and new, does not add up to pluralism. 'Pluralism' and 'diversity' are sometimes used as if they were synonyms, but diversity is just plurality, plain and simple – splendid, colourful, perhaps threatening. Pluralism is the engagement that creates a common society from all that plurality.

Pluralism is only one of the possible responses to this diversity. Some people may feel threatened by diversity, or even hostile to it. The pluralism that would engage people of different faiths and cultures in the creation of a common society is not a 'given', but an achievement.[7] Pluralism is not the sheer fact of plurality or diversity alone, but is active engagement with that diversity. One can be an observer of diversity. One can 'celebrate diversity', as the cliche goes. Or one can be critical of it or threatened by it. But real pluralism requires participation, engagement. Diversity can and often has meant isolation and the creation of virtual ghettoes of religion and sub-culture with little traffic between them.

Pluralism is more than the mere tolerance of differences; it requires some knowledge of our differences. There is no question that tolerance is important, but tolerance by itself may be a deceptive virtue. Sometimes an attitude of tolerance may stand in the way of engagement. Pluralism is also not simply relativism, but makes room for real and different religious commitments. Some people are wary of the language of pluralism, insisting that it effectively waters down one's own religious beliefs by acknowledging that others believe differently. Some mistakenly think that a pluralist perspective assumes that there is no real difference among various religious traditions and their values:

> India is believed to be the most culturally, linguistically and genetically diverse geographical entity and India's democratic republic is premised on a national belief in pluralism, not the standard nationalist invocation of a shared history, a single language and an assimilationist culture.[8] State boundaries in India are mostly drawn on linguistic lines. In addition India is the most religiously diverse country in the world, with significant Hindu (80.5%), Muslim (13.4%), Christian (2.3%), Sikh (1.9%), Buddhist (0.8%), Jain (0.4%) and Others (0.7%).[9]

> India is at the threshold of momentous changes in its society, polity and economy. Like most other colonial societies, India is facing a constant dilemma, i.e. how to come to terms with the paradoxical tendency to simultaneously emulate and reject the Western culture.[10] Since culture is one way in which a community distinguishes itself from other communities by constituting, regulating stabilizing and legitimizing its practices and institutions as specific as its identity, every community seeks to preserve and perpetuate its indigenous cultural identity.[11] Yet, this is also a fact that all communities and cultures keep changing continuously. The change occurs on the basis of the endeavor of each new generation to confront the previously unresolved issues and the new problems perceived by its members. Thus, over the centuries cultures in different societies

have changed gradually yet significantly. The pace is a bit faster in contemporary times because in this era of globalization, no society can evolve its culture in relative isolation or independent of others which was the pattern in earlier times. Colonialism and imperialism hastened this process and resulted in cultural encounters which produced simultaneous postures of submission and assertion, resistance and acceptance as in India.

The contemporary Indian cultural situation is an inevitable consequence of changes in the social structures, institutions and values which have damaged the indigenous cultural identity of Indian society and lead to a pan-Indian culture which would enable us to resolve all tensions and conflicts presently being faced by our society. The 'Indian identity is sought to be achieved despite the plurality of religious faiths, diversity of linguistic and ethnic groups, customs, rituals and food-habits. The official conception of this identity is usually articulated in terms of a professed recognition of diversity and pluralism, i.e. unity in diversity. However, we have not been able to evolve any workable comprehensive conceptual framework which could help in reconciling the diverse strands of the past and the conflicting demand of the present. Consequently, we continue to face the constant tension between the homogenizing Universalist tendency, superimposed by the ruling elite and the heterogeneous particularizing tendencies rooted in the patterns and strategies of mass mobilization adopted by the leadership during the struggle for Independence and later.

In such a scenario, the cultural fabric of our life is so perforated that our ruling elite and middle classes have neither been able to resist the charm and power of consumerist lifestyle of the West nor muster the capacity to assimilate and practice the norms which are pre-supposed by that lifestyle. It would be a wishful thinking that the process of decolonization or cultural reorientation and renaissance can be achieved in India merely by taking a collective decision not to get trapped or lured by the Western world-view and striving for re-establishment or revival of 'indigenous' belief systems and values as discovered or invented and projected by the Western scholarship. As long as recognition by the West to think, write and publish in the Western languages about issues and problems that are of contemporary interest in the West, to participate in their conferences and seminars, to get their grants and support is going to remain the criterion of success in the academic, cultural, social, political, and economic spheres, we cannot expect Indian mind to aspire for intellectual and cultural autonomy.

In contrast to India, a civilizational society, Canada is a settler society with immigrants constituting a key resource for its nation-building. While the 1988 Canadian Multicultural Act celebrates cultural diversity, the 1950 Constitution of India promises to create and sustain a multicultural India with unity and integrity of the nation intact. It is argued that the Constitutional stipulations have reduced – though not eliminated – cultural majoritarianism and assimilationist tendencies in Indian society.[12] While, Canada's model of Multiculturalism provides for integration of immigrants and refugees to participate in the public domain and extends equal citizenship rights to all,[13] the Indian constitution provides for equality and dignity while celebrating unity in diversity and is aiming at developing all through inclusive growth.

Yet, many common concerns with regard to unity, diversity, equity, access to political power and economic resources, minority and citizenship have been and are being raised in India and Canada. These states face greater challenges in the post-9/11 era with its clash of civilization ideology promoting cultural intolerance and ethnic tensions.[14] Although normative positions on the management of diversity may differ, the challenge and its emergence as a global phenomenon cannot be avoided or missed. Internal and international migrations are increasing all over the world under the combined effects of industrialization, globalization and resulting gross socio-economic inequalities. Moreover, competing paradigms to the recognition of pluralism, such as assimilation, segmentation or exclusion, have been largely delegitimized. In some instances they were clearly incompatible with our renewed human rights commitments and, in the other, they have failed to insure the very objectives – such as producing an integrated and united society – they were aiming at. So, to paraphrase a well-known dictum, 'multiculturalism may well be at the same time a bad option and the best among all other worst'.[15]

Against this general framework, one still needs to justify the relevance of examining the policy issues and problem areas linked to multiculturalism in two countries as different and as similar as Canada and India. The first one is a relatively recent settler society where immigration has been used consistently over almost two centuries in a conscious nation-building process. The other, a civilizational nation-state, where diversity is the product of layers and layers of processes largely historical that can be traced back as far as two millennium ago. The issue of difference in scale between the two cannot and should not be overlooked. Around or above 35 millions Canadians often consider that their country is rather complex to manage with 10 provinces and three territories, two official languages, some 600 recognized First Nations, more than 100 immigrant ethnic communities and, since 2007, a nation within a united Canada, Quebec. On the other hand, India, with its more than one billion and 300 million citizens, 29 states, seven Union Territories, 22 official languages with hundreds of spoken languages and thousands of dialects, more than 533 recognized scheduled tribes and five major religious minorities, wins the bid of complexity.[16] It is also worth remembering that because of unequal level of human and economic development, priorities regarding diversity may differ in each country.

Nevertheless, as will be seen in many scholarly contributions on the subject, Canada and India share a strong political commitment to pluralism, unity and equality as much as the numerous challenges in the management of diversity at the national, local, institutional and civil society levels. Although circumstances and thus possible solutions to problems are not the same, the issues currently debated in both societies are often framed rather similarly. Indeed, after more than 30 years of official multiculturalism policy in Canada and 60 years of evolution of the constitutional rights to various minorities and marginalized groups in India, many common questions are now being raised: Has the right balance between the unity and diversity equation been achieved or should more stress be put on shared citizenship and intercultural relations? Do concepts such as multiculturalism or the protection of minorities adequately address the needs of all sections of society? To what extent have various affirmative programmes targeting inequality been successful or have they just increased class differences within target groups and in the wider society? And how can we ensure that culturally sensitive practices be compatible with liberalism and human rights?

The fact is that multiculturalism was adopted as the official policy of the Canadian government during the premiership of Pierre Elliot Trudeau in the 1970s and 1980s. The Canadian government has often been described as encouraging multicultural ideology because of its public emphasis on the social importance of immigration. Multiculturalism is reflected in the law through the Canadian Multiculturalism Act and section 27 of the Canadian Charter of Rights and Freedoms.[17] However, the relationship between diversity and Canadian culture is also believed to be pervasive. In a number of ways, the evolution of Canadian culture has been away from a centred, unitary vision, and ethnic diversity has contributed in important ways to this centrifugal pattern. Canada is known as the nation of immigrants. In 2001, approximately 2,50,640 people immigrated to Canada. During the 1990s and 2000s, the largest component of Canada's immigrants came from Asia, including the Middle East, South Asia, South-East Asia and East Asia and the Canadian society is often depicted as being very progressive, diverse and multicultural.[18]

The broader context of such development is the worldwide existence of culturally plural societies, many of which are products of international phenomena such as colonization, slavery and refugee and immigration movements. Culturally plural societies are those in which a number of different cultural or ethnic groups reside together within a shared political and social framework.[19] Most, if not all, contemporary societies are now culturally plural; no society is made up of people having one culture, one language, and one identity. There was an assumption that such cultural diversity within societies will eventually disappear due to contact between cultures is a creative and reactive process, generating new customs and values, and stimulating resistance, rather than simply leading to cultural domination and homogenization.[20]

Simultaneously, it is believed that placing culture at the heart of development policy constitutes an essential investment in the world's future which may be a pre-condition to successful globalization processes.[21] It can become a means to achieve a more satisfactory human existence. As such, development is inseparable from culture. Strengthening the contribution of culture to sustainable development is a goal that was launched in connection with the World Decade for Cultural Development (1988–1998).[22] In this regard, the major challenge is to integrate the principles of cultural diversity and the values of cultural pluralism into all public policies, mechanisms and practices.

Historically, cultural pluralism has often been used in various political systems to accommodate linguistic, ethnic and religious diversity. First, there are systems which believe that political power and cultural autonomy can be given to at least larger concentrated minorities through federal (Canada, India), regional (Spain, Italy), or other forms of political autonomy. Studies have shown that when aspirations for cultural autonomy and calls for religious or linguistic rights go unanswered, threats of separatism begin to appear.[23] Within such settings, religious and linguistic rights guarantee and support the cultural identity of at least the largest minorities, and ensure the integrity of the state in which they live. Second, where political autonomy is neither feasible nor refused, political systems may still have in place certain religious or linguistic rights for specific minorities under the traditional majority/minority model of governance. Third, traditional immigration societies, such as the US, Australia, Canada and Brazil, often attempt to deal with the question of cultural freedom predominantly within the private sphere.[24] However, despite such attempts, tensions may arise, for example, between indigenous minorities and the majority population as well as between long-established immigrant communities and newcomers.

Further developments in internal and international migratory movements tend to challenge these settings in many ways and can lead to diverse permeable societies with new and ever changing arrangements with respect to cultural freedoms and rights. In an attempt to address different forms of oppression and exclusion, the term minority has been broadened and claimed by various groups.[25] The definition of minority itself is, in fact, historically contingent and has been frequently challenged.

It is well known that multiculturalism as a public policy approach for managing cultural diversity in a multiethnic society, officially stresses mutual respect and tolerance for cultural differences within a country's borders. As a policy, multiculturalism emphasizes the unique characteristics of different cultures. The word was first used in 1957 to describe Switzerland, but came into common currency in Canada in the late 1960s.[26] It quickly spread to other English-speaking countries.

Looked at broadly, the term is often used to describe societies (especially nations) which have many distinct cultural groups, usually as a result of immigration.[27] This can lead to anxiety about the stability of national identity, yet can also lead to cultural exchanges that benefit the cultural groups. Such exchanges range from major accomplishments in literature, art and philosophy to relatively token appreciation of variations in music, dress and new foods.[28] Multiculturalism became incorporated into official policies in several nations in the 1970s for reasons that varied from country to country.

In Canada, it was adopted in 1971 following the Royal Commission on Bilingualism and Biculturalism, a government body set up in response to the grievances of Canada's French-speaking minority (concentrated in the Province of Quebec).[29] The report of the Commission advocated that the Canadian government recognizes Canada as a bilingual and bicultural society and adopt policies to preserve this character. However, biculturalism was attacked from many directions. It was the same time which marked the emergence of the multicultural movement in Canada and Australia and then in the USA, UK, Germany and elsewhere. Since the multicultural movement sprang up unplanned in many different political contexts, attracted a diverse cluster of groups, and has so far failed to throw up a coherent philosophical statement of its central principles, it lacks a clear focus and identity.

In fact, the term multiculturalism generally refers to the acceptance of various cultural divisions for the sake of diversity that applies to the demographic make-up of a specific place, usually at the scale of an organization such as a school, business, neighbourhood, city or nation. Some countries have official, or *de jure* policies of multiculturalism aimed at recognizing and allowing members of distinct groups within that society to celebrate and maintain their different cultures or cultural identities as a way to promote social cohesion. In this context, multiculturalism advocates a society that extends equitable status to distinct ethnic and religious groups, with no identifiable ethnic, religious, and/or cultural community values around which to unite.[30]

From a multiculturalists perspective the good society cherishes the diversity of and encourages a creative dialogue between its different cultures and their moral visions. Such a society not only respects its members' rights to their culture and increases their range of choices but also cultivates their powers of self-criticism, self-determination, imagination, intellectual and moral sympathy, and contributes to their development and well-being.

In a multicultural society different communities have different needs, and some might be structurally disadvantaged or lack the skill and the confidence to participate in the mainstream society and avail of its opportunities. Both justice and the need to foster a common sense of belonging then require such measures as group-differentiated rights, culturally differentiated applications of laws and policies, state support for minority institutions, and a judicious programme of affirmative action.[31]

Although equal citizenship is essential to fostering a common sense of belonging, it is not enough. Citizenship is about status and rights; belonging is about acceptance, feeling welcome, a sense of identification. The two do not necessarily coincide. One might enjoy all the rights of citizenship but feel that one does not quite belong to the community and is a relative outsider, as do some groups of African-Americans in the United States, Afro-Caribbeans and Asians in Britain, Arabs in France and Israel, and Muslims and, for some time, Sikhs in India.

Multicultural societies in their current form are new to our age and throw up theoretical and political problems that have no parallel in history. The political theories, institutions, vocabulary, virtues and skill that we have developed in the course of consolidating and conducting the affairs of a culturally homogeneous state during the past three centuries are of limited help, and sometimes even a positive handicap, in dealing with multicultural societies. The latter need to find ways of reconciling the legitimate demands of unity and diversity, of achieving political unity without cultural uniformity, and cultivating among its citizens both a common sense of belonging and a willingness to respect and cherish deep cultural differences.

This is a formidable theoretical and political task and no multicultural society has so far succeeded in tackling it. The erstwhile Soviet Union and Yugoslavia perhaps lacked the requisite imagination and wisdom and so disintegrated. Even such affluent, stable and politically mature democracies as the USA and the UK and France have so far had only a limited success, and show signs of strong moral and emotional disorientation in the face of increasing minority demands for recognition and equality. Thanks to the wisdom of its founding fathers, and the judicious balance between unity and diversity embodied in the Indian Constitution, India has managed to persist for five decades as a territorially intact and moderately successful polity.

The political context in which the Constitution of India was drafted has however altered considerably. The Constitution presupposed a much higher rate of economic growth and a much greater degree of equitable distribution of resources among the diverse communities than has proved to be the case. It took full account of religious and a rather limited account of cultural diversity, but none of ethnic self assertion. Assuming, paradoxically, that India had minorities but not a majority, it sought to nurture the former's cultural self-expression but not the latter's and allowed the minorities to act as collective agents while ignoring the real and fraught possibility of the majority becoming integrated and acting as a collective subject.

It also assumed a culturally neutral and socially transcendental state, able to ensure political impartiality, and did not anticipate that a determined majority might culturally monopolise the state and use it to enforce its own vision of India. Now that these and other possibilities have materialized, we need to undertake a radical reconsideration of some of the constitutive principles of the Indian state, and find a historically more sensitive and realistic way of evolving political unity out of the newly emergent forms of diversity.[32]

From the 1970s to mid-1990s, there was a clear trend across Western democracies toward the increased recognition and accommodation of diversity through a range of multiculturalism policies (MCPs) and minority rights. These policies were endorsed both at the domestic level in some states and by international organizations, and involved a rejection of earlier ideas of unitary and homogeneous nationhood. Since the mid-1990s, however, we have seen a backlash and retreat from multiculturalism, and a reassertion of ideas of nation building, common values and identity, and unitary citizenship – even a call for the 'return of assimilation'.[33] This retreat is partly driven by fears among the majority group that the accommodation of diversity has 'gone too far' and is threatening their way of life. This fear often expresses itself in the rise of nativist and populist right-wing political movements, such as the Danish People's Party, defending old ideas of 'Denmark for the Danish'.[34]

But the retreat also reflects a belief among the centre-left that multiculturalism has failed to help the intended beneficiaries – namely, minorities themselves – because it has failed to address the underlying sources of their social, economic and political exclusion and may have unintentionally contributed to their social isolation. As a result, even the centre-left political movements that initially championed multiculturalism, such as the social democratic parties in Europe, have backed away from it and shifted to a discourse that emphasizes 'civic integration', 'social cohesion', 'common values', and 'shared citizenship'.[35]

The social-democratic discourse of civic integration differs from the radical-right discourse in emphasizing the need to develop a more inclusive national identity and to fight racism and discrimination, but it nonetheless distances itself from the rhetoric and policies of multiculturalism. The term *post-multiculturalism* has often been invoked to signal this new approach, which seeks to overcome the limits of a naïve or misguided multiculturalism while avoiding the oppressive reassertion of homogenizing nationalist ideologies.[36]

Important government multicultural policies can include: dual citizenship, government support for newspapers, television, and radio in minority languages, support for minority festivals, holidays, and celebrations, acceptance of traditional and religious dress in schools, the military, and society in general support for arts from cultures around the world and programmes to encourage minority representation in politics, education including the work force. While multiculturalist policies are sometimes seen as opposing cultural assimilation, the policies of countries such as Canada do support structural assimilation. Immigrant groups are encouraged to participate in the larger society, learn the majority languages, and enter the labour force.

In Canada, the most noted critics of multiculturalism are Kenneth McRoberts, Neil Bissoondath, Daniel Stoffman, and Reginald Bibby. As a young man, McRoberts worked for the Royal Commission on Bilingualism and Biculturalism and his career as a political scientist has roughly coincided with the policy of multiculturalism. While some argue that it was disastrous for Canadian nationalism, as it offended Quebeckers and their dualistic vision of Canada as a bilingual and bicultural society. He seems to represent the French Canadians, who thought that multiculturalism threatened to reduce them to just another ethnic group. Of all Canadian provinces, Quebec has been the least supportive of multiculturalism, due in part to a widespread view that multiculturalism was implemented at the federal level to dilute the 'two founding peoples' philosophy which had preceded it, thereby diminishing the place of the province's French majority within Canada, and due in part to Quebec's policy internally of welcoming people of all origins but insisting that they assimilate into Quebec's French-speaking society.

Recently, however, the more assimilationist aspects of this policy have been tempered with recognition that Quebec is a de facto pluralist society and understanding of pluralism as a feature of modern Quebec society or any other society that welcomes immigrants. The Quebec government has therefore adopted a form of multiculturalism termed an 'interculturalism policy'. This policy seeks to integrate immigrants into the mainstream French-speaking society of Quebec on the basis of French, the language of the majority, as the common public language of all Quebecers; all citizens are in this way held to be invited to participate in a common civic culture. Similarly, the Trinidad and Tobago born Bissoondath argues that official multiculturalism limits the freedom of minority members by confining them to cultural and geographic ghettos. He also argues that cultures are very complex and must be transmitted through close family and kin relations. To him, the government view of cultures as being about festivals and cuisine is a crude oversimplification that leads to easy stereotyping.

Daniel Stoffman's book *Who Gets In* also raises serious questions about the policy of Canadian multiculturalism. Stoffman points out that many cultural practices, such as allowing dog meat to be served in restaurants and street cockfighting, are simply incompatible with Canadian and western culture.[37] He also raises concern about the number of recent immigrants who are not being linguistically integrated into Canada, (i.e. not learning either English or French). He stresses that multiculturalism works better in theory than in practice.

Public Policy Approach in India and Canada

Public policy is the principled guide to action taken by the administrative executive branches of the state with regard to a class of issues in a manner consistent with law and institutional customs. In general, the foundation is the pertinent national and substantial constitutional law and implementing legislation such as the US Federal code. Further substrates include both judicial interpretations and regulations which are generally authorized by legislation. Other scholars define it as a system of 'courses of action, regulatory measures, laws, and funding priorities concerning a given topic promulgated by a governmental entity or its representatives'.[38] Public policy is commonly embodied 'in constitutions, legislative acts, and judicial decisions'.

Shaping public policy is a complex and multifaceted process that involves the interplay of numerous individuals and interest groups competing and collaborating to influence policymakers to act in a particular way. These individuals and groups use a variety of tactics and tools to advance their aims, including advocating their positions publicly, attempting to educate supporters and opponents, and mobilizing allies on a particular issue. Often, the need for public policy develops over time. Public Policy is often easier to make and implement when it affects smaller groups of people.[39]

In any policy area, be it national defence, health care or education public policy is the joint product of what might be termed domain-specific and environmental determinants. In the case of Indian affairs in the Canadian context, domain-specific determinants include such socio-demographic characteristics as high levels of Indian unemployment and poverty, low levels of formal education, chronic housing shortages, and high rates of infant mortality, along with growing demands for greater social, cultural and political autonomy. Environmental determinants refer to broader political constraints which are imposed upon any specific policy domain. In the case of Indian affairs in Canada, these would include a governmental commitment to liberalism and the protection of individual – as opposed to group – rights, fiscal constraints, public opinion, and competing demands from other policy domains, such as an interest in developing energy resources in areas where there are unsettled land claims.

In most cases groups have greater control over public policies that impact upon them when those policies are shaped by domain-specific determinants. Conversely, control is weakened to the extent that environmental determinants are dominant; the clientele of public policy are left exposed to environmental forces beyond their political capacity to control. It is believed that a decade of constitutional flux in Canada has strengthened the environmental determinants of public policy towards Indian affairs. As a consequence, while the search for a new constitution appeared at first to be an important opportunity for Indians, many believe that it has turned out to be a policy trap.

The constitutional debate in Canada brought a new set of environmental factors to bear upon Indian affairs which were largely beyond the control of Indian political organizations, and which threatened to constrain severely Indian policy options in the years ahead. Canadian public policy in the field of Indian affairs is concentrated within a single government (the Government of Canada) and a single piece of legislation (the Indian Act, last subjected to any comprehensive revision in 1951). While most federal departments have some programmes which are tailored for native peoples, Indian policy *per se* is primarily lodged in one department, the Department of Indian Affairs and Northern Development. The 1970s has witnessed intense and often productive interaction between the federal government and Indian organizations across a myriad of domain-specific concerns.

A critical study of the policy processes in both the countries illustrates the enormous importance of its review. It is believed that the policy-making is dominated by a strong leader, while local politicians are very important actors in policy implementation. Policy-making processes are shaped by concerns of regime legitimacy, and policy implementation is shaped by concerns with party building. Finally, it should be stressed that the process is not without contradictions. This is because on the one hand, the regime claims to keep politics away from policy implementation, while on the other; the whole process is fundamentally political. This leads, in any case, to three related contradictions.

First, the developmentalist discourse produces expectations. If it is true, as Harshe and Srinivas claim, that even when the schemes fail and are criticized, there is still 'the fact that the people are willing to debate the development agenda'.[40] The new discourse may also help in empowering people to stake their claims. Second is the contradiction between modern management and party building. The political regimes work on both – but at some point, of course, they are no longer compatible. But the contradictions are emerging already. Party building involves money and the diversion of funds. In many programmes, it seems this can be contained to an acceptable level: party workers and others take a share, but there is not too much protest against this practice. In the Food for Work programme in India, however, it has been brought out that the rent-seeking behaviour went out of hand.

Third is the contradiction between centralization and participation. Policy-making is centralized, but policy implementation is supposed to be participatory. People are supposed to become 'partners in development'. But partnership requires ownership, and this requires some kind of say in processes of agenda setting and local policy design. This is not happening. How these contradictions will develop over time is still to be awaited. There are openings for making the policy process more participatory and transparent and the government more responsive and accountable.

There is a political leadership that claims to be modern, performance-oriented, in favour of participation and committed to making a difference. But given the compulsions of the electoral system as well as the rent-seeking behaviour at all levels within the bureaucracy, there are obvious limits to the changes that can be achieved by actors from within the government itself. This means it now depends to a large extent on non-state actors and their capacity to make use of the openings and take the government to task. It is in this light that empirical studies of specific policy processes in the two countries are potentially useful and should be encouraged. They may show windows of opportunity for an engagement from outside with the policy process in the State which always remains desirable.

Notes

1. See Christopher Raj and Marie Mc Andrew (eds), *Multiculturalism Public Policy and Problem Areas in Canada and India*, New Delhi: Manak Publications Pvt. Ltd., 2009.
2. http://www.wikipedia.culture.in; http//en.wikipedia.org.
3. Ibid.
4. See for instance, Adamson Hoebel, *Anthropology of the Study of Man*, New York: McGraw-Hill, 1966, p. 492.
5. Angus Reid, *Multiculturalism and Canadians: Attitude Study 1991*, survey report, Ottawa: Minister of Supplies and Service, Canada 1991.
6. Y. Abu-Laban and D. Statisiulis, 'Ethnic Pluralism under Siege: Popular and Partisan Opposition to Multiculturalism', *Canadian Public Policy* 18.4 (1992): 365–386.
7. http://www.pluralism.org.pluralismessays, from diversity to pluralism, p. 2.
8. M.G. Smith, 'Social and Cultural Pluralism in the Caribbean', *Annals of the New York Academy of Sciences* 83 (January 1960): 761–791.
9. Census of India, 2011.

10. See Milton B. Singer, *When a Great Tradition Modernizes: An Anthropological Approach to Indian Civilization*, New York: Praeger, 1972 and Upendra Baxi and Bhikhu Parekh (eds), *Crisis and Change in Contemporary India*, New Delhi: Sage, 1995.
11. See T.G. Azarkanyan, 'Culture and Civilization', *Journal of World History of Culture* 3 (1961): 65–66.
12. Gurpreet Mahajan, *The Multicultural Path: Issue of Diversity and Discrimination in Democracy*, New Delhi: Sage, 2002, p. 14.
13. Howard Adams, *Alberta Culture and Multiculturalism*, Penticton, BC: Theyhes Publishers, p. 67, quoted in Richard J.F. Day, *Multiculturalism and History of Canadian Diversity*, Toronto: University of Toronto Press, 2000, pp. 12–14.
14. Raj and Andrew, op. cit., p. 2.
15. Himani Bannerji, *Essays on Multiculturalism, Nationalism and Gender*, New Delhi: Creative Publications, 1996.
16. Ibid., p. 10.
17. Adams, op. cit., p. 68.
18. Bhikhu Parekh, *Rethinking Multiculturalism*, New York: Palgrave, 2000, pp. 20–21.
19. Richard J.F. Day, *Multiculturalism and the History of Canadian Diversity*, Toronto: University of Toronto Press, 2000, p. 82.
20. J.W. Berry, 'Integration and Multiculturalism: Ways Towards Social Solidarity', Papers on Social Representations, in online journal, Vol. 20, 2011, page 2.2. Also see Berry, J.W., 'Globalisation and Acculturation', *International Journal of Intercultural Relations*, Vol. 32, 2008, pp. 328–336.
21. Raj and Andrew, op. cit., p. 47.
22. E. Kallen, *Ethnicity and Human Rights in Canada*, Toronto: Oxford University Press, 1995, p. 10.
23. Grant H. Cornwell and Eve Walsh Stoddard (eds), *Global Multiculturalism: Comparative Perspectives on Ethnicity, Race and Nation*, Lanham: Rowman and Littlefield Publishers Inc., 2001, p. 204.
24. Ibid.
25. Ibid., p. 205.
26. Multiculturalism, http://martinfrost.ws.multi_cultures.com.
27. Ibid.
28. Bannerji, op. cit., p. 19.
29. Ibid.
30. B. Berry, *Race Relations*, New York: Houghton Mifflin, 1951.
31. J.S. Furnivall, *Netherlands India*, Cambridge: Cambridge University Press, 1939.

32. W. Kornhauser, *The Politics of Mass Society*, London: Routledge and Kegan Paul, 1960.
33. M. Chand, 'Diasporas as Drivers of National Competitiveness in Emerging Economies', in T.M. Devinney, T. Pedersen and L. Tihanyi (eds), *Advances in International Management: The Past, Present and Future of International Business and Management*, Vol. 23, New York: Emerald, 2010, pp. 583–602.
34. For an overview of the attitudes of European social democratic parties to these issues, see René Cuperus, Karl Duffek and Johannes Kandel (eds), *The Challenge of Diversity: European Social Democracy Facing Migration, Integration and Multiculturalism*, Innsbruck: Studien Verlag, 2003.
35. R. Rangaswamy, 'Immigrant and Refugee Cultures around the World', in M. Ember, C. Ember and I. Skoggard (eds), *Encyclopedia of Diasporas*, New York: Springer, 2005.
36. For references to 'post-multiculturalism' by progressive intellectuals, who distinguish it from the radical right's 'anti-multiculturalism', see, regarding the United Kingdom, Yasmin Alibhai-Brown, *After Multiculturalism*, London: Foreign Policy Centre, 2000 and 'Beyond Multiculturalism', *Canadian Diversity/Diversité Canadienne* 3.2 (2004): 51–54; regarding Australia, James Jupp, *From White Australia to Woomera: The Story of Australian Immigration*, 2nd edition, Cambridge: Cambridge University Press, 2007; and regarding the United States, Desmond King, *The Liberty of Strangers: Making the American Nation*, Oxford: Oxford University Press, 2004 and David A. Hollinger, *Post-ethnic America: Beyond Multiculturalism*, revised edition, New York: Basic Books, 2006.
37. See, Daniel Stoffman, *Who Gets In: What's Wrong with Canada's Immigration Programme and How to Fix It*, Macfarlane, Walter & Ross, Toronto, Canada, 2002.
38. Dean Kilpatrick, 'Definitions of Public Policy and Law', https://mainweb-v.musc.edu/vawprevention/policy/definitions.html.
39. David B. Audretsch, Isabel Grilo and A. Roy Thurik, 'Explaining Entrepreneurship and the Role of Policy: A Framework', in David Audretsch, Isabel Grilo and A. Roy Thrik (eds), *Handbook of Research on Entrepreneurship Policy*, UK: Edward Elgar Publishing, 2007.
40. R. Harshe and C. Srinivas, 'Andhra Pradesh: Dilemmas of Development', *Economic and Political Weekly*, Vol. 35, No. 23, 2008, pp. 1886–9. Also see Jos Mooij, 'Smart Governance? Politics in the Policy Process in Andhra Pradesh, India' Working Paper 228, October 2003, Overseas Development Institute, London.

5

Gender, History and Historiography in India and Canada

Some Reflections

Amrit Kaur Basra

It can be observed that the knowledge, power and resources of dominant groups, everywhere have shaped and determined the process of history writing. It was evident both in case of India and Canada. In the context of colonial India, beginning was made by the colonial rulers and when by 1960s, with the opening of the National Archives to the researchers, pace of historical research was quickened, then 'recorded narrations' only brought out the vision and role of those who in many ways were responsible for constructing it. For a long time, historical perspectives remained elite in nature. Gradually change emerged as researchers came to use 'new sources' and analytical tools. The break through in hitherto 'male perspectives' on Indian history came in 1980s, with the emergence of feminist writings. These writings backed by extensive researches questioned the existing knowledge, exposed its male centric narrations and showed the role of women in the ongoing historical processes.

Identical trends can be seen in the case of Canadian history, encompassing period between pre-contact days to 1970s. The emergent themes in Canadian history, initially focused more on political strands and role of men but gradually feminist historians provided reinterpretation of produced historical narration by focusing on gender.

The present paper makes an attempt to study some themes that have emerged in the historiography of both countries. For this purpose the paper is divided into four segments. The first two segments provide an overview of historiographical strands connected with the history of Canada and India. After situating feminist writings within above mentioned narration, the remaining two strands highlight the role of feminist researchers in modifying and alternating pre-existing conclusions. The paper on the basis of above narrations shows that by focusing on gender perspective, not only the role of women as the 'makers of history' can be shown but at the level of research, new sources and analytical frameworks can be provided.

I
From Colonial Construct to Subaltern Studies in India

The establishment of British Colonial rule in India with the battle of Plassey in 1757 was followed by introduction of administrative, legal and political changes. While the rulers denied any sense of history to Indians, they themselves began the process of writing it. The establishment of Asiatic Society of Bengal in 1784 marked that process. The colonial ideologies of orientalism, occidentalism, liberalism, utilitarianism, and evangelicalism went on to maintain that Indian society was degenerate. It were the British whom divine providence had sent to India to introduce reform and civilize Indians. James Mill in his writings divided Indian history into Ancient, Medieval and Modern period. He equated Ancient with the rule of Hindus and Medieval with that of Muslims. He identified British with the Modern (Metcalf, 1996).

These imperialist assumptions were challenged and rejected by Indians. However, at both levels, historical facts were not analysed. The professional basis of history writing became discernible, when, with the opening of the National Archive of India in 1960s, researchers got an access to colonial records. Initially, the focus remained on political and economic histories. The Imperialist writings found expression in Cambridge and New Cambridge histories. In these writings as represented by historians like Anil Seal, C.A Bayly and Judith Brown, nationalist consciousness was denied to Indians and even the role of Mahatma Gandhi in leading mass nationalism leading to freedom of India was trivialized (Sarkar, 1983).

Over the period of time, focus shifted to regional studies. Extensive writings emerged on themes like the uprising of 1857. There remained little focus on social history and various social groups.

It was in 1983 that Ranajit Guha published *Elementary Aspects of Peasant Insurgency in Colonial India*. It marked the beginning of Subaltern Studies. Based on the retrieval of voices of peasants and tribal from 'colonial discourses'; Ranajit Guha outlined dominant features of peasant insurgency. Based on the Gramsci's notion of hegemony, he showed that Subalterns were not as much conscious of their own subjectivity as they were about the power and position of dominant groups. For him, insurgents possessed negative consciousness (Guha, 1983: 1–17). His views on negation were critiqued by many historians and neglect of women and lower caste groups was also pointed out. However, the advent of Subaltern Studies marked a distinct change at the level of textual analysis. Presently, there is focus on varied social groups.

One of the major themes in Indian historiography is connected with socio-religious reform movement. The concept of Bengal Renaissance about which more details will be provided in the next segment has also engaged the attention of historians.

The issue of communalism, its genesis and partition of India has also engaged the attention of historians (Pandey, 1990).

In this way, historiographical trends on Indian history have moved away from political to social history, from leaders to masses. The initial focus on broad processes has given way to local histories. In the process, different kinds of sources have been used.

At the level of gender studies, distinct changes were seen in 1980s.

II
From Native Indians to Immigrants

When Jacques Cartier came to Lawrence Valley in 1534, the land was inhibited by various indigenous groups. His explorations paved the way for the establishment of 'New France'. The British merchants, explorers and missionaries were also active in the eastern parts of Canada and the treaty of Paris signed in 1763 marked the end of French colonial rule and the beginning of British supremacy in Canada. Alongside, there also began a process that led to codification of information about the country by the settlers. The basis of history writing can be traced to several such writings. It was shaped by the ongoing historical changes leading to emergence of Canada as a nation.

By late 19th century, the basis of professional history writing was laid. It was in 1897 that the first volume of the Annual Review of

Historical Publications on Canada was published. Professor George M. Wrong, head of the department of history in the University of Toronto from 1894 to 1927 was responsible for its publication. The publication and growing interest in history was the product of national consciousness. The tradition of historical enquiry has been carried forward by Canadian Historical Review (Wrong, 1936: 1–8).

Presently several dominant themes can be identified in Canadian historiography. Initially, the focus was on the British and the French who were seen as the 'Founding Fathers' (Berger, 1987). The role of historical geography and economic resources was also highlighted and these two themes still engage the attention of historians (Krueger, 1982: 11–78). The issues of the 'French Survival, the domination of Ontario and the subordination of West' have shaped several historical works (Morton, 1967: 44–49).

The role of leaders in shaping the politic of Canada has been explored in several biographies. The role of John Macdonald in strengthening Canada during the Confederation has been stressed by historians like Creighton. He has been seen as the maker of modern Canada (Creighton, 1967: 50–62). Within regional studies, role of local leadership and political parties has also been explored (Schultz, 1967: 1–27).

Initially, the writings on indigenous people negated their role in shaping the history of Canada but gradually focus shifted on them. It was evident in 1980s. Several studies focused on their exploitation during the 'period of contact'. Bruce trigger, on the basis of documented records and oral testimonies mapped the history of Hurons (Basra, 2002: 142). He showed that the foothold gained by the French in the Lawrence Valley was made possible by the Native Indians. They established trading and social relations with them but remained unaware about their imperialist objectives (Trigger, 1985).

The focus on social history and various ethnic groups can be seen in several works. In his celebrated work, John Potter identified Canadian society as hierarchal. His focus remained on elite social groups (Potter, 1965).

The writings on South Asians also show several trends. The celebrated work of Hugh Johnston on Komagata Maru has focused on political strands connected with policies of Canada and Britain toward Indians. He has shown, how immigration laws of Canada were contested by passengers on board and latter were helped by local (Johnston, 1979).

The experiential aspects of South Asians have also been mapped. Sadhu Singh Dhami in his autobiography has reflected on his relationship with motherland, that he left behind and Canada (Dhami, 1997).

On the whole, history writings in Canada have progressed over the period of time in mapping past and present. However, it also remains a fact that historian's' craft focused only on males perspective. It is only with the emergence of women's writings connected with women's movement in Canada, that a new perspective emerged. The role of women in shaping Canadian history came to the forefront.

III
Women in Indian History

An overview on Indian historiographical trends shows that initially women were used as a reference point in many works. The male perspective remained dominant. The voices of women can be seen from available records dating back to early history on India but analysis of texts remained at the level of males. The women were treated as objects and not subjects. There was no attempt to write history from their perspective. Yet there did occur many changes that brought women into public spaces and into the realm of history.

During colonial period, it was the social religious reform movement that brought focus on women. Latter also added to the processes of changes. Indian women obtained education and participated in the national movement. The emergence of 'social feminism' gave way to political feminism (Forbes, 1996). It also marked the beginning of women's movement in India. In the post independent India, the process continued. There was realization that women have been left behind as they were denied their share in ongoing progress of India (Kumar, 1993).

The need to focus on women's studies entered academic institutions in 1980s. It was in 1974 that the first research unit on women's studies was set up in S.N.D.T University, Bombay. It became a centre in 1985. It brought together social scientists who on the basis of their researchers showed the presence and role of women in historical processes over the period of time. It led to the emergence of women studies as a distinct discipline (Majumdar, 1986: 23–33).

The use of Gender as a tool of analysis has resulted in modification and changes in the very mode of history writings. The historiographical traditions, which hitherto were accepted, have been challenged.

The role of patriarchy in subordinating women through social structures and socio-religious norms has been explored in several canonical texts. These texts have shown that how women within familial domains were located and were assigned duties as daughters, wives and mother. Uma Chakravarti has talked about brahmanical patriarchy. She has brought out the role of women in negotiating with patriarchal traditions (Chakravarti, 2006).

It has been underlined that women were not mere subject but they were also objects. Texts like Mahabharat have been studied to highlight experiential aspects of women (Shah, 1995: 13–28). J.S. Grewal's analysis of AdiGranth has thrown light on position of Sikh women (Grewal, 2011: 133–162).

Women's question emerged in the 19th century. It revolved around the issues relating to practice of Sati, imparting of education to women and plight of women. Initial writings and researches focused only on male reformers and their visions having bearing on women. Latter were located within domestic spaces whose status could be improved only by them. Their voices were not the focal point of analysis. It were feminist researchers that came to challenge it and provided new perspectives.

For instance, writings on social religious reform movements in 19th century India have revolved around the theme of 'Bengal renaissance'. The contestation between oriental and occidental intellectual ideas has been explored. Raja Ram Mohan Roy, in particular has been seen as the 'Father of Modern India'. His role in the enactment of law banning sati in 1829 has been applauded (Joshi, 1975: 13–15). There has been an overwhelming emphasis on intellectual ideas of Raja Ram Mohan Roy (Ray, 2000).

There have been critiques of modernity and dichotomy between colonial modernity and Indian traditions has been questioned. It has been shown, how in the historical context of 19th century India, there were multiple responses. The imposition of colonial ideology in forms of administrative, legal, political, and cultural changes on subject population was also contested. In fact, at one level, both colonial rulers and Indian reformers carried identical patriarchal notions (Sangari, 1999: XXIV–XXIX).

It was more than evident in the debate that surrounded the issue of Sati in 1820s in India.

Lata Mani in her brilliant analysis has shown that discourse on 'Sati' as it emerged in form of debate did not mark a sharp break between Anglicists and Orientalists. In fact importance was given to brahmanical texts and the issue of banning Sati was discussed in context of existing orientalist knowledge. In the process women only became a site for discussion. The Indian society was essentially discussed by men (Mani, 2007: 53–79).

There have been several works that have looked at the status of women within households and have focused on their consciousness.

The institution of marriage has been a focal point of analysis. The status of women as married wives and mothers and their plight as widows has engaged feminist scholarship. There is extensive use of works produced by women reformers in form of texts. The experiential aspects as evident in autobiographies have also been explored.

Some illustrations can be discussed. Periyar E.V. Ramasamy, reformer from South India held strong views on the institution of marriage. According to him:

In the matter of marriage between man and woman, that is, in life as husband and wife, it can be said that in no other country such atrocities are committed, as in our own. If it is to be expressed in short, the philosophy of marriage here, is nothing but that which leads to the enslavement of women by men (Ramasamy, 2009: 21).

Rashsundari Debi in her autobiography *Amar Jiban* recounted her life as a married woman in Bengali household. Married to a rich landlord, she spent her time in domestic chores. Her life changed, when she became a widow. Her only vocation, then was to spend time in doing religious rituals (Sarkar, 2001: 130–141).

One of the pioneer woman reformers in Western India was Pandita Ramabai. She wrote *The High Caste Hindu Woman* in 1888. Based on her own experience, she located the life journey of Hindu woman from childhood to widowhood in religion and social customs of the Hindu nation. Drawing attention towards the deprivations suffered by woman within domestic spheres, she warned that if former were suffering, then it was bound to affect men also. She strongly advocated self-reliance, education of Hindu women in order to improve their condition. For this purpose, she stressed the need to have women teachers (Ramabai, 1888: 55).

She encountered numerous difficulties in her own life. She was extolled for her knowledge of Sanskrit literature and religious texts but when she married a low caste man, she was shunned by male reformers. Worse followed, when she became a widow and also accepted Christianity. She remained firm in her decision to help other widows and founded Sewa Sadan. Uma Chakravarti in mapping her life has clearly shown, how brahmanical norms shaped by caste and religion affected her life. Pandita Ramabai not only spoke against them but also charted her own path (Chakravarti, 2007).

Parvati Athavale, widowed sister of Anandibai Karve wrote in her autobiography *My Story: The Autobiography of a Hindu Widow*:

> Among the many difficulties experienced by widows, one of the greatest is that of the rites that compel them to the renunciation of all worldly things. As I was subjected to those rites, I had a personal experience of them. And I have had to make journeys from place to place as one who had been subjected to those rites, with my shaven head and widow's garbs (Athavale, 1928: 159).

The focus on above mentioned researches clearly shows that while male reformers had their own agenda in addressing women's question, women wanted changes on the basis of their experiences. They wanted equity and freedom in leading their daily lives. Sushila Devi in her essay that was published by the civil and military Gazette in 1907 advocated education for widows (Devi, 1907: 105).

The relationship between religion and gender occupied the attention of reformers of Arya Samaj and its followers. One of its main paper 'Panchal Pandita' dedicated to the issues of women's education and plight of widows published numerous articles on the subject. Many of them were written by women themselves. The value of education was upheld and it was argued that women who had not received education had virtually done nothing in their lives. Women were urged to lead their lives in accordance with religious norms. It was argued that educated women were bound to get more respect from their husbands as they could look after finances of their households (Pandita, 1900: 3–6). In this way, discourse on domesticity was strengthened and endorsed by women.

The value of education for women was underlined. It was noted that widows who had obtained education and had dedicated their lives to serve others and to follow religion were praise worthy (Pandita, 1901: 1–2).

The feminist scholarship has also marked its presence in studying partition of India. For a long time, scholars focused on structure and inbuilt politics of communalism, resulting in partition of India. It were women's writings that used written records and orality to point out the experience of women who were raped and kidnapped. While both the nations fought over the issue of kidnapped women and tried to recover them as part of nation's identity, it was feminist scholarship that showed that partition was inscribed on the bodies and souls of women. Leaders like Mridula Sarabhai who disregarded political directives, did her best to recover kidnapped women (Basu, 1996: 122–144), it were latter whose silence spoke about their trauma. The impact of violence on the lives of women who experienced partition and thereafter tried to relive their lives, have been brought out in the scholarly works of Urvashi Butalia, Kamla Bhasin, Menon, and others. While in her work, by focusing on family narration, Urvashi Butalia highlights the memory of partition, Ritu Menon and Kamla Bhasin have brought the issue of gender and nation. The experiences of women who fell victim to violence during partition of India has been focus point of analysis to underline that while men remained caught with political narrations leading to independence of India, women recounted those days at the level of 'self' and their surroundings. Above all, both works focused on value of memory in recovering silenced voices of Indian women (Butalia, 1998; Menon and Bhasin, 1998).

The use of memory through orality as an analytical tool for writing women's histories has been a hallmark of such works. The focus on violence also shows that how in day-to-day life also women are impacted by it. Communal riots and domestic violence are major hindrances and deny human and civic rights to woman. While recording voices of Sikh women, victims of anti-Sikh riots of 1984 in Delhi, Uma Chakravarti and Nandita Haksar found that many recounted trauma of partition riots (Chakravarti and Haksar, 1987: 18–21).

Prem Choudhary in her many scholarly works has studied the position of women in Haryana. During colonial times, many widows were denied right to inherit property both by the community and state in the name of upholding tradition (Choudhary, 1994). In present day Haryana, Khap Panchayats threaten the lives of young couples who have married as per their own choices. The relationship between women and state, between caste groups and law enforcing agencies has been analysed (Choudhary, 2007).

The relationship between caste, class, religion at the level of gender has been a subject of feminist scholarship. The aim is to understand inbuilt processes that deny social and economic equity to women in Indian society. The denial of resources to women, even when they generate it, is a major impediment in the progress of Indian women (Agarwal, 1994: 1–4).

The focus on history in bringing out women's perspective is a part of women's movement. The feminist scholarship has not only shifted focus on the role of women in shaping historical processes but it has also shown that presence of women was evident in both domestic and public spheres (Ramaswamy, reprint, 2013: 199–217).

The methodological frameworks within the discipline of history use interdisciplinary approaches in highlighting experiences of women (Roy, 1993: 68). Chandra Talpade Mohanty has talked about 'Feminism without borders', which is not 'borderless feminism'. It recognizes differences located in specific spaces but 'envision change and social justice' (Mohanty, reprint, 2006: 2)

IV
Feminist Historical Writings in Canada

The role of gender perspectives in Canadian history writings can be traced in the growing consciousness of Canadian women that found expression in organized women's movement. Initially, the lead was taken up by Anglo-phone women and distinct phases of Anglo-phone and Franco-phone women's movement could be seen. However, the second phase of feminist movement in 1960s saw coming together of leaders. There was demand for equal rights for women in public spaces. The issues like education, health, wages came to dominate organizations working for women. Feminism emerged both as an ideology and a movement (Burt, et al., 1991).

The feminist writings, while highlighting the role of women across time and space in Canada, also demanded justice and equity for women. In this way, rightful place of women both in domestic and public was sought. The varied experiences of women also brought out themes of 'womenhood'. In this regard, mention can be made of the book *Rethinking Canada: The Promise of Women's History*, edited by Veronica Strong Boag et al. The book is a compilation of various articles mapping plural voices of women. The book underlined that no comprehensive history of Canada is possible, if women constituting half of Canadian population are excluded (Boag et al., 2002).

Several works have highlighted the role of ethnicity, class, religion, politics and spaces in shaping lives of women and their responses. These writings have challenged pre-existing generalization about Canadian history. The gender perspective cannot be negated.

The role of native Indians as the 'First Nation' has been underlined in several work. From gender's perspective, Sylvia Van Kirk made significant contribution. She analysed the activities of Hudson Bay Company and North West Company in Western Canada. She showed that in establishing trading linkages, British sought help from native Indians. There was active role of women in organizing trading transactions. For instance Thanadelthur was active in negotiating trading transactions between Europeans and tribes of Ojibwa, Cress and Chipewyan. In the words of Sylvia Van Kirk, such woman acted as 'women in between' males of ethnic groups. They also took care of physical comforts of Europeans. Many native women married them. However, over the period of time, when European women started coming to British Columbia, many married native Indian women with their children were abandoned (Van Kirk, 1980).

The roles of French women over the period of time and their responses at levels of family, religion and political identity have been explored in several ways. During the period of 'New French', French women remained engaged in responsibilities within familial domain. Marie Rollet, wife of Louis Hebert, a farmer was the first European woman to settle in New France (Dumont, et at., 1987: 17). These women endorsed patriarchal domination. French women resented the domination of British Canadians in polity of Canada since 1763 and they identified their national identity within the parameters setup by French men. The issue of children came to dominate French families. It was stressed that, there was need to have more children so that numerical strength of French could be increased (Trofimenkoff, 1982). While French women responded to their nurturing role as mothers and supported the cause of French nationalism, it also remains a fact that during the second wave of feminist movement in Canada, French women came to play an important role and demanded many rights in 'politics'. Leaders like Marie Gerin-Lajoie, Therese Casgrain Lise Payette and Jeanne Sauve played an important role in public spaces. There was demand for equal rights for women and even Parti Quebecois had to respond to it. The researches on these aspects clearly show the role of Quebec women in private and public domain. These works are reflective of growing consciousness at the level of womanhood (Prentice, et al., 1988).

The process of migration and settlement of Sikhs in Canada, especially in British Columbia has been underlined by several works. Unfortunately there is little focus on experiences of women (Verma, 2002). Kamala Elizabeth Nayar in her article has studied the impact of immigration on such women. Based on interviews of three generations of women, she has focused on their experiences. She has shown that when Sikhs moved and settled in Canada, then they brought their culture in new country. The role of religion remained important. In the initial stages, women responded more at the level of familial spaces but it is the third generation women, who are finding it difficult to response to their culture, religion and modernity. While Sikhism extols virtues of women and accords them equality, young women feel that community leaders are not practicing it. For them culture is defined and experienced in day to day life but within modern society, where they are located, it is becoming difficult for them to live in accordance with traditional value system (Nayar, 2010: 253–272).

On the basis of above-mentioned strands, it can be observed that feminist writings have made significant interventions in the process and nature of history writing.

Conclusion

It can be concluded that determined by spaces and historical processes, nature of historiography in India and Canada has been distinct. However in both countries, male voices and their perspectives dominated history writing, women being part of historical processes, remained either hidden or on the periphery of history. This was and has been challenged by feminist writings in both countries. Not only the role of women in the 'making of history' has been proved but also history has been written from their perspectives. The use of multiple sources is also evident. The very meaning of archives has been modified. Not only the voices of women have been recovered from written sources but also the use of orality has provided a new perspective in feminist writings. The complexities of historical changes and impact of caste, class, ethnicity, religion, and education, politics to name few in shaping responses of women has also been explained.

References

Agarwal, Bina, *Gender and Command over Property: An Economic Analysis of South Asia*, New Delhi: Kali for Women, 1994.

Agarwal, Gyan P. (ed.), *New Horizons of Globalization: India and Canada*, New Delhi: Deep and Deep Publications Pvt. Ltd., 2007.

Athavale, Parvati, *My Story: The Autobiography of a Hindu Widow*, New Delhi: Zubaan, an imprint for Kali, 1928, pp. 158–162.

Basra, Amrit Kaur, 'Voyages of Jacques Cartier: Narration, History and Historiography of Canada', in K.R.G. Nair and R. Borges (eds), *Discovering French Canada*, New Delhi: Allied Publishers Pvt. Ltd., 2002.

Basu, Aparna, *Mridula Sarabhai: Rebel with a Cause*, New Delhi: Oxford University Press, 1996 (Paperback edition 2003).

Berger, Carl, *The Writing of Canadian History: Aspects of English Canadian Historical Writings since 1900*, Toronto: Oxford University Press, 1987.

Boag, Veronica Strong, Mona Gleason and Adele Perry, *Rethinking Canada: The Promise of Women's History*, Toronto: Copp Clark Pitman, 1991.

Burt, Sandra, Lorraine Code and Lindsay Dorney (eds), *Changing Patterns: Women in Canada*, Toronto: McClelland and Steward, 1991.

Butalia, Urvashi, *The Other Side of Silence: Voices from the Partition of India*, Delhi: Kali for Women, 1998.

Chakravarti, Uma and Nandita Haksar, *The Delhi Riots: Three Days in the Life of a Nation*, New Delhi: Lancer International, 1987.

Chakravarti, Uma, *Pandita Ramabai: A Life and A Time*, New Delhi: Critical Quest, 2007.

——, *Everyday Lives, Everyday Histories: Beyond the Kings and Brahmins of 'Ancient India'*, New Delhi: Tulika, 2007.

Choudhary, Prem, *The Veiled Women: Shifting Gender Relations in Rural Haryana, 1880–1990*, New Delhi: Oxford University Press, 1994.

——, *Contentious Marriages, Eloping Couples: Gender Caste and Patriarchy in Modern India*, New Delhi: Oxford University Press, 2007.

Creighton, D.G., 'Sir John Macdonald and Canadian Historians', in Ramsay Cook, Craig Brown and Carl Berger (eds), *Approaches to Canadian History*, Toronto: University of Toronto Press, 1967.

Devi, Sushila, 'The Ideal of Hindu Womanhood with Practical Suggestions from its Realization', in Uma Chakravarti and Preeti Gill (eds), *Shadow Lives: Writings on Widowhood*, New Delhi: Zubaan, an imprint for Kali, 1907, pp. 105–106.

Dhami, Sadhu Singh, *Maluka: A Novel*, Publication Bureau, Patiala: Panjabi University, 1997.

Dumont, Micheline, Michele Jean, Marie Lavigne and Jennifer Stoddart, *Quebec Women: A History*, Translated by Roger Gannun and Rosalind Gill, Toronto: Women's Press, 1987.

Forbes, Geraldine, *Women in Modern India: New Cambridge History of India*, Cambridge: Cambridge University Press, 1996.

Grewal, J.S., *Recent Debates in Sikh Studies: An Assessment*, New Delhi: Manohar, 2011.

Guha, Ranajit, *Elementary Aspects of Peasant Insurgency in Colonial India*, New Delhi: Oxford University Press, 1983 (reprint 1992, 1997).

Joshi, V.C. (ed.), *Rammohan Roy and the Process of Modernization in India*, Delhi: Vikas Publishing House Pvt. Ltd., 1975.

Johnston, Hugh, *The Voyage of the Komagatu Maru: The Sikh Challenge to Canada's Colour Bar*, New Delhi: Oxford University Press, 1979.

Krueger, Ralph R., 'A Geographical Perspective: The Setting of the Settlement', in William Metcalf (ed.), *Understanding Canada: A Multidisciplinary Introduction to Canadian Studies*, New York: New York University Press, 1982, pp. 11–78.

Kudchedkar, Shirin (ed.), *Post Modernism and Feminism: Canadian Contexts*, New Delhi: Pencraft International, 2005.

Kumar, Radha, *The History of Doing: An Illustrated Account of Movements for Women's Rights and Feminism in India, 1800–1990*, New Delhi: Zubaan, an imprint for Kali, 1993.

Lerner, Gerda, *The Creation of Patriarchy*, Oxford: Oxford University Press, 1986.

Mani, Lata, 'Production of an Officer Discourse on Sati in Early Nineteenth Century Bengal', in Sumit Sarkar and Tanika Sarkar (eds), *Women and Social Reform in Modern India*, Vol. I, New Delhi: Permanent Black, 2007.

Menon, Ritu and Kamla Bhasin, *Borders and Boundaries: Women in India's Partition*, Delhi: Kali for Women, 1998.

Metcalf, Thomas R., *Ideologies of the Raj: The New Cambridge History of India*, Vols 3 and 4, Cambridge: Cambridge University Press, 1996.

Mohanty, Chandra Talpade, *Feminist without Borders: Decolonizing Theory, Practicing Solidarity*, New Delhi: Duke University Press, published in South Asia by Zubaan, 2003 (reprint 2006).

Morton, W.L., 'Clio in Canada, the Interpretation of Canadian History', in Ramsay Cook, Craig Brown and Carl Berger (eds), *Approaches to Canadian History*, Toronto: University of Toronto Press, 1967, pp. 1–27.

Nayar, Kamala Elizabeth, 'Sikh Women in Vancouver: An Analysis of their Psychosocial Issues', in Doris R. Jakubsh (ed.), *Sikhism and Women: History, Texts and Experiences*, New Delhi: Oxford University Press, 2010.

Pandey, Gyanendra, *The Construction of Communalism in Colonial North India*, Delhi: Oxford University Press, 1990.

Potter, John, *Vertical Mosaic: An Analysis of Social Class and Power in Canada*, Toronto: University of Toronto Press, 1965.

Prentice, Alison, Paula Bourne, Gail Cuthbert Brandt, Beth Light, and Wendy Mitchinson (eds), *Canadian Women: A History*, Toronto: Harcourt Brace Jovanovich, 1988.

Raj, Maitreyi Krishna (ed.), *Women's Studies in India: Some Perspectives*, Bombay: Popular Prakashan, 1986.

Ramabai, Pandita, *The High Caste Hindu Woman*, New Delhi: Critical Quest, 1888 (reprint 2013).

Ramasamy, Periyar E.V., *Women Enslaved*, New Delhi: Critical Quest, 2009.

Ramaswamy, Vijaya, 'Gender and the Writings of South Indian History', in Sabyasachi Bhattacharya (ed.), *Approaches to History: Essays in Indian Historiography*, New Delhi: ICHR in association with Primus Books, 2011 (reprint 2013).

Ray, Sibnarayan, *Bengal Renaissance: The First Phase*, Calcutta: Minerva Associates, 2000.

Roy, Kumkum, 'The Challenge of Women's History', in A. Suryakumari (ed.), *Women's Studies: An Emerging Discipline*, New Delhi: Gyan Publishing House, 1993.

Sangari, Kumkum, *Politics of the Possible: Essays on Gender, History, Narratives, Colonial English*, New Delhi: Tulika, 1999.

Singh, Upinder, *A History of Ancient and Early Medieval India: From the Stone Age to the 12th Century*, Delhi: Pearson Longman, 2009.

Sarkar, Sumit, *Modern India*, New Delhi: Macmillan India Ltd., 1983.

Sarkar, Tanika, *Hindu Wife, Hindu Nation: Community, Religion and Cultural Nationalism*, New Delhi: Oxford University Press, 2001.

Schultz, Harold J., 'Portrait of a Premier: William Aberhart', in Ramsay Cook, Craig Brown and Carl Berger (eds), *Politics of Discontent*, Toronto: University of Toronto Press, 1967.

Shah, Shalini, *The Making of Womanhood*, New Delhi: Manohar, 1995 (2nd edition 2012).

Trigger, Bruce G.T., *Natives and Newcomers: Canada's 'Heroic Age' Reconsidered*, Toronto: McGill-Queen's University Press, 1985.

Trofimenkoff, Susan Mann, *Dream of Nation: A Social and Intellectual History of Qubec*, Qubec: McGill-Queen's Press, 1982.

Van Kirk, Sylvia, *'Many Tender Ties': Women in Fur-Trade Society, 1670–1870*, Winnipeg: Watson and Dwyer Publishing, 1980.

Verma, Archana, *The Making of Little Punjab in Canada: Patterns of Immigration*, New Delhi: Sage, 2002.

Wrong, George M., 'The Beginning of Historical Criticism in Canada: A Retrospect, 1896–1936', *The Canadian Historical Review* XVII (1936): 1–8.

II

Gender Perspectives

6

Narratology as a Tool in Gender Discourse

Devika Khanna Narula

Narratology is associated with the structural and narrative techniques employed in a discourse to foreground a certain perspective/vision/ retrospective analysis. It is not narration but the devices that constitute narration, and through their deployment, the writer brings out certain socio-cultural and psycho-analytical facts that may otherwise have been overlooked in the attention to the linear story. Thus through the tools of narratology, a story changes into a discourse. Roland Barthes in the chapter on 'Introduction to the Structural Analysis of Narratives' (*Image/Music/Text*) states 'it is evident that discourse itself (as a set of sentences) is organized and that, through this organization, it can be seen as the message of another language, one operating at a higher level than the language of the linguists' (84). Thus the narrative becomes a signifier of something more than the simple story so that the narratives of women writers, using the tools of narratology, no longer remain stories of their suffering and endurance but significantly become signifiers to signify the underlying currents, to create a new and fresh awareness of the signified, that is their marginalization, invisibility and lack of voice, as realities across cultures, time and space.

Please pardon my use of the term *women writers* repeatedly but this is a signifier that the writings by women about women differ from those by men in the sensitivity involved in experiencing the emotions of the woman. Women writers generate a social awareness of the situation of women in their psychological as well as socio-cultural reality. It is a matter of 'voice' of a feminine consciousness exploring and expressing the nuances of sensitive reflexive reaction to the casual unnoticeable insensitivities of a patriarchal society. Women have been controlled by the ideas that patriarchal codes have formulated about them, imposing a straight-jacket of the 'correct' and the 'acceptable' codes for women. The formation of women's character is conditioned by ideas of male approval or disapproval and by male censorship. Analysing the facts around us, we realize what a deceptive illusion of freedom and choice has been created by patriarchy that implodes on being disturbed even slightly. Consequentially, feminine resistance becomes an ongoing reaction, obvert or covert, to salvage her own dignity and to assert her position. The objective of the women writers is to create and disseminate this awareness which then would in itself become an instrument of resistance. Narratology, then, becomes a tool in gender discourse to explore ways/methods of resisting the persistent problem of feminine oppression. The interpretation and presentation of behaviour or events, through narratology, brings it to a new level of awareness, leading to a social change that is evolving, slowly but definitely.

Thus, feminist struggle is a constant effort on the part of an individual or a group to retain its dignity, to protest against oppression/exploitation, and to retaliate against 'non-recognition'. It is predominantly the expression of the need to be 'recognized' as co-contributors in the process of 'life' and not just as 'facilitators', implying that the oppression suffered by women is not only physical and abusive but also psychological. The 'voice' or even the 'silence' of women is pre-dominantly raised in protest against such reduction as she is viewed only through the lens of the male perspective which defines her in terms of his needs, his gaze and his projection of her personality, thereby defining her in terms of her body and duties/service. However, in the domain of art, whether literature, painting, sculpture or the film media, the representation of the feminine, especially by women writers, assumes certain complexities and problematization as modes of depiction are used to project and negotiate nuances underlying the 'seen' reality. Thus what a work of art does not 'say' often becomes as important, or even more so, than what it says. In fact, the narratology in gender discourse foregrounds and explores possibilities and ways of resistance to feminine oppression, and in this context 'silence' becomes one of the tropes used as a resonating device to achieve the objective. The narratives under consideration, *Chittacobra* by Mridula Garg, situated in an urban contemporary context of an educated middle class, *Under The Shadow of Kamakhya* by Indira Goswami, located in a rural traditional society bound by religious rites, and some Canadian short stories of immigrant South Asian Canadian women resisting non-recognition in their specific urban situations, will be used to explore and develop the distinctive ways in which women retaliate and assert their real selves. The focus will be on the techniques of narratology used in these narratives to highlight the distinctive treatment given by the authors to the subject and specifically the use of the trope of 'silence' as a tool of retaliation.

However, before I start I would like to draw your attention to the famous painting *Bani-Thani* as an entry point for my discussion. *Bani-Thani* is a most well known and symptomatic piece of the Kishangarh School of painting of Rajasthan. *Bani-Thani* is the portrait of the personal maid of Raja Sawant Singh's(1748–1764) stepmother Bankawatiji, who was intelligent and lucky enough to have the opportunity to study literature because of her proximity to the queen. She had a natural flair for poetry and composed and sang beautiful songs to Krishna. Bani Thani was an enchanting beauty, tall and slim, with a queenly smile. Raja Sawant Singh fell in love with her and ordered the court painter Nihal Chand to paint Radha, the consort of Lord Krishna, taking inspiration from Bani Thani and the painting, ironically, came to be named after her. *Bani Thani* is the epitome of the Kishangarh style of painting, projecting the graceful in a woman with its stylized depiction of an elongated face, high arched eyebrows, half open heavy lidded lotus eyes, sharp pointed nose, thin curved sensuous lips, and a pointed chin over a long narrow neck, with a curl of the hair near the ear lobe, adding to her feminine grace. She is resplendent in her jewellery as she delicately holds her gauze like odhni as a foil to her profile, creating an impression of the individual Bani Thani as a sensuous beauty with eyes, eyebrows and lips that denote her sensuality, a projection through the male gaze and as per the male perception, of what is 'desirable' in a woman. One significant feature of the Kishangarh school of painting is the depiction of the subject in profile; it never portrays the frontal view of a face. This is an intriguing fact and it leads one to dwell on the fact that by such depiction a multifaceted personality is submerged into a single dimensional personality. In the painting *Bani*

Thani, too, the stylized portrayal does not reflect the many dimensions of Bani Thani's personality, her intelligence or her devotion for which she later came to be called Rasik Bihari, but only the sensuality and grace that must have first caught the eye of Raja Sawant Singh. Thus, for a viewer who is not aware of the history behind the painting, it is merely a beautiful stylized aesthetic piece. But for a seeker of answers, the question arises as to why did the Kishangarh school of painting depict only profiles and never frontal views? Is it not a reduction of the complexity of a human personality to a stylized simplification? Does it not depict an imposition of a viewpoint and filtration of a human personality as per the requirements of the person in control? And taking this argument into the context of narratology and gender, is it not true that feminism is resisting such reduction of the feminine by the male gaze? Prabha Ganorkar in her essay 'A Language of My Own: Language, Self and Representation' has voiced the concern and one of the main preoccupations of women writers. She says:

> To be the Other is to be the non-subject, the non-person, the non-agent – in short, the mere body. In law, in customary practice, and in cultural stereotypes, women's selfhood has been systematically subordinated, diminished, and belittled, when it has not been outright denied. ... The creation of the self takes place at various levels. One is that which is created by the individual herself, the second is that created by people around and the third is created through representation. ... Within the politics of culture and of gender, the feminine self realizes that she is being othered at different levels. It is through literature that she finds a tool to express herself, her ideas about her 'self', define what she is and also rebel against a representation that is problematic.
>
> (Jain, 370–371)

The sign of social change referred to above is seen in different devices of narratology that are used to reflect a greater awareness and articulation of the fact that 'silence', 'invisibility' and 'subjugation' are tropes that have always signified the 'feminine'. This is true of diverse cultures though here we shall focus only on the South Asian writers in Canada and contemporary women writers in India whose work reflects the subtle ways in which male control is exposed and resisted. The important role of 'sisterhood' and female bonding in supporting and motivating resistance to oppression also needs to be looked at since the new social context of living away from the family, whether within India or as a migrant in Canada, more often than not, entails living on one's own, and in many cases NGOs replace the conventional emotional support extended by female relatives. Traditionally, women would support the patriarchal system because the ideas of 'security', 'home' and 'social status' are all linked to a woman's positioning with reference to the male. The NGOs, on the other hand, create a sense of an independent identity of the woman herself as an individual, an entity in herself, and often give her the courage to break through the mists of 'socialization' to see herself in a new light. Thus, women writers use the tools of narratology to disseminate this awareness and turn a simple story into a discourse of the feminine. The volume of short stories *Her Mother's Ashes* by women writers of the South Asian Diaspora in Canada as well as *Tamarind Mem* by Anita Rao Badami, the stories by Indira Goswami and the novella *Chittacobra* by Mridula Garg are all excellent examples of the use of techniques of narrative to create an awareness of methods of resistance and the redemption of one's own dignity. Barthes has stated, that 'all narratives share structural features that each narrative weaves together in different ways'.

The socio-cultural space of women has its location within the parameters of control dictated by the patriarchs. Challenging the patriarchs would mean being left out in the open without 'social protection'. In such a situation, how does a woman retaliate against the injustice of society, or against an onslaught on the dignity of her 'self', while keeping herself within the folds of society? Mridula Garg in her essay on 'Women as Society in Literature' refers to the initial victim and guilt syndrome viz-a-viz men that women suffered in their protest against social mores, but then they moved on:

> Women quickly assimilated the fact that the real war was not between the sexes or genders but between an oppressive value system and the forces demanding an equality of opportunity. The oppressive value system was an adjunct of the inequitable class and caste systems ... once this was understood, it was easy to see that the so-called women issues were, in fact social issues. The female protagonists that the women writers then chose to write about, dealt with the bigger picture. They emphasized the changes needed in the economic and political systems, to deal with the degradation of environment and of the human psyche.
>
> (Jain, 359)

In the Preface to the Second Edition of *Feminist Theory: From Margin to Center*, bell hooks explores feminist theory in the context of the struggle of black women against discrimination and states as follows:

> Significantly what we know from charting the history of contemporary feminist movement is that individual women were rebelling against sexism all over the place. When those women began to meet and talk together, that collective rebellion came to be known as women's liberation and would later evolve into feminist movement. Feminist struggle takes place anytime anywhere any female or male resists sexism, sexist exploitation, and oppression. Feminist movement happens when groups of people come together with an organized strategy to take action to eliminate patriarchy.
>
> (hooks, xi)

Thus, feminist struggle has been an ongoing process, and a consistent resistance, though the ways of doing so may differ and where the individual is depressed by her circumstances, the sisterhood of other women helps restore her confidence. The significance of this discourse is to define women's position in socio-political terms, by going beyond the cliché that men are women's enemies. Further, women themselves inadvertently carry the burden of patriarchy and contribute to their own exploitation. Hence, it is necessary 'to examine systems of domination and our role in their maintenance and perpetuation' (hooks, 27). Creating the awareness of such a tendency in different situations becomes the feminist writer's objective as she explores various possibilities both of context and of retaliation. In Mridula Garg, and Indira Goswami's book, though the contexts are different, yet the questions raised are similar. One of the most pertinent questions is: are we contributing and facilitating our domination by patriarchy? And if we want to break away, what are the negotiating terms on which we can retain our foothold in society and yet liberate ourselves?

Mridula Garg's *Chittacobra* is a narrative that describes the situation of an urban educated woman in an arranged marriage. She is a perfect wife, in every respect, and participates fully in her sexual relationship with her husband Mahesh. Thus, she fulfills her part of the code of the institution that is marriage. However, Mahesh has married her for convenience and not for love. In the initial years of marriage, Manu tries her best to win his love but fails to do so. In their social circle, nobody can doubt that they are not a 'happily married' couple because there are no differences between Mahesh and her, she lives the same kind of life that couples all around her are living. Mridula Garg uses dialogue as the mode of narration and exposes the gap between the façade outside and the truth within, through the use of the tropes of prison, illusion and the disjunct between the 'social' life that one is forced to live and the experience that creates a true sense of being. The narrator in her social identity of 'Mrs Goyal' is an educated woman apparently well placed in her social urban setting, with a husband who apparently cares for her. My use of the word 'apparently' is intentional because it denotes the 'appearance' of things, and not the reality of the narrator's hidden life. The constant jostling of the past with the present, of memories of her friend Richard with the reality of her husband with whom she has no emotional bonding, reveal the confluence of the two in her consciousness so that even if she is living life as Mrs Goyal, her truth lies in the moments she has spent with Richard, and still living those moments in her memories. Manu, however, finds her love in Richard with whom she finds reciprocity of emotional bonding and an acknowledgement of her as an individual. Thus it is in her sexual union with Richard that she finds fulfillment. An indication of how unimportant her interaction with Mahesh is for her is reflected in the 'silence' that surrounds her relationship with him and her acquiescence in everything that he says as she does not waste her energy in unnecessary protest, since her life with Mahesh has no significance for her. She lives two parallel lives, one of her fulfillment and flowering into a woman who experiences love, the other as the dutiful wife in every respect, fulfilling her societal, sexual and maternal role of a model wife and mother. Thus, for Manu the real world is not the social world of Mahesh's friends and acquaintances and of parties or even her 'home' but the time that she spends with Richard in Delhi and which is what she always keeps alive within her. Manu exists on two planes of spatial and temporal reality, where the normal concept of the 'real' is reversed.

The narrator is actually a rebel who refuses to give herself to her husband without being in love with him. On the exterior, she carries on all her duties of the traditional wife as expected by society but within herself she lives a secret life that is extremely painful but fulfilling at the same time. All these are narrative techniques used by Mridula Garg to expose the sham of the so-called successful and happy arranged marriages, where there is no emotional bonding but only a co-existence as per social norms. Another narrative technique employed by Garg to convey the difference in Manu's relationship with Richard and Mahesh is the mode of narrative presentation that she employs in the two cases. There is more of dramatization and less of narration in the Richard sequences and vice-versa when she is with Mahesh. This technique signifies her coming alive with Richard as against her enactment of an 'expected' conventional role with Mahesh. Though apparently accepting the conventional, Manu rejects the diktat of society where loveless bonding is held up and admired as the perfect loving couple. Her silent protest at and rejection of the expected submergence of her identity into that of Mahesh's identity is a rebellion against something that is conventionally implicit in the patrimonial lineage of families:

> I shall make you mine by giving you my name. You will cease to be.
> I alone will have an identity and you shall merely bear its name.
> Even your creative faculties will be usurped by my name.
>
> ... Someone had said that ... years ago ... no, he had not said it, only wanted it to be so. An unspoken order had demanded a mute surrender every moment, every minute. Two persons with but one name. Where was the scope for asking and arguing?
>
> But I did not acquiesce. I revolted against the silent hegemony.
>
> I wanted my name. Even if no value was attached to it, I wanted it. I wanted my freedom. I had to have control over my right to surrender.
>
> (Garg, 55–56)

Her submission to her 'role' as a 'wife' is evident in her sexual act with Mahesh where she submits herself as a body, responding to Mahesh's touch but at the same time stands apart and views the act objectively:

> ... my body was familiar with each stroke and shot of the game being played on it. To make love was a game, an art, a need, a demand of the body. To love was ... stupid?
>
> (Garg, 87)

Instead of being reduced to a sexual object by the man, she chooses to present herself as such to him to play with, but this detachment takes away his mastery over her, as he himself is reduced to a programmed 'doer' whose every move is anticipated by her. The 'silence' that surrounds her, as she abides by her expected role, is her tool of resistance.

Mridula Garg also uses the motif of the mirror extensively in *Chittacobra* to depict the inner self as against the social self. The 'blue circle caught in the mirror' is an image that reflects the romance in her life, and reminds her of her time with Richard as opposed to the later scene where she sees the reflection of her pale face in the mirror and wonders how she can make it into a wrinkled ageing face to discourage her husband from carrying her to parties as a trophy-wife. 'Make-up' is another trope for hiding the truth, it is the mask that covers and protects her true self, the inner self, and denotes the social self. The jubilation with which she uses powder to create a false wrinkled image of herself or the 'slashing' of her lips with a dark purple lipstick shows the created social face of 'Mrs Goyal' reflected in the mirror. The instances also reflect what Lacan calls the 'play' with the mirror-image, creating different selves through posturing. Thus, the techniques employed and the mode of presentation determine the impact of the discourse. As Roland Barthes in his chapter on 'Introduction to the Structural Analysis of Narratives' states:

> Is everything in a narrative functional? Does everything, down to the smallest detail, have a meaning? Can narrative be divided up entirely into functional units? We shall see in a moment that there are several kinds of functions, there being several kinds of correlations, but this does not alter the fact that a narrative is never made up of anything other than functions: in differing degrees, everything in it signifies. This is not a matter of art (on the part of the narrator), but of structure; in the realm of discourse, what is noted is by definition notable.
>
> (Barthes, 88–89)

Mridula Garg has taken pains to present us with a dramatized narration that speaks for itself and that highlights social issues of marriage, the relationship between man and woman and the question of the inner self as opposed to the socially created one. The issue of the 'real' is problematic – is the social world, however stifling, 'real' or is it the free world where one can express oneself, the 'real' one? In the chapter on 'Introduction to the Structural Analysis of Narratives', Barthes rejects the idea of 'reality' presented in a narrative as he says:

> Claims concerning the 'realism' of narratives are (therefore) to be discounted. In all narrative imitation remains contingent. The function

> of narrative is not to 'represent', it is to constitute a spectacle still very enigmatic for us but in any case not of a mimetic order. The 'reality' of a sequence lies not in the 'natural' succession of the actions composing it but in the logic there exposed, risked and satisfied.
>
> (Barthes, 123–124)

The 'logic' of events becomes more significant than temporal and spatial faithfulness because the scenes created are being created for a specific effect on the audience.

Indira Goswami, too, uses signifiers and narrative devices to convey her intended meaning. One of these is the trope of 'silence' as used in her narrative *Under the Shadow of Kamakhya* where the situation of the protagonist is different from that of Manu in *Chittacobra*. Where Manu is an educated urban woman, confident and apparently independent, Padmapriya is a quiet, withdrawn rural persona from a Vaishnavaite clan which keeps total control over a woman's sexuality. However, in this narrative the 'silence' of the woman produces reverberations all around her in the protesting voices of the mother, the priest-father, the jajman Brahmins and other women. Nothing can be private here, even her so called 'shame' of being rejected by her husband and its cause, the tiny white mark, is to be exposed before everyone else. However, sister bonding is used by Goswami to depict how it is Lawonya who plans the revenge and gives the confidence to Padmapriya that transforms her into a new personality. Lawonya teaches Padmapriya to make her sexuality an avenging tool rather than a victim, and to use it to subdue the priest Sambhudev as well as her husband, Bhuvaneshwar. Lawonya advises Padmapriya to use her body language instead of words to entice and use Sambhudev as a tool in her revenge on Bhuvaneshwar.

Indira Goswami uses the device of parallelism to correlate and contrast two events totally distinct from each other. The parallel of the sacrifice of the buffalo, so deftly handled by Sambhudev, is established first with Padmapriya who offers herself willingly for seduction, and then with Bhuvaneshwar when she informs him that the child in her womb is not his but Sambhudev's. The juxtaposition of Padmapriya and the image of the Devi Kamakhaya on the one hand, and that of the buffalo and Bhuvaneshwar on the other hand, is a signifier of the justification and the jubilation of the revenge. Goswami uses cinematic technique as a narratology device throughout the narrative but in this last scene it is used most effectively, constantly fluctuating between the two scenes taking place simultaneously, with the drums and cymbal of one signifying the other:

> The sound of drums and cymbals floated down from the temple. Preparations were probably being made for the sacrifice of a buffalo.
>
> (75)

And this leads to the climax

> Bhuvaneshwar collapsed in a heap near the door.
>
> (76)

The two are intricately linked, with the first signifying and giving meaning to the second action.

The 'silence' of Padmapriya is exploited to great effect because she is neither questioned about her actions nor is she expected to supply any answers. The 'silence' becomes a potent device of narratology. It is used as a protective mantle that surrounds her and is a part of her personality. This is the reason no one realizes the change that has been effected in her by Lawonya's words and support. This is reflected in the transformation of the stigma of the white spot on her body into the beauty of the small white flowers. Goswami uses this motif of the white dots (as the flowers appear from a distance) to project the way in which thinking differently can change the perspective, innocence can be used deftly like the *khargah* of Sambhudev and slaughter effected through words. Bhuvaneshwar is surprised to see Padmapriya transformed into a sinuous fulsome beauty in the two years of their separation and is led unresisting to the altar as he is engulfed by the carnal pleasures that Padmapriya's body now offers. The trope of the 'body' is used by Goswami, too, to reverse the typical. Here, too, instead of being reduced to a mere body as a sexist object, Padmapriya uses her body to entrap the two men, one who becomes her partner in her revenge and the other who is the object of her revenge, thereby inverting the patriarchal 'control' over woman's sexuality. Further, Goswami also uses the motif of 'space' very effectively when the darkness of Padmapriya's room, into which she retreats due to fear of social stigma, is transformed into the womb-like space in the hillside of the Devi's temple, hidden by the entangled branches of plantation and giving off a peculiar blood smell, clearly a symbolic representation of the vagina, where she allows herself to be willingly led by Sambhudev, in defiance of social ostracism. The way Goswami presents the case of Padmapriya, the planning and execution of her revenge, shows a certain schematization that reflects the theory of structural analysis of narratives as expounded by Roland Barthes:

> From the start, meaning must be the criterion of the unit (here Barthes refers to the smallest segment of narrative as a unit): it is the functional nature of certain segments of the story that makes them units – hence the name 'functions' immediately attributed to these first units. ... the essence of a function is, so to speak, the seed that it sows in the narrative, planting an element that will come to fruition later – either on the same level or elsewhere, on another level.
>
> (Barthes, 88–89)

Thus, 'silence' as a trope uses a rich repertoire of other metaphors of the body, space and the colour white juxtaposed with red, to negotiate and punish the patriarchal subversion of the female. The assault on her dignity is countered by incapacitating the male through 'apparent' compliance with patriarchal codes, so that there can be no criticism of Padmapriya. Hence, the narratology employed by Goswami in her narration gives added depth and a larger meaning to what appears on the surface. Roland Barthes explains the significance of the 'meaning' in the story:

> Narrative does not show, does not imitate; the passion which may excite us in reading a novel is not that of a 'vision'(in actual fact, we do not 'see' anything). Rather it is that of meaning, that of a higher order of relation which also has its emotions, its hopes, its dangers, its triumphs.
>
> (Barthes, 124)

The writers of the South Asian Diaspora in Canada often write about the experience of the migrant wives. Most of the short stories in the collection *Her Mother's Ashes* and in the novels by these women writers deal with the husband's 'non-recognition' of his wife as an individual, an entity in herself. This becomes a difficult situation because of their being immigrants and away from the emotional social support of their families. Most of these women find 'recognition' and love outside marriage, a person who acknowledges them as an individual and respects their dignity. However, mostly this love remains unfulfilled since social bonds always manage to cast a stranglehold on relationships that cross the socio culturally defined borders and cross over into free realms. In Anita Rao Badami's novel, *Tamarind Woman,* the mother Saroja is one who has been forced into marriage with a man who cannot give her emotional sustenance and treats her only as a 'body' during the short time he spends with her because of his extensive touring. There is no compatibility between the husband and wife but then she finds love with the car mechanic. However, once it is discovered, the man dies under mysterious circumstances. Has society stepped in to prevent the status quo being disturbed? Saroja's shrillness and bitterness are an outlet for her frustration with her meaningless relationship, and it is only later after her husband's demise that she gradually returns to normalcy again. Her emotions are reflected in most of the women characters of the short stories in the collection *Her Mother's Ashes.* In Vidyut Aklujkar's short story 'Behind the Headlines' Lakshmi is a disgruntled wife who has been reduced to a robotic commodity working with efficient precision to make life comfortable for her husband. She suffers in silence as the husband is engrossed in his consumption of 'news', and has no contact with her except in a businesslike manner; he, in fact, does not recognize her as an individual but only as an instrument to make life smooth and comfortable for him. Eventually, she leaves him but the last thing she does is to stuff newspapers into his overnight bag instead of clothes as she had been instructed to do by her husband's secretary. This is her form of revenge, before she walks out on him. In Lakshmi Gill's 'Altered Dreams' Magdalena is a picture of gender-disadvantage. She is studying for her Ph.D. to get a firmer hold on her profession, to match her husband's qualification, and to fulfill her parents' dream. Her Canadian husband's attitude is that of the privileged male who gets worked up if things are not according to his convenience; at every point where Magdalena tries to put her convenience forward, he threatens her with a divorce. Similarly, 'Lekythos', the other story by Lakshmi Gill in the second volume, has a similar situation where the husband does not co-operate with the wife's desire to write a novel and yet she accomplishes her task by working on it daily, after completing all her duties as a 'wife' in the patriarchal home.

Women are seen only as 'bodies' or 'commodites' in the way that is typical of the patriarchal mindset, where all blame always lies with the woman and no blame accrues to the man. In 'Why Am I Doing This?' by Hema Nair, Vijaya's husband marries her only for her dowry-in-cash which his father needs to expand his business and which cannot be given by the woman he loves. Once this is done, Vijaya is sent back and the other woman accepted. No one blames her husband, not even her own father, for his manipulation of the woman. Uma Parameswaran's 'Freeze Frame' succinctly puts this aspect into words when she describes Sunda's feelings of becoming a non-entity: 'You know what kills me...(is) that he has twisted my spirit so much, I used to be so independent, so confident before he took over my life and now I have no identity; no spirit; I hate myself for what I have allowed him to do to me' (96). The interesting point to note here is the realization 'what I have allowed him to do to me' i.e. she is as much responsible for her predicament because she has accepted her traditional role in the patriarchal system and acquiesced in his domination.

Thus, what and how a story unfolds depends on the devices of narratology used to create a discourse out of a simple story by highlighting and foregrounding hidden nuances lying beneath apparently normal behaviour, incidents and relationships. The narratives are merely a few illustrations of the way feminist struggle and resistance work to counter the indignity imposed on them. What is true of these narratives and the layers of meaning submerged within them, is also true of other narratives of women, across culture and space, as they assert their own sense of dignity. The notable fact, however, is that a commonplace story, typical and common to many other instances, is transformed into a powerful narrative with the use of various techniques of narratology. Clearly it is the *structural devices* rather than the simple story-line that impact the reader. Rather than see a story in its simplicity, or a situation as limiting, the plurality of signifying codes of narratology should be considered as an invitation to read a text in a pluralistic way to bring out its multiple meanings and connotations. According to Barthes, 'the writerly text is *ourselves writing*, before the infinite play of the world (the world as function) is traversed, intersected, stopped, plasticized by some singular system (Ideology, Genus, Criticism) which reduces the plurality of entrances, the opening of networks, the infinity of languages' (182).

Thus, rather than read a text for its simplistic linear plot (this happens, then this, then this), rather than be constrained by either genre or even temporal progression, Barthes argues for what he terms a 'writerly' rather than a 'readerly' approach to texts, through signifiers and devices of narratology.

References

Primary

Aziz, Nurjahan, ed., *Her Mother's Ashes*, Vol. 1 and 2, Toronto: TSAR Publications, 1994.

Garg, Mridula, *Chittacobra*, New Delhi: Books India International, 2006.

Goswami, Indira, *The Shadow of Kamakhya*, New Delhi: Rupa & Co., 2001, reprinted 2005.

Secondary

Barthes, Roland, *Image, Music, Text*, English translation by Heath, Stephen, New York: Noonday Press Edition, 1988, copyright by Barthes 1977, by Stephen Heath 1977.

hooks, bell, *Feminist Theory: From Margin to Center*, Cambridge, MA: South End Press; 1984, 2nd ed. 2000.

Jain, Jasbir, ed., *Growing Up as a Writer*, New Delhi: Sahitya Akademi, 2007.

7

LGBTQ Community

Canada and India

Garima Gupta

In 2010, in a speech marking Human Rights Day, UN Secretary General Ban ki-moon said that, 'as men and women of conscience, we reject discrimination in general, and in particular discrimination based on sexual orientation or gender identity'. On 15 December 2011, the first ever United Nations report on the human rights of lesbian, gay, bisexual and transgender (LGBT) people detailed how around the world people are killed or endure hate motivated violence, torture, detention, criminalization and discrimination in jobs, health care and education because of their real or perceived sexual orientation. This report was presented as part of human rights violations against LGBT people. The report noted that 'Violence against LGBT persons tends to be especially vicious compared to other bias-motivated crimes', citing data indicating that homophobic hate crimes often included, 'a high degree of cruelty and brutality'. Violent acts were often not reported as the victims often did not trust the police or feared reprisal or were unwilling to reveal their sexual orientation publicly. In the report, Navi Pillay, the UN High Commissioner for Human Rights called on countries to repeal laws that criminalized homosexuality. There are 76 countries still where it is illegal to indulge in same-sex activities and in at least five countries the death penalty prevails (http://www.un.org).

LGBT, now referred to as LGBTQ (Q for Queer) though by no means a homogenous group is rendered homogenous by the most unlikely shared characteristic – the kind of victimization and discrimination they face. However, in the recent years this minority group has begun to struggle for their very own piece of the sky and the earth and it has borne fruit with the shifting of the international attitude towards this community. Some 30 counties have decriminalized homosexuality in the last two decades or so. Thus in this article I attempt a comparison between the status of LGBTQ community in Canada and India, given the culturally plural character of the two nations. However, before doing so we need an appraisal of the policies followed by the two nations to manage their variegated character and the concepts that we come across is that of cultural pluralism and multiculturalism.

Cultural pluralism was a term first coined and used by Horace Meyer Kallen who expressed his idea regarding cultural pluralism in 1915 in an essay, entitled 'Democracy *versus* the Melting-Pot' published in *The Nation.* The term is used when smaller groups within a larger society maintain their unique cultural identities, and their values and practices are accepted by the wider culture provided they are consistent with the laws and values of the wider society. Today, Kallen's cultural pluralism has been recognized by many as an insightful prescience into today's multicultural society. For example, David Hollinger (1995) argued in his book on the study of multiculturalism that '[t]he 'cultural pluralism' associated with the name of Horace Kallen is an important precursor to multiculturalism'(*Postethnic America*, 11).

Multiculturalism is the appreciation, acceptance or promotion of multiple cultures, applied to the demographic make-up of a specific place usually at the organizational level. All the prominent features of multiculturalism can be summed up in the words of Prof. Caleb Rosado. According to him:

> Multiculturalism is a system of beliefs and behaviours that recognizes And respects the presence of all diverse groups in an organization or Society, acknowledges and values their socio-cultural differences, and Encourages and enables their continued contribution within an inclusive cultural context which empowers all within the organization or society. (http://www.edchange.org)

In a political context the term is used for a range of meanings, ranging from the advocacy of equal respect to the various cultures in a society, to a policy of promoting the maintenance of cultural diversity, to policies in which people of various ethnic and religious groups are addressed by the authorities as defined by the group they belong to. A common aspect of many such policies is that they avoid presenting any specific ethnic, religious, or cultural community values as central (*Stanford Encyclopedia of Philosophy*).

Though multiculturalism came in for scathing criticism, in particular after 9/11 attacks as redundant, inadequate and defunct, even dangerous, its relevance cannot be denied or overlooked. As Tariq Madood (2007) puts it, 'Contrary to all those who think that the time to speak of multiculturalism is over, I think it is most timely and necessary, and that we need more not less' (*Multiculturalism,* 13).

Multiculturalism: Canada and India (Wikipedia)

Multiculturalism in India and Canada is of very different hues as it owes its origin in the two countries to very different conditions. In India, the cultural diversity is an inherent condition of the nation whereas in Canada it grew out of the immigration policies of the nation. Now there is a rich critical discourse available analysing the concept and different aspects of 'Multiculturalism' both as a theory and practice but for the present purpose I would like to dwell upon its evolution in the political scene of the two countries.

In the context of Canada, multiculturalism cannot be ignored as it is followed as a conscious policy by the government. Lord Tweedsmuir the 15th Governor General of Canada was an early champion of multiculturalism; from his installation speech in 1935 onwards, he maintained in speeches and over the radio recited his ideas that ethnic groups 'should retain their individuality and each make its contribution to the national character', and 'the strongest nations are those that are made up of different racial elements'.

The beginnings of the development of Canada's contemporary policy of multiculturalism can be traced to the Royal Commission on Bilingualism and Biculturalism, which was established on 19 July 1963 by the Liberal government of Prime Minister Lester B. Pearson in response to the grievances of Canada's French-speaking minority. The report of the Commission advocated that the Canadian government should recognize Canada as a bilingual and bicultural society and adopt policies to preserve this character.

The recommendations of this report elicited a variety of responses. Former Progressive Conservative Prime Minister John Diefenbaker, viewed them as an attack on his 'One Canada Policy' that was opposed to extending accommodation to minority groups. The proposals also failed to satisfy those Francophones in the Province of Quebec who gravitated toward Québécois nationalism. Additionally, Canadians of neither English nor French descent (so-called 'Third Force' Canadians) advocated that a policy of 'multiculturalism' would better reflect the diverse heritage of Canada's peoples.

Paul Yuzyk, a Progressive Conservative Senator of Ukrainian descent, referred to Canada as 'a multicultural nation' in his influential maiden speech in 1964, creating much national debate, and is remembered for his strong advocacy of the implementation of a multiculturalism policy.

On 8 October 1971, the Liberal government of Prime Minister Pierre Elliot Trudeau announced in the House of Commons that, after much deliberation, the policies of bilingualism and multiculturalism would be implemented in Canada. When the Canadian constitution was patriated by Prime Minister Trudeau in 1982, one of its constituent documents was the Charter of Rights and Freedoms, and section 27 of the Charter stipulates that the rights laid out in the document are to be interpreted in a manner consistent with the spirit of multiculturalism.

The Canadian Multiculturalism Act was introduced during the Progressive Conservative government of Brian Mulroney, and received Royal Assent on 21 July 1988. On a practical level, a result of the multiculturalism Act was federal funds began to be distributed to ethnic groups to help them preserve their cultures, leading to such projects as the construction of community centres. On 13 November 2002, the government of Liberal Prime Minister Jean Chrétien designated, by Royal Proclamation, 27 June of each year Canadian Multiculturalism Day.

Canadian multiculturalism is looked upon with admiration outside the country, resulting in the Canadian public dismissing most critics of the concept. Multiculturalism is often cited as one of Canada's significant accomplishments and a key distinguishing element of Canadian identity. In a 2002 interview with the Globe and Mail, Aga Khan the 49th Imam of the Ismaili Muslims described Canada as 'the most successful pluralist society on the face of our globe, without any doubt in my mind .... That is something unique to Canada. It is an amazing global human asset.' Critics of multiculturalism in Canada often debate whether the multicultural ideal of benignly co-existing cultures that interrelate and influence one another, and yet remain distinct, is sustainable, paradoxical or even desirable. Canadian Neil

Bissoondath in his book *Selling Illusions: The Cult of Multiculturalism in Canada* (1994), argues that official multiculturalism limits the freedom of minority members, by confining them to cultural and geographic ethnic enclaves (social ghettos).

Multiculturalism in India is quite different in character from that of Canada in the sense that it is not followed as conscious policy of the government though it is not entirely absent as there are certain provisions of the Constitution which are intended to protect the cultural distinctness of the minorities, the relevant provisions being, articles 29 and 30. However, these concerns have been placed by the government in two neat and distinct categories – the public and the private.

To gain a better understanding of the issue, it is important to draw a clear-cut distinction between the public sphere and the private sphere. Gurpreet Mahajan (1998) has noted that the Indian Constitution devised a 'two-fold' policy. According to her, on the one hand it tried to ensure that no community is excluded or systematically disadvantaged in the public arena, on the other it provided autonomy to each religious community to pursue its own way of life in the private sphere. In order to manage the cultural, ethnic and mostly religious diversity, the Indian Constitution and Polity has focused more on those aspects of minority protection that lie within the domain of the private sphere like the religious and community practices. However, the same effort has not been put in the aspects of the public sphere and thus one finds that the public sector is not as sensitized to the minority groups as it should be. Thus though the domain of private sphere remains sacrosanct, inviolable by the State in an effort to ensure a peaceful coexistence of all, in the public sector this is not so. The diversity of India is not reflected in its public spheres. This may be the reason, that despite the sensitization of the state and polity to the demands of the private sphere, it has been unable to contain the linguistic, regional, ethnic, and religious confrontations within. Thus though Indians are a heterogeneous group, the Indian state and polity appears homogenous.

In addition to this distinction, between the private and the public spheres it was further assumed that the individual upon entering the common public sphere was capable of leaving behind fundamental commitments and constitutive attachments (Bhargava, 1999: 170). Further, Gurpreet Mahajan (1998) feels that in the west provisions for the protection of minority rights were advanced at a time when religion and the church had ceased to be parallel sources of authority to the state and their influence had significantly declined. This was obviously not the case in India where the hold of religion continues to be profound. This difference, she feels, explains why provisions for minority rights have often had perverse effects in this country (7). Yael Tamir (1993) has pointed out that minority disadvantage arises when members of the minority community are prevented from carrying their distinctive practices into the public sphere (53), and it is thus not difficult to see the reason why minorities have suffered marginalization in this country. As Amir Ali (2000) puts it, 'In any attempts to place multiculturalism on the agenda in India, the public sphere must thus be made more conducive to the expression of cultural diversity, rather than protecting religious and cultural practices of the private sphere' (2503).

This difference in the management of the cultural plurality by the two countries and the difference in the attitude to multiculturalism to my mind is reflected in the difference of status accorded to the LGBTQ community within each, as will be seen subsequently.

LGBTQ Rights: Canada and India

Lesbian, gay, bisexual, transgender and queer (LGBTQ) rights in Canada are some of the most advanced in the Americas and in the world as can be seen in the following timeline of the important milestones in lesbian/gay/bisexual rights in Canada (http://www.religioustolerance.org).

1965: Everett Klippert was arrested. He acknowledged to the police that he has been gay for 24 years and is unlikely to change. Two years later, he was sentenced to an indefinitely long term in prison as a 'dangerous sex offender'.

1967: Reviewing Klippert's case, the Supreme Court of Canada upheld a lower court ruling that mandated life imprisonment as the maximum penalty for homosexual behaviour.

1967: Within a few weeks of the Court's decision, Attorney General Pierre Trudeau introduced bill C-150 to Parliament to liberalize the Canadian Criminal Code. One aim of the amendments was to decriminalize homosexual behaviour between adults.

1968: Trudeau's amendments to the Criminal Code become law.

1969 (14 May): C-150 permitting any consensual sexual activity by a maximum of two adults was decriminalized, was signed into law.

1971: Everett Klippert was released from prison.

1977: Quebec became the first province in Canada to include sexual orientation in its Human Rights Act. Discrimination against heterosexuals, homosexuals and bisexuals was prohibited.

1978: The Canadian Immigration Act was altered so that it no longer prohibited homosexuals from immigrating into the country.

1986: The Ontario Human Rights Code was amended to include sexual orientation as a protected class. Ontario is the most populous province in Canada. It was the second province to do so.

1987: Manitoba became the third province to add sexual orientation to its human rights code.

1989: The Canadian Human Rights Commission ruled that same-sex couples, and their children should be considered a family.

1992: The military lifted its previous ban of promotions, postings and career training for homosexuals, as a result of a lawsuit initiated by Captain Joshua Birch and others.

1995: The Province of Ontario extended family benefits to its gay and lesbian employees in same-sex relationships.

1995: An Ontario Court judge ruled that same-sex couples must be allowed to bring joint applications for adoption. The judge rules that four lesbians have the right to adopt their partners' children. Ontario becomes the first province to make it legal for same-sex couples to adopt. British Columbia, Alberta and Nova Scotia follow suit, also allowing adoption by same-sex couples. Other provinces are looking into the issue.

1996: Bill C-33 passed in the Federal Parliament. The term 'sexual orientation' was added to the Federal Human Rights Act as a protected class.

1999: In the 'M v. H' case, the Supreme Court of Canada ruled that same-sex couples were to have the same rights as opposite-sex unmarried common-law couples.

2001 (14 January): Two same-sex couples were married in a church service in Toronto. They could not obtain a marriage license, and so went through the ancient ritual of the reading of the bans. The Ontario government refused to register their marriages. However, two and a half years later, on 10 June 2003, the Ontario Court of Appeal retroactively recognized the marriages, thus making them the first same-sex couples in the world – at least in recent centuries – to be legally married.

2003 (February): New Democrat MP Svend Robinson unveils a private member's bill that would allow same-sex marriages. The federal government has already changed several laws to give same-sex couples the same benefits and obligations as heterosexual common-law couples.

2003 (10 June): The Ontario Court of Appeal unanimously ordered the Ontario government to issue marriage licenses to same-sex adult couples, and to register their marriages. Michael Stark and Michael Leshner made North American history by obtaining a marriage license and being married a few hours later.

2003 (17 September): Bill C-250 was passed. It added sexual orientation to the existing list of four protected classes in Canada's hate propaganda legislation. Hate speech against persons on the basis of their sexual orientation is now a criminal offense. Exceptions are made in the law for religious hate speech.

2004 (November): The Ontario Court of Appeal rules that gays and lesbians in the province are entitled to survivors' benefits under the Canada Pension Plan dating back to 1985.

2005 (June): New Brunswick's Court of Queen's Bench finds the province's current definition of civil marriage violates the rights of gay people. The ruling makes New Brunswick the eighth province where a court has opened the door to legal same-sex unions.

2005 (20 July): Bill C-38, which theoretically made same-sex marriages available across Canada was signed into law.

The provinces of Ontario (Kathleen Wynne, George Smitherman, Glen Murray), British Columbia (Tim Stevenson, Lorne Mayencourt, Ted Nebbeling), and Manitoba (Jim Rondeau, Jennifer Howard) have had openly gay provincial cabinet ministers. On 26 January 2013, Kathleen Wynne became the leader of the Liberal party of Ontario and premier of that province (the largest of the country's 13 provinces and territories, with approximately 39 per cent of the country's population).

In 2013, the organization Proud Politics, dedicated to providing networking and fund-raising assistance to LGBTQ people in politics, launched in Toronto. Thus Canada displays a long and glorious history of attempts to incorporate the LGBTQ community in its mainstream.

In India, however, the status of LGBTQ has always been dubious. Though the Indian culture is replete with mythological references to this group, the society as a whole and the government has been unsympathetic to their plight. In India, transgender people are called hijras. They were legally granted voting rights as a third sex in 1994. Hijras face heavy employment discrimination due to their transgender status, and thus frequently earn their income through sex work, which means they are criminalized due to the illegality of kerb-crawling, soliciting in a public place, etc. Because of the legal ambiguity of the procedure, Indian transgender individuals do not have access to safe medical facilities for sex reassignment surgery (SRS). According to a report by the United Nations Development Programme, India, hijras have a high prevalence of HIV, and most hijras have low socio-economic status and literacy levels, posing barriers to seeking health care.

Homosexual intercourse was a criminal offence until 2009 under Section 377 of the Indian Penal Code, 1860. This made it an offence for a person to voluntarily have 'carnal intercourse against the order of nature'. This law was struck down by the 2009 Delhi High Court decision *Naz Foundation v. Govt. of NCT of Delhi*, which found Section 377 and other legal prohibitions against private, adult, consensual, and non-commercial same-sex conduct to be in direct violation of fundamental rights provided by the Indian Constitution. Though laws to protect the community have been recently formulated by the Indian government, at the ground level the story is entirely different and with the social derision faced by these people they still have a long way to go.

The difference in the status of the LGBTQ community in India and Canada can be adequately judged by the following table (Wikipedia).

Summary Table

CANADA	
Same-sex sexual activity legal	since 1969
Equal age of consent	Since 1993, the age of consent explicitly do not distinguish based on sex of partners, but there is different age of consent for anal sex.
Anti-discrimination laws in employment	✓ since 1998
Anti-discrimination laws in the provision of goods and services	✓ since 1998
Anti-discrimination laws in all other areas (incl. indirect discrimination, hate speech)	✓
Same-sex marriage(s) nationwide	✓ since 2005
Adoption by same-sex couples	✓
Gay, lesbian, and bisexual people allowed to serve openly in the military	✓
Transgender and transsexual people allowed to serve in the military	✓
Right to change legal gender	✓
Access to IVF for lesbians	✓
MSM allowed to donate blood	Since 2013, but donors must have been celibate for more than 5 years.
Commercial surrogacy	✓ (banned for heterosexual couples as well)

INDIA	
Same-sex sexual activity legal	✓ (since 2009)
Equal age of consent	×
Anti-discrimination laws in employment	×
Anti-discrimination laws in the provision of goods and services	×
Anti-discrimination laws in all other areas (incl. indirect discrimination, hate speech)	×
Same-sex Legal Unions	× (one single case in 2011)
Recognition of same-sex couples	×
Both joint and step adoption by same-sex couples	×
Gays allowed to serve in the military	×
Right to change legal gender	×
Access to IVF for lesbians	×
MSMs allowed to donate blood	×

Conclusion

LGBTQ is an integral part of the human civilization in general all across the globe. It is not a new phenomenon that has recently come into being but always existed in human civilizations. Today when all the countries are recognizing the diversity, the cultural plurality, within them and trying to preserve and celebrate them recognizing their essentially enriching value to the nation, it becomes imperative not to confine the definition of diversity to the categories of ethnicity, religion, language or culture but to expand it to include all form including that of sexual orientation. The attitude of the governments towards managing their inherent plurality becomes a pertinent factor as well as can be seen in the preceding discussion. The difference in the status of LGBTQ community in India and Canada is reflective of this expansion and difference in diversity management.

References

Ali, Amir, 'Case for Multiculturalism in India', *Economic and Political Weekly* 35.28/29 (15–21 July 2000).

Bhargava, Rajeev, 'Should We Abandon the Majority-Minority Framework?', in Gurpreet Mahajan and D.L. Sheth (eds), *Minority Identities and the Nation State*, New Delhi: Oxford University Press, 1999.

Bissoondath, Neil, *Selling Illusions: The Cult of Multiculturalism in Canada*, Toronto: Penguin Books, 1994.

Hollinger, David, *Postethnic America: Beyond Multiculturalism*, New York: Basic Books, 1995.

Mahajan, Gurpreet, *Identities and Rights: Aspects of Liberal Democracy in India*, New Delhi: Oxford University Press, 1998.

Modood, Tariq, *Multiculturalism*, USA: Polity Press, 2007.

Tamir, Yael, *Liberal Nationalism*, Princeton, NJ: Princeton University Press, 1993.

Web References

http://en.wikipedia.org/wiki/LGBT_rights_in_Canada.

http://en.wikipedia.org/wiki/Multiculturalism_in_Canada.

http://en.wikipedia.org/wiki/Multiculturalism_in_India.

http://plato.stanford.edu/entries/multiculturalism.

http://www.religioustolerance.org or from http://www.cbc.ca important milestones in lesbian/gay/bisexual rights in Canada.

http://www.edchange.org/multicultural/papers/rosado_managing_diversity.pdf.

http://www.un.org/apps/news/story.asp?NewsID=40743#Uifld.

8

Woman's Body

The Gender Question in Fiction and the Media

Vinita Gupta Chaturvedi

The paper seeks to study how in two works of art – a novel, *Ice-Candy-Man* written by Bapsi Sidhwa and Deepa Mehta's *Earth 1947*, a screen adaptation of the same novel, the horror and brutality of communal passions is brought out when a nation is split along the lines of religion and when women become its greatest casualty. The division of India leading to the birth of two nations caused immense suffering to women on both sides of the border, women who suffered abduction and extreme violence because in the minds of the marauding rioters they were symbolic of the other nation which needed to be subjugated and conquered. Sidhwa, who was a witness to the carnage of partition and who later worked for the rehabilitation of the traumatized victims, was aware of the brutal fact that 'victory is celebrated on a woman's body, vengeance is taken on a woman's body'.[1] Her novel is one long searing exploration of one such brutalized woman who is emblematic of the spirit of undivided India in the way she holds together her admirers of diverse faith and is the gravitational centre of communal harmony in the days previous to partition but who suffers violation at the hands of these very admirers because for them, now, she is symbolic of the newly formed other nation. The novel depicts the peaceful years preceding partition, the abduction of the ayah, her subsequent marriage to one of her violators and finally her rescue and rehabilitation in India.

Deepa Mehta's film on the other hand depicts the pre-partition peace, subsequent turmoil but ends chillingly with the betrayal of trust, the abduction of the ayah and the extreme violence wreaked upon her body. Justifying the finale of the cinematic adaptation, which ends at the mid-point of her novel, Sidhwa comments, 'But the film had to end the way it did: the impact would have weakened otherwise.'[2] For the filmmaker the violence perpetrated on the woman's body is of more importance than the subsequent weak efforts at her integration into society which the other half of the novel depicts.

Bapsi Sidhwa's poignant and heart-rending novel about the division of the Indian sub-continent and its horrible aftermath was originally published in 1988 under the title *Ice-Candy-Man* and later changed to *Cracking India* for its American publication in 1991. The novel is set in Lahore shortly before the partition of India and Pakistan in 1947 and recalls in horrifying details the effect of the historical event on the lives of a motley group of individuals. The novel was closely adapted by the Indo-Canadian filmmaker Deepa Mehta in 1997 and released under the title *Earth 1947* in the year 1998. Both the works of art are highly autobiographical in nature. Bapsi Sidhwa, an eminent diasporic writer/activist from Pakistan was born in Karachi in 1938 and spent her childhood in Lahore before migrating to the USA. She witnessed the partition of India from close quarters and the novel's protagonist Lenny, a young child of eight years, records the chain of events leading up to the partition and the horrible consequences that are played out in its wake.

Deepa Mehta, the renowned Indian born director of Hollywood films such as *Sam and Me* (1990), the trilogy *Fire*, *Earth* and *Water*, and the more recent *Midnight's Children* was born in Amritsar in 1950 to a family that had fled Pakistan at the time of partition and relocated to New Delhi where she spent her formative years. She is now married to a Canadian documentary maker and settled in Canada. In her many interviews Deepa Mehta has admitted to being deeply affected by the horrifying tales of partition related to her by the members of her family. She migrated to Canada in 1973 and thereafter her directorial ventures began. Her widely acclaimed film, *Earth 1947* is based on Bapsi Sidhwa's novel and the entire film is recounted by a grown up Lenny who recalls her childhood in the salubrious town of Lahore where citizens of all faiths existed in peaceful harmony till the cleaving of the country in the year 1947. The film follows the novel with complete fidelity except that its climactic end – the abduction of the

Ayah – is an event that occurs only midway through the novel. For both the artists the violence perpetrated on the ayah's body by the violent band of rioters is the most significant incident in their works – in Sidhwa's novel it occupies an undeniable centrality of position while the film's action relentlessly hurtles towards it.

The novel *Ice-Candy-Man* is set in a hitherto cosmopolitan and peaceful Lahore and unfolds in chilling detail the sequence of events leading up to and the partition of India. The novel is told entirely from the point of view of the polio-stricken girl-child Lenny Sethi, who accompanied by her ayah Shanta, often perambulates the streets of Lahore, making mental note of the people they meet and the conversations they hold. The novel bears many autobiographical elements – like Lenny, Sidhwa too was afflicted by polio and both the writer and her protagonist were confined to home for the first fifteen years of their lives and were largely self-taught. The author chooses to narrate the story from the perspective of an eight-year-old child who is located, like herself, in the Parsee community. The Parsees constituted an extreme minority section of the Indian population and this standpoint also gives a certain objectivity and neutrality to the narratorial voice. By reposing the central consciousness of the novel in a child of eight the author enjoys the freedom to concentrate more on the domestic aspect of a historical event as cataclysmic in proportion as the Partition. Hence even though the writer has chosen a vast historical canvas the focus is not so much on politics as on the changing personal relationships. While listening to the ice-candy-man's ceaseless expatiation on the current political developments, Lenny wonders why they do not rather talk about their immediate surroundings: 'Sometimes he quotes Gandhi, or Nehru or Jinnah, but I'm fed up of hearing about them. Mother, Father and their friends are always saying Gandhi said this, Nehru said that. Gandhi did this, Jinnah did that. What's the point of talking so much about people we don't know?'[3]

Against this colossal backdrop of political upheaval the domestic tragedy, chiefly that of women, is played out. It is almost like Jane Austen choosing to write on her two inches of ivory or 'two or three families of county England', where fine miniature like depiction of society takes place, relegating the larger political debate to the background, consciously choosing the personal over the political. Sidhwa too portrays a small cast of Parsee, Hindu, Sikh and Muslim characters in a realistic setting, delineating each of them in vivid detail and suffusing this world, in equal measure, with humour and pathos.

The landmark political milestones in the history of India, from the year 1942 when the novel opens, up till 1947, are undoubtedly dotted through the novel but Sidhwa's focus is concentrated more on the position of women in this society, their strength and travails and especially foregrounds the theme of violence wreaked on women against the immensity of this political canvas. The historical developments recede into the background to give the tragedy a human face – it is the tragedy of common people and chiefly that of women which takes precedence over it.

The novel is narrated entirely through the eyes of the highly observant and inquisitive child, Lenny. Because she suffers from polio and is advised not to attend school it gives her ample time to traverse the city and observe the changing complexion of the pre-partition and post-partition developments in the city. She is frequently taken out by her ayah for walks through the city of Lahore which gives her an opportunity to interact with and observe people. A string of characters are introduced, the most important of who are Lenny's feisty Godmother, her sisters the Electric-Aunt, Minny aunty and so on who constitute the Parsee community to which Lenny belongs. During her walks with the ayah, they are joined by a disparate crowd of domestic staff that represents the ayah's social circuit. This group comprises an utterly believable and life-like set of characters – the reticent Muslim masseur Hassan, the Chinaman, the Pathan knife-sharpener Sharbat Khan, the faithful Sethi retainer Imam Din, Sher Singh the Sikh zoo-keeper, the Hindu gardener Hari and the boisterous Dilnawaz, the fun-loving ice-candy-man. The group often assemble in parks, courtyard and street-corners to genially discuss the day's affairs, politics and to casually flirt with the ayah. The ayah is the gravitational centre of this ensemble who attracts and holds together these men belonging to different religious faiths. But out of this group the ayah's favoured suitors are the masseur and the ice-candy-man. In the beginning of the novel they are a cheerful, peace-loving group and even though there are continuous reports of growing tension in other parts of the country, Lenny takes pride in their placid meetings and muses that the group around Ayah remains unchanged. Hindu, Muslim, Sikhs, Parsees are always unified around her. The Ayah can be seen as a harmonizing principle holding men of diverse faith together and in a sense she becomes symbolic of the Nation that holds its constituent elements together and her body transmogrifies into that of the nation-state. But this harmony is fragile and short-lived and Lenny slowly becomes aware of their religious differences: 'One day everybody is themselves – and the next day they are Hindu, Muslim, Sikh, Christian. People shrink, dwindling into symbols. Ayah is no longer just my all encompassing Ayah – she is also a token. A Hindu' (93).

During the course of these walks Lenny also becomes aware of her Ayah's sensuality and the perils of the male gaze that she attracts so easily: 'The covetous glances Ayah draws educate me. Up and down, they look at her. Stub-handed twisted beggars and dusty old beggars on crutches drop their poses and stare at her with hard, alert eyes. Holy men, masked in piety, shove aside their pretences to ogle her with lust. Hawkers, cart-drivers, cooks, coolies and cyclists turn their heads as she passes, pushing my pram with the unconcern of the Hindu goddess she worships' (3). This clearly indicates early on in the novel that there is a certain deification of the Ayah's body that makes its defilement at the hands of this crowd later in the novel even more reprehensible. These men gather around the ayah, vying for her attention and trying to outbid each other in gaining her affection. During the course of the novel these innocuous exchanges and good-natured banter assume sinister proportions as the ominous clouds of partition gather over the land threatening to rend relationships asunder. Finally in the event of partition unspeakable horrors are unleashed and the worst sufferers are the women. These very men who had befriended the ayah, including the genial, fun-loving prankster, ice-candy-man pounce and prey upon the ayah, who represents the newly formed Hindu nation to them and in their minds violating her is conjoined with the idea of an intended aggression on the nation. For the rioters the woman's body becomes a metaphor for the nation.

The leader of this rampaging mob is the ice-candy-man whose turning into a social deviant is plausibly delineated in the novel. He is presented as a carefree, happy go lucky trickster who regales this crowd with his antics, dupes the white memsahibs, and pursues the ayah with a dogged determination. He keeps changing his appearance, chameleon-like, from a bird man to a begging fakir to an ice-cream vendor with equal ease. The facility with which he slips into these roles eerily foreshadows his transformation into a diabolic, rabble-rousing bigot. His transformation comes about after he is witness to the gruesome act of violence perpetrated on his sisters on the other side of the border. He goes to the railway station to receive his relatives arriving on the train from Amritsar but is shocked to find the train compartment filled with mutilated corpses wallowing in blood and a sackful of women's dismembered breasts. This is the turning point in his life and the thought of imagined atrocity on his sister's bodies completely unhinges him. After this incident his words and actions towards the ayah become increasingly abrasive till the point where he leads this mob of former friends into the Sethi residence, tricks the innocent, trusting Lenny into revealing the ayah's hiding place, carrying her away and handing her over to the lustful mob. Not content, he sells the ayah into prostitution, changes her religion and rechristens her Mumtaz. That is his ultimate revenge on the ayah's body. In appropriating her body he and the mob are assuaging their collective desire for vindictiveness on the new nation.

The novel presents a wide array of women characters under various degrees of male oppression, domestic abuse and sexual assault, the most depraved and humiliating one being the attack on Shanta. There is an unspoken air of patriarchy prevailing upon this society, across the class divide, even the upper echelon of the Sethi household and the eminent doctor attending to Lenny are not insulated against the male impulse to dominate. Sidhwa herself remembers growing up in a controlled environment where she got married at nineteen, bore children, and had to keep her creative energies suppressed before others. During childhood her physician recommended a complete abstention from physical activity on account of her polio and stopped her from attending school. Recalling this narrow prescription for herself she humorously said in a recent interview: 'You see the irony is that the doctors told my parents she's not going to become a professor or a doctor. She's going to get married and have kids maybe. So don't send her to school. But the irony is I did become a professor.'[4] Early on in the novel, the genteel doctor Colonel Bharucha, treating Lenny for her polio gives a similar advice to her mother 'She is doing fine without school, isn't she? She doesn't need to become a professor ... She'll marry – have children – lead a carefree, happy life. No need to strain her with studies and exams'(15).

Lenny's mother, the elegant Mrs Sethi is a picture of grace and altruism. Throughout the novel she comes across as a dignified, devoted wife, an expert caregiver and a sociable, efficient hostess. She along with Lenny's godmother tirelessly help their Hindu friends by supplying them with fuel and provisions during the time of riots. But early on in the novel vignettes of the simmering tension in the Sethi couple's married life is offered through the now innocent now sinister fights that they have over money and through the reticence and sullen non-communicativeness of Mr Sethi. The crisis in their married life deepens with the worsening social and political scenario till it finally erupts into infidelity and physical abuse. Bapsi Sidhwa dextrously presents these microcosmic scenes of domestic violence which reflect the rampage outside. Lenny has a fragmented understanding of this violence when she hears the agonized cries outside her house: 'And closer, and as upsetting, the caged voices of our parents fighting in their bedroom. Mother crying, wheedling. Father's terse, brash, indecipherable sentences. Terrifying thumps. I know they quarrel mostly about money. But there are other things they fight about that are not clear to me. Sometimes I hear Mother say, 'No, Jana; I won't let you go! I won't let you go to her!' Sounds of a scuffle. Father goes anyway. Where does he go in the middle of the night? To whom? Why ... when Mother loves him so? Although Father has never raised his hands to us, one day I surprise Mother at her bath and see the bruises on her body' (212). What makes the context even more horrifying is the fact that the scene is juxtaposed with the rehabilitation of the helpless, destitute women victim of riots who are seeking shelter in the open courtyard.

Sidhwa borrows immensely from biographical experience of watching the plight of these traumatized victims during her childhood and it gets reflected in the novel. In her review of the novel, Laurel Graeber informs us, on Sidhwa's authority that: ' Her home city of Lahore became a border city in Pakistan, and was promptly flooded by hundreds of thousands of war refugees. Many thousands of these were victims of rape and torture. Due to lasting shame and their husbands' damaged pride, many (female)victims were not permitted entry into their homes after being 'recovered'. There was a rehabilitation camp with many of these women adjacent to Sidhwa's house, and she states that she was inexplicably fascinated with these 'fallen women' as they were described to her at that time. She realized from a young age that 'victory is celebrated on a woman's body, vengeance is taken on a woman's body. That's very much the way things are, particularly in my part of the world'.[5] Critic Malmberg attributes Bapsi Sidhwa's social activism and her identification and championing of women's cause to this early sensitization to women's plight.[6] It is reported that the agonized cries of the traumatized rehabilitated victims of partition remained powerfully sketched in Sidhwa's memory and are recalled in a recent article: ' the dread roar of mobs has ceased, terrible sounds of grief and pain erupt at night. They come from the abandoned servant's quarters ... why do these women cry like that? Because they're delivering unwanted babies, I'm told, or reliving hideous memories. Thousands of women were kidnapped.'[7]

Lenny echoes this empathy when she hears the wails coming from the courtyard at night and Hamida explains that they emanate from the 'fallen women': 'My heart is wrung with pity and horror. I want to leap out of my bed and soothe the wailing woman and slay her tormentors'(214). Lenny's second nanny Hamida is Shanta's replacement and is described as one such fallen woman by her Godmother. Hamida, a picture of devastation was abducted by a Sikh mob and her attempts at rehabilitation failed when her own family refused to take her back. She feebly accepts her misfortune as the decree of Fate, but Lenny, a witness to Shanta's abduction has learned a lesson that it is not Fate but Men who are the perpetrators of atrocity on women: 'I have seen Ayah carried away – and it has less to do with fate than with the will of men'(214).

One of the lessons that young Lenny has to learn in life is to successfully withstand such an assault on her body. She admits that she has benefited in life from two teachers – her feisty Godmother who is a true source of strength and action, a reservoir of native wisdom, and her 'adenoidal' Cousin whose groping of her body is something she has to successfully learn to thwart. This precocious cousin who, on the threshold of adolescence, is discovering his sexuality provides the most 'illuminating tutorials' (254) to Lenny on growing up. He is worldly-wise and educates her on what exactly has happened to the ayah and how she has ended up in the brothel. Even though they share a camaraderie and childishly unravel what appears to them mysteries of the adult world, there are disturbing scenes where he makes tentative explorations of Lenny's developing physique. His straying hands are reminiscent of the 'disappearing toe' of the ice-candy-man whenever he is playfully tormenting the voluptuous ayah. Whenever Lenny and the Cousin are alone, at the slightest pretext, he indulges in exhibitionism and this relentlessly carries on till at the end of the novel when Lenny brings his overtures to a close with a resounding slap:

> 'I draw back, slapping his hands till my hands sting, feeling sick and all shrivelled up.
>
> Cousin looks at me, lovesick and sheepish, his spanked fingers quivering guiltily on his thighs.
>
> 'If you ever do that again, I'll break your fingers, knuckle by knuckle,'I say severely' (231).

Even though they are both young children, on the verge of discovering themselves, for Lenny it is a learning experience to counter such attacks in future and put an end to the 'Cousin's carnal cravings' (252).

Deepa Mehta's film *Earth 1947* closely follows the novel, the initial frames depicting the even tenor of life in the city of Lahore on the eve of partition. The camera languorously captures the many outings of the child Lenny and her Ayah through the parks, monuments and alleys of the city to lilting musical strains. Discourse on history and politics takes place in the conversations that Lenny overhears among her ayah's circle of admirers. In the film the wooing of ayah by her two suitors, the masseur and the ice-candy-man, takes precedence over other sub-plots of the novel. Ranna's story which is a terrifying record of carnage perpetrated on the Muslims by the Sikhs in Pir Pindo village is expended with in the film. The harrowing account of Ranna, based on a real life victim whom Sidhwa knew, is offered as a counterpoint to the atrocities committed by the Muslims in the novel in order to balance out the evil on both the sides. But Mehta sacrifices the story, as she does other episodes, to the exigencies of film-making where her focus is more on what comes across as a triangular love story, ice-candy-man's terrible feeling of being slighted, his overnight transformation into a monster after witnessing the gruesome sight in the train and his resolve to wreak similar vengeance on the Ayah. The film is one such relentless movement towards this horrific climax. Justifying the end of the film at the point of Shanta's abduction and about doing away with certain episodes, this is what Bapsi Sidhwa has to say about the film:

'I love *Earth*, the film adaptation of my book *Ice-Candy-Man*. Novels are notoriously difficult to adapt to the screen, and this was perhaps the most difficult of my novels to make into a film .... Deepa had to jettison many characters and subplots to give shape to her cinematic vision of my book and fit it into a two and a half hour film. But the film stands firmly on its own, as a work of art apart from the book. It has its own intrinsic integrity and logic.'[8]

Rarely does a film adaptation do full justice to a work of fiction, no matter how utterly faithful it remains to the original. In this case too adapting only half the novel shows Mehta's constrains in telling a story that deals with a large canvas in around two hours so as to make it cinematically viable. Bapsi Sidhwa herself understands the nuances of film-making which makes selection of events so critical to the film director: 'The differences between a script and a novel are enormous. A script is a working document; because of variables such as locations and the introduction of actors a script is a changeable entity. The only constants are the story and the characters. The plot and dialogues are subject to continuous change. Further the final shape of the film depends to a large extent on camera angles, the imagination of the director and, all important, editing. The director fleshes out the script and moulds it to the cinematic images she has envisioned. I learned this, and much more, during my presence on the sets of Earth.'[9] Thus Mehta selects one of the major themes in the novel – the gradual moral down slide of the ice-candy-man from an amiable, gregarious fun-loving person into a beast which also parallels the deteriorating political and religious affairs of the country and makes his heinous act the culminating point of the film because for her, like for Sidhwa, the woman's body is emblematic of the nation on which male branding is the supreme act of subjugation.

Little Lenny's circumscribed world revolves around three characters: Shanta, Hassan and Dilnawaz. She rejoices in Dilnawaz's tomfoolery, dotes on her ayah and watches Hassan make surreptitious advances towards the ayah. Both of them take turns to woo the inscrutable ayah but it is finally the masseur who gets chosen over the ice-candy-man. Dilnawaz's discovery of the physical intimacy between Shanta and Hassan is coterminous with his shocking discovery of the mutilated bodies in the train. The camera work lingers caressingly over the explicit love making scene between the ayah and the masseur, clandestinely watched over by the lustful ice-candy-man. It is one of the most diabolic scenes in the film where Dilnawaz's expression betrays extreme anger, lust and desire for retribution. Henceforth the film traces the moral degradation of the ice-candy-man who confesses to a self consuming hatred towards the Hindus, much to the horror of his audience, makes Shanta and Lenny witness the riotous killings on the streets of Lahore, brutally murders the masseur and finally abducts and appropriates Shanta for himself.

For Deepa Mehta, like Sidhwa, the personal tragedies where relationships are torn asunder are a microcosm of the cataclysmic severing of political relations on the national level. But as a successful Indo-Canadian filmmaker, Deepa Mehta's film-making is governed by various other exigencies as she explains in an interview: 'Film is a powerful medium and my hope is that Earth will produce a dialogue and force people to think more deeply about the cost of such divisions … . I wanted to tell this really large story from the standpoint of an intimate group of friends from different ethnic groups and trace out the process of partition through them.'[10] Mehta's agenda of film making becomes a little bigger because even as she is directing a film on Indian partition she is abrogating to herself the task of clearing some popular western misconceptions about India:

> I have my own theory about why there has been such a silence about this tragedy by western filmmakers, and it is just a theory. I think it is bound up with a number of attitudes that prevail in the western countries about India .... There is firstly the spiritual India – a place where you go and find nirvana. Secondly, there is the conception that India is entirely poverty stricken, with a permanent kind of begging bowl attitude. There is the India of Maharajas, princes and queens, and the India that comes from nostalgia for the Raj. And there is always the prevailing pressure that people should feel superior to some other place: look how bad India is with all the beggars, aren't we lucky to be better off. It is uncomfortable and difficult for some filmmakers to produce works that destroy these perceptions. India brings specifically fixed images in many western minds, and the minute you start de-exoticizing that, you have your deal with Indians as real people, and there is a pressure not to do that .... Finally, there are many dark political questions about partition that the British establishment doesn't want brought to light. When you know the real history of partition and the responsibility that lands in the laps of the British, obviously you understand why it is a very uncomfortable subject for them.[11]

In this interview Mehta's various ideas about making a film on the sensitive issue of partition come to light which get reflected in the film. Perhaps that is why she does not carry the novel's story further – Shanta's ignominous marriage to the ice-candy-man, his turning into a dotard lover and finally Shanta's rescue and rehabilitation in India. She chooses to end her film at the point where the most brutal attack gets carried out on Shanta's body and the film's narrative moves inexorably towards this end.

Notes

1. Laurel Graeber quotes Bapsi Sidhwa in 'The Seeds of Partition', review of *Cracking India, New York Times Book Review*, 6 October 1991.
2. Bapsi Sidhwa's interview in *The Hindustan Times*, 19 May 2000.

3. Bapsi Sidhwa, *Ice-Candy-Man*, London: Penguin Books, 1988, p. 29. Subsequent references to the text will be cited in the body of the paper.
4. *Dawn Books and Authors*, Dawn.com. Azhar Jaffri, 15 April 2013.
5. Graeber quotes Sidhwa, op. cit.
6. 'It appears as if realizations such as this inspired Sidhwa's later activism for the cause of women's rights', Malmberg. http://voices.cla.umn.edu/newsite/authors/SIDHWAbapsi.htm.
7. Bapsi Sidhwa, 'New Neighbours', *Time*, 11 August 1997.
8. Bapsi Sidhwa's interview in *The Hindustan Times*, 19 May 2000.
9. Ibid.
10. Deepa Mehta in an interview with Richard Phillips on World Socialist Website, 6 August 1999. http://www.wsws.org/en/search.html.
11. Ibid.

9

Feminist Mythology and 'Cultural Capital' in Nabaneeta Dev Sen and Louky Bersianik

Mohar Daschaudhuri

Louky Bersianik, whose name by birth was Lucile Durand, admitted in an interview, that she owed her sound education to her mother, who insisted on admitting all her daughters in a Convent which, at her time, was the only means to a good education in Quebec, Canada. In a predominantly Catholic Montreal, she grew up in a deeply religious household, and went to a school administered by the devout nuns. That may partly explain why at college, Bersianik chose to work upon the incomplete biography of Jesus by Bernanos, which made her delve into Christian theology. This early inculcation of religion, however, had an unexpected effect on her, as she mentions, 'quite strangely, this research took me away from religious faith. He [Jesus] helped me unfold myself ...' (Dupré, 1991: 12). 'Bersianik's training and degrees in French, the classical literatures, music, and linguistics have clearly contributed to her keen sense of the past ... she is both a virulent desecrator of the old patriarchal world she has inherited and a jubilant visionary of an emerging culture au feminine', remarks Karen Gould (Gould, 1990: 151). *Le Pique-nique sur l'Acropole,* the francophone novel which will be studied here, as its author claims, 'is a text centred upon Philosophy and Psychoanalysis .... The woman narrator is Ancyl, not myself .... This book is more of theory-fiction' (Dupré, 1991: 13).

Bengali poet, writer and academician Nabaneeta Dev Sen also admits to be greatly influenced by her mother, Radharani Devi, a self-educated poet and writer. The all women household described in the second part of the book which will be the subject of this study, *Sita Theke Shuru* (*Beginning from Sita*), is almost autobiographical, she confesses in an interview. Sen admits that she enjoyed her single motherhood: 'Since my divorce [with Amartya Sen] in 1975, after sixteen years of marriage, I have headed an all-woman household. My mother, who passed away in 1989, was a widow, I am a divorcee and my two daughters were two single women ... I enjoyed my motherhood ...' (http://www.calcuttaweb.com). As the author explains, the stories in the second part of the book, 'Matriarchy', are not just any humorous family saga, but a conscious effort to show that amongst women, they can lead 'a healthy happy life', and that, 'a working Bengali single mother, need not be necessarily angry and stressed out'.

The two novels chosen for this study were written in the 1990's, though situated in two different continents. Bersianik published *L'Euguélionne* in 1976, *Le Pique-nique sur l'Acropole* in 1979 and *Maternative* in 1980, the last work being the shortest of all. Dev Sen who completed her Ph.D. in the United States grew up in a similar academic environment as Bersianik when the second wave of feminist movements were changing the norms of family in the West while in India it was the period of social development after independence which incorporated both men and women who had fought together in the freedom movement. *Sita Theke Shuru* published in 1996 bears the trace of her deep roots in the post-structuralist French feminist tradition.

While *Le Pique-Nique sur l'Acropole*, reads more as a treatise on feminism: redefining the parameters of history and ideology, as if the ancient mothers of civilization have come together to reconstitute collective memory of women, in a parody of the famous *Banquet* of Plato, *Sita Theke Shuru* is a collection of tales centring upon historical, mythological as well as modern women. However, an undercurrent of feminist thought, solidarity, assertion of individuality runs through the warp and woof of these apparently humorous and cynical portrayals. The common thread linking up the two novels is an effort to re-write patriarchal myths from a woman's view-point. There has been a great hole, an unexplained silence about the history and mythology as experienced by women, 'trou de mémoire' or 'a hole in the memory', as says Ancyl in the first chapter of the *Pique-nique*, and the two writers present alternative readings of classical texts sometimes exposing the gaps, sometimes presenting other possible readings of mythology. Their language based on folk songs (as in the case of Dev Sen) or on gossip, chants the praise of life, the woman's body which can create and transform the world by touch.

From the third concerto of *Le Pique-nique*, (chapters are called concertos as they are the songs composed in harmony by the women narrators in unison) the women members who belong to various continents, age-group, classes, gather and the picnic begins. Xanthippe, the wife of Socrates, plays the lead, and retells the myths of Clytemnestra and Iphigenia, mother and daughter separated by the ambitious and selfish motive of their father Agamemnon, remembered as a great King in Greek history. Xanthippe, young and neglected wife of the great philosopher Socrates, along with Ancyl, Aphelia and five other women gather for a picnic near the Acropolis and recount their experiences of sexuality. As opposed to the grand Banquet of Socrates where famous theologians of ancient Greece had gathered to understand and discuss at great length the finer intellectual questions concerning life and death, knowledge, God and nature, the women speak in simple language, with humour and irony about lived experiences. The topic chosen is 'sexuality'. Ancyl describes the process of body-writing, inhaling air and churning creation out from the very pores of female body. She recounts farces: ironic interpretations of mythological stories around women which are interpreted by her in two, three or four different ways (Bersianik, 1992: 40–41). While they discuss, a young girl Avertine transgresses the written instruction on the statues of the Caryatides, touches them and brings them to life. Symbolically it implicates the reawakening of ancient mothers, the originators of History by the loving touch of a woman.

Similarly, in *Sita Theke Shuru*, Dev Sen recounts the story of women from ancient to present times. The book is divided in three parts: (a) *Pouraniki*: re-telling of the story of the *Puranas*, (b) Matriarchy: recounting personal story of the mothers: mother of the author, author as mother and (c) *Adhuniki*: the story of modern women. 'Pouraniki' demystifies the story of Lord Rama, and puts forth the reflections of Sita on her exile, demonstrates her clarity of purpose, her determination to bring up her twin sons alone in the hermitage of lord Valmiki, her love of nature which obeys her and of a people who have put her chastity to test. It portrays the maturity of Amba who by her force of love, and sexuality coerces the promise of union with Bhishma, in death if not in life. The second part 'Matriarchy' is the writer's autobiography, as the daughter of a voracious reader and scholar Radharani Devi and mother of two intelligent, witty, and loving daughters, the friendship and love that binds them, the humour in their everyday life. The third part, 'Adhuniki' consists of stories woven around the live experiences of women in modern times. A few common strands link the three otherwise varied stories. Whether in the historical, or in the personal and constructed fiction, we see women protagonists questioning and redefining womanhood, cultural practices and social values.

Pierre Bourdieu, French sociologist proposes the theory of cultural capital. Similar to economic capital, cultural capital is a baggage of knowledge, art, crafts, rites and rituals which get embedded in the human mind through the process of socialization and fashions our worldview, cultural capital seeps deeply into our subconscious mind and moulds our personality, our way of thinking, our associations and preferences (Bourdieu, 1998: 24). According to Pierre Bourdieu writing in the 20th century, man has developed a culture of domination by incorporating symbols of domination in the prevalent culture. 'Cultural capital' which is similar to economic capital, penetrates and influences all our systems of education, religion, language, etc. In his book *La Domination Masculine*, he elaborates on how the relationship of domination and subordination penetrates our ways of thinking, speaking, reacting and our notion of the world at large. Thus particular seasons, certain natural phenomena, parts of the human body, certain ways of walking, naming, special markers in the language, they all display this relationship of domination and subordination where the dominated or the inferior part is associated with the feminine and the dominant or the superior is identified with the masculine (ibid.: 16). The alienation of the woman is therefore complete and becomes unalterable because the very tools with which she must think and perceive of herself are biased against femininity. All history, all accounts of religion, social thought and philosophy reflect woman as 'the other' even while speaking for them.

Masculine domination may be defined as, 'that which impels us to obey an order to which we feel morally bound ... the apparently objective dispositions which makes this obedience possible are the very effects of these dispositions'[1] (Champagne et al., 2004: 224–225).

In this article I propose to explore how mythology which can be considered as a 'cultural capital', propagating a male-centric view of human values, of nature and culture, has been questioned and re-interpreted by the two women writers. Patriarchal myths inculcate in the subject, a fear of the unalterable Law of the Father. They construct a 'cultural capital', which has these three characteristics:

- is symbolized as the Phallus and is supposed to be the origin of life and creation,
- functions through two binary categories of good/evil, man/woman, spirit and body,
- institutionalizes knowledge through textual writing proceeding from a central subject which relies predominantly on visual experiences and linear reasoning.

Bersianik appears to be engaged consciously in the act of liberating women from the burden of phallocentric mythology. She states:

> I would like to return to the source of patriarchy. Reopen the process of Orestes...We are not conscious that reality starts from mythologies. If we do not understand this there are a lot of things we cannot grasp. We must absolutely come out of the mental categories which have emerged from the patriarchal system and all our reasoning operate from out of patriarchy from within it.[2] (*Voix et Images*, Vol. 49, 17)

Dev Sen recounts the story of Sita, Amba, Shakuntala as it might have been, from the subjective viewpoint of the women. Unlike Bersianik who reconstructs another story, Dev Sen retains the principal axes of the Pouranic tales, leading the reader to only fill up the unspoken gaps in the story. However, both writers clearly delineate an alternative cultural capital, at the level of ideology, narrative and style. The scope of this paper being limited, the main focus will be on the act of re-writing or re-interpretation of ancient texts by the two women writers as they define the changes in the 'cultural capital' associated with God and creation in these three aspects.

Primarily both Bersianik and Dev Sen re-interpret phallocentric mythology with women protagonists who are in control of their lives and assert their will and identity against a patriarchal historical and philosophical tradition. Secondarily, binary values of good/evil, spirit/body, writing/speech, are interrogated and the unipolar value system de-constructed in order to embrace a vision of life that encourages multiplicity and multiple ways of sensing and experiencing. Finally I shall try to demonstrate the techniques of style by which the two writers, aware of the fact that language itself is a trap, appropriate it and palliate its dissymmetry to create the discourse of 'difference'/woman – an oral discourse, fluid, corporeal, multiple, playful, which Suzanne Lamy defines as 'rooted in the community of women. The themes: the body, experiences and gestures which are specifically female' (Lamy, 1979: 56).

Phallogocentrism and Creation

Freudian theory establishes the priority of the phallus, defining the female in reference to the male, as she 'who is not', and who must be content with substitutes, (clitoris, breasts, child), expression of her envy of the penis. Bersianik's protagonist Euguélionne makes cynical subversions of Freud's theory, 'No liberation outside of the Phallus'[3] (Bersianik, 1976: 213). Oedipus' murder of his father and subsequent punishable act of incest are situated at the base of Freudian psycho-analysis. They consist of a trickery that hides the female – in particular, the mother. Luce Irigaray questions this myth, 'when in *Totem and Taboo* Freud theorizes about the murder of the father, the founder of the primitive horde, he omits a more archaic murder, that is of the woman-mother called for by the institution of a certain order in society … . The father forbids any bodily contact with the mother.' In *Le Pique-nique,* the women in chorus take up the story of the repeated murder of the daughters. The murder of Iphigenia recurs as a leitmotif, 'Father! Father!' ('Père! Père!'), cries Iphigenia (Bersianik, 1992: 90–101). It is followed by the repeated murder of women all over the world, '… those six lakh women …' (ibid.: 101). They weep and wail, the women and children such as the little Aditzetu (a pun on the word, 'Ah! disais-tu!' which, in French means, Oh!-you said so!). She is the nine-year-old mutilated African girl who interrogates thus, 'Does Aga love me? No'. The 'Non' in French, is a homonym of the word 'name' (nom). Thus the writer subverts the name (nom) with the no (non) of the Father. Thus Bersianik, as Maroussia Hajdoukowski-Ahmad observes – 'knots a dialogical solidarity, both diachronic and synchronic, between the daughter/victims, from one era to the next, from one continent to the other, and from one book to another'. (Gilbert Lewis, 1985: 209).

Luce Irigaray, in *Sexes and Genealogies*, states that man can exist because he can define his finitude by the ideal of God or the 'infinitude' in the masculine gender. God represents an ideal which man may imitate. In order to become, it is necessary to have a gender or an essence. Patriarchal mythology provides this essence of masculinity, which I postulate as the 'symbolic capital', which creates a certain *habitus*, a way of thinking, acting, which gives man the authority to create as the son of God. On the contrary, says Irigaray, the woman lacks a horizon, and therefore she cannot attain her plenitude[4] (Irigaray, 1987: 73).

Bersianik's *Le Pique-Nique sur L'Acropole*, like Mary Daly's book, [*Gyn/ecology*], seems to concern itself with '... mind/spirit/body pollution inflicted through patriarchal myth and language at all levels' (Daly, 1976, 9). In *Le Pique-nique* the Banquet of Socrates represents a gathering of learned men with power to create laws, texts, and a body of knowledge which will act as a 'cultural capital' to the intelligentsia. The author questions this idea of authority which the man as the Son of God, or the possessor of the Phallus, takes as his birthright. As opposed to the Banquet, the women gather informally and as in contrast to the intellectual exposition based on a false cultural capital of phallogocentrism, love expressed by the desire of the body, felt through sensual experiences become the basis of creation – of truth and life. Bersianik and Dev Sen, in their anachronistic texts, traverse time, denouncing repeatedly the referential phallic system from which monolithism has obscured the female: mythically (Oedipus, Agamemnon, Zeus, Rama, Indra); philosophically (Plato, Thomas Aquinas, Marx, Manusmriti); psychoanalytically (Freud, Lacan); religiously (Hinduism, Judeo-Christian religions). As Xanthippe proclaims, '... upon each Inconscience begotten from the uterus, this is engraved: the mother's body, the only memorable and fundamental signifier for every living-being-in-the-world when it is about to complete its journey to the centre of the earth, when it resurfaces, after a long immersion from beneath *Twenty Thousand Leagues Under the Sea*'[5] (Bersianik, 1992: 55).

Xanthippe asks her friends, Ancyl and Aphélie, to touch her: 'Touch me and you shall give me birth ... I shall be re-born, who has realised everything' (ibid.: 56).

On a similar vein, Lord Rama, the re-incarnation of the great Hindu deity of creation, has been portrayed as a selfish, ambitious, weak and indecisive person by Nabaneeta Dev Sen in *Sita Theke Shuru*. Even Rishi Valmiki, the creator of the epic and thus, like Socrates, the man with the power to create the world, trembles in fear before Sita. For instance, when Sita escapes from Lanka on the back of Hanumana, Valmiki is scandalized as the war between Ravana and Rama is essential to defeat Evil and restore Truth. He admonishes her in no polite terms; 'Did you not hesitate to embrace another man, to cling by his body, it would entail sin, or did your stay with the monster Ravana ...' before he may complete his crude thoughts, Sita interrupts his crude thoughts; 'Control your tongue, O respected Muni! He is not a human being. Since childhood I rode on the horse, after marriage I have mounted on elephants, that was not a sin! If today I flew on the back of Hanuman, who is like my son, who addresses me as Janani, the mother, how could you call it sin! O prejudiced mind!' (Dev Sen, 1996, 20–21). Sita's power over all of nature and her ability to revive the dead Rama and his brothers as Luv Kusha massacre the royal army is an act of love and adoration. She derives her power not from God, but from mother Earth, who has given her birth, who sustains her through the tests of fire and of ignominy. She too revives them 'by the touch of Sati' or chastity. Here, chastity does not imply faithfulness towards one's husband but being true to one's *dharma*, or intrinsic nature.

Love brings back the Caryatides, the ancient mothers of creation, who had been frozen in time, (like the collective memory of women) and therefore had to act as blind agents of patriarchal laws, such as the goddess Athena, the warrior goddess, 'it is she the War-goddess and not any God, she is the symbol of the Greek civilization and yet she proclaims that she has no mother to whom she owes her birth as she has emerged out of the head of Zeus as Eve of Adam's breast .... Phallus for Uterus. Avertine approaches the porticos crying out: 'Caryatides ! Wake up.' (... c'est elle la déesse guerrière et non pas un dieu, qui est le symbole de la civilisation grecque ... elle proclame qu'elle n'a pas de mère à qui elle doive la vie puisqu'elle est sortie de la tête de Zeus comme Eve de la côte d'Adam ... le Phallus pour l'Utérus. Avertine s'avance vers le portique en criant: 'Caryatides, éveillez vous!')' (Bersianik, 1992: 206).

Love can transform death to life, as in the case of the Caryatides, so in the case of Bhishma. Unshakable in his pledge to never marry, he is moved by the love and desire of Amba. For a moment he loses his self-control. Yet he cannot break his promise not to marry but instead assures her that he shall give in to her, in death if not in life. Amba likewise does not hesitate to end her life in order to be reborn as Drupada's son, Draupadeya, whom the stern Bhisma embraces before he dies in the moonlit battlefield of Kurukshetra (Dev Sen, 1996: 59–71).

Multiciplicity in Subject Positions – Multiple Interpretations of Mythology

As Joseph Campbell emphasizes, mythological symbols oriented towards the patriarchy influence the mental structures of our thought process much more profoundly than coercive laws or social dictats: 'Mythological symbols touch and exhilarate centres of life beyond the reach of vocabularies of reason and coercion' (Campbell, 2001: 4). The Phallocentric mythologies proceed by dividing existence into binary oppositions, where the values attached to the masculine occupy a superior place than those that are attached to the feminine other.

Pierre Bourdieu in his study of the Kabyle society conducts an empirical study on how most social structures in patriarchal societies are based upon binary divisions of space and time, 'The social order functions like an immense machine which upholds and sustains the masculine domination and structures the vision of time and space into two categories, the superior with the masculine and the inferior with the feminine' (Bourdieu, 1998: 16). Simone de Beauvoir in her *The Second Sex* says, 'The terms masculine and feminine are used symmetrically only as a matter of form, as on legal papers. In actuality the relation of the two sexes is not quite like that of two electrical poles, for man represents both the positive and the neutral, as is indicated by the common use of man to designate human beings in general, whereas woman represents only the negative, defined by limiting criteria, without reciprocity' (Beauvoir, 1953: 115). She adds to this stating, 'Thus humanity is male and man defines woman not in herself but as relative to him; she is not regarded as an autonomous being … . She is defined and differentiated with reference to man and not he with reference to her; she is the incidental, the inessential as opposed to the essential. He is the subject, he is the Absolute, she is the Other' (Moi, 1987: 212).

In order to undo the binary oppositions of good/evil, life/death, both Dev Sen and Bersianik, intermingle in their texts, a patriarchal version of mythology along with all other possible interpretations thereby destabilizing the relationship of the subject with space and time, with the values of right and wrong. For example, the sacrifice of Iphigenia to the Gods is associated in Greek mythology with selflessness of Agamemnon, his ability to efface his family ties for the good of the nation. The murder of Agamemnon by Clytemnestra becomes an act of adultery and grave sin. In the version of Xanthippe, Agamemnon murders his daughter and inhumanly distributes her flesh to be consumed by the Oracle. It demonstrates the ruthlessness of the Phallic order, the cruelty which a mother could never forgive, and explains the revenge of Clytemnestra as punishing an act of pre-meditated infanticide, which only a mother's love could avenge' (Bersianik, 1992: 99).

Similarly, Lord Rama's decision to follow his people's wish and send Sita in exile even after her test of walking unscathed through fire, is generally eulogized as an act of selflessness, courage and love for the nation. Not only Sita, but Laksmana, Bharat, Kaushalya, and even Valmiki seem to regard Rama's decision painfully. Dev Sen portrays him as a king without authority, without conscience, blinded by his ambition to be remembered by posterity. In the story 'Sita enters the underworld', Rama revived by Sita, is grateful to her but is still unwilling to take her back to Ayodhya for fear that his people may not accept her. He appears cowardly when he confesses that he would rather commit suicide. Similarly in the story entitled, 'Rajakumari Kamaballi' Rama enamoured by the illusive charm of Surpanakha, he is almost ready to marry her, he does not reveal his married status.

It would be unjust however to presume that these writers have replaced the phallocentric mythology with a feminine principle. In Dev Sen as in Bersianik, the new interpretations of mythology do not claim to be unique or truer than previous versions of the story. In fact each speaker in *Le Pique-nique*, presents us three or four versions of the story at the same time. For example, in the story of the sacrifice of Iphigenia, Bersianik first gives us the version of the *Iliad* (Bersianik, 1992: 64). Then in the myth itself a small girl appears at the place of Iphigenia who resembles her exactly but all of a sudden we have moved from the time of mythology to real journalism, she says: 'I am Adizetou, a small girl from Africa who has undergone clitoridectomy at the age of seven'(137). In her turn at the story telling session of the pick-nick, she recounts how a big cat, her friend always tells her to run away from gathering of old men and women, to beware of mats unfolding behind her, to not let women sit on her. Pain will be a part of all her awakened moments, integral to life. She may never know pleasure, sexually and conceptually. As Suzanne Lamy remarks, 'Feminist spirituality proclaims wholeness, healing, love and spirited power not as hierarchical, as power over, but as power for, as enabling power. Thus Bersianik's texts end in reunion, in sisterly equality, whereas in Dev Sen, mother, daughter, friend, are united in pain and laughter, and refuse to live in the fear of the law of the father.

Mythology is rendered real and living by juxtaposing the ancient myths with modern practices, translated into lived experiences. If myths recount the story of our ancestors, they are also a part of our subconscious, and reproduce its structures and processes in individual and collective life.

Translinearity and Dialogism

Concurring with many contemporary feminist linguists such as Julia Kristeva and Helene Cixous, Bersianik has argued that men have been the esteemed 'proprietors of language' and have therefore defined, ordered, and classified language for their own purpose invested it with their own interests (Gould, 1990: 154). Dev Sen's book mocks at traditional language with irony, humour and passion. Bersianik's style is replete with sarcasm and satirical humour. Thus they set the stage for a veritable human comedy of negativity viewed through feminist eyes. Bersianik parodies the Bible's triple emphasis on parable, gospel and sermon in *Euguelionne*, and in *Le pique-nique*, her wrath turns upon the Platonic philosophy that validates the reproduction of Self (the Cave Myth). Dev Sen's stories provide alternative versions of the Pouranic tales. As Aarti Kaul Dhar, remarks, 'Each story depicts a picture where the plot can turn any which way. Though in the epics the women characters as Ahilya, Shurpanakha, Tarka and Seeta are eternal sufferers (as if born to suffer) these modern sets of tales paint a different picture altogether with newer and fresher perspectives examining and analysing characters and the situations they are placed in. In *Sita Theke Shuru* the modern woman traces the Indian woman's journey from Seeta to herself, from the Pouranic times to the modern threshold' (Kaul Dhar, 2010).

Thus intermingling what we may call experiences in the memory of a people with the individual's lived experiences, Bersianik's texts abound in references, from Greek mythology to current journalism. *Le Pique-nique* can hardly be considered as a novel, it has footnotes and a bibliography, showing the consciously constructed text. In fact Bersianik admits that she wanted to create pure poetry (Dupre, 1991: 14) and therefore she works on the visibility of the words rather than their legibility. As in the text of Iphigenia (first reading the text of the Iliad, then the version of Aeschylus, and later a version by the author) is a kind of weaving of text-textile, but not as in palimpsest, superimposed one upon the other. Bersianik says it is like the spider's web: by following one line at once the lines above and the lines below are visible. Actually one can pin point at which one comes first and which one follows: 'one can see both the past and the future of the text .... My writing becomes the spider's house. My text is a house' (Bersianik, *Voix et Images*, Vol. 59, 15).

The text of *Le Pique-nique* is itself a treatise on new ways of writing or body-writing, 'c'est enjamber des murs, des morts, des mers, des siècles', (Bersianik, 1992: 86). It is a song, a chant, as she calls her chapters. Each chapter begins with an inscription on the stone: implying the scriptures written by patriarchal texts in white and black. The song, on the contrary, mingles syntaxes, registers, plays on onomatopoeia, forms neologisms, uses irony, allusions, metaphors, and is full of suggestive silence. For ex: soit le corps-producteur-traceur-tracteur-tourneur-de-mots, soit le corps-producteur-lecteur-becheur-bequeteur de mots (ibid.: 36). The word play on producer-tracer-tracker (tracteur)-churner of words, used for describing the female body, becomes an alliterated chant of weaving words. For Bersianik a book is like a glass house, one can see through, and the invisible is rendered visible, the wall intermingle, 'Un livre est-il un château de verre? Il le serait si on arrivait à y voir au travers. Et que l'invisible soit rendu visible. Et que ce qu'il y a hors les murs traverse les murs et soit devant' (39). It is a malleable, suggestive, changing text, a house which has no walls, or transparent ones, from which the elements of life may flow, where the undercurrents of our subconscious mind may surface on the waters of the oscillating script.

In *Sita Theke Shuru*, the three sections, 'Pouraniki', 'Matriarchy' and 'Adhuniki' clearly interlink the three aspects of knowledge: collective memory as portrayed in mythology, personal experience of the author, and interpretations of lives of women around her, as fiction-writing. Though varied in their style and theme, stories in all the three sections continuously play and create new language structures and a narration which proceeds by interconnections. It also suggests: are the concerns and problems of Sita, Amba, Shakuntala, whose chastity is continuously put to test, who must forego their own pleasures for the greater social order, are they not the same as those of present day women? That though we read of jealousies and hatred among women, real bonds of friendship too may exist between mother, daughter, sisters, as Shalbhya and Shakuntala, both daughters of Meneka come to rescue each other from the treachery of Dyushyanta. Mythological time and space are embedded in our everyday life and the structure of the books emphasizes on the simultaneous reading of the two spaces – textual and conceptual space. Irony and humour play their part in questioning. However here I shall talk of one procedure of personalizing the text, which can be observed in both the writings of Bersianik and Dev Sen.

Emile Benveniste in his article 'Man in Language' (Benveniste, 1966: 230–255) talks about two principal modes of pronouns, and tenses. The first and the second person imply a direct rapport between the speaker and the listener, implies the presence of both at the time and space of discourse. Whereas the third person is impersonal, it is therefore used in historical and mythological texts in order to create a sense of universality and detachment of the authorial voice from the narration. Similarly here the tense used in French is simple past. However in the mythology personalized as in the two works in question, the tense is historical past. In Dev Sen there is also a constant shift between 'sadhu bhasha', or the literary formal language and 'chalitbhasha', the language of familiarity. The language mixes up chaste Bengali with English vocabulary, genres and dialects. Serious philosophical statement with ironic turn of phrases. When Rishi Valmiki, or the authorial voice speaks it is in chaste Bangla. The character of Sita and Rama have been contemporized by giving them modern day mentality, practicality and not presented as an ideal. Common sense and not noble ideology is the guiding principle behind their action.

Conclusion

Dev Sen and Bersianik never lose sight of the past and remind us constantly of the lies that tradition has repeatedly told women. Both Dev Sen and Bersianik challenge the idea of a centre/God/which may create binary values. To them, values are created and they change in time, context, in the play of life. Love does not function to a specific purpose. Experience and creation are simultaneous processes. By their narrative style, these authors destabilize the textual linearity of patriarchal mythology by using humour, irony, subversions, and other stylistic tools. Narration proceeds through multi-centred, multi-layered texts and inter-texts enforcing conscious participation of the reader.

Women's sexuality, pleasure and friendship, spirituality and their confrontation with patriarchal values are some of the common themes of the two texts. Real and imagined worlds intermingle. The culture which gives us identity, structures our thought, has left its indelible traces on our memory; is it possible to recreate it? Who defines the 'other' and who has the legitimacy to speak for it? These are a few challenges and debates of post-modernism.

Distinction between mythology, reality and history become more and more undefined. A close look at the two texts may shed some light on this. Though the two novels destabilise the existing symbolic patterns, question the phallocentrism of mythology through a trans-linear vision and a multi layered writing, there remain some distinct points of divergence in the vision and in the treatment of mythology by the two women writers. For example, Dev Sen retains the traditional values and sensitivity attributed to women characters in Hindu mythology. Even in exile, Sita continues to adore Lord Rama and shows him due respect (we are touched by the love she feels while she gazes at the unconscious Rama after Luv and Kush make him unconscious at the battlefield). Her Sita may refuse to obey the whims of husband Rama, but she cannot belie her *dharma*. She finally returns to Ayodhya. Dev Sen also recognises Sita's godliness as well as her humanity, bestowing her, at the same time, with practical common sense which makes her a dutiful yet a questioning wife.

Unlike in the West, not all writers and feminists in India see the rejection of patriarchal culture as a solution to the women's question. There is another great difference between feminism in India and in the West. Madhu Kishwar underlines: 'Western feminism is an offshoot of individualism and liberalism. Individualism is an ideology which posits that the rights of the individual are the foundations of all human rights. They consider each individual ultimately responsible primarily to herself or himself' (Kishwar, 2004: 31). Sita returns not to satisfy herself, but because her sense of duty to her society impels her to it. Thus most stories in Dev Sen's collection end with reconciliation, harmony even at the cost of loss of individuality, while in Bersianik women form an alternative order, though the order may not be women-centric, the salvation lies in the touch of love between and amongst women. However, in the final count, it must be remembered that the present study is an Indian reading of two very subjective texts, in the light of a limited theory. There may be as many readings of the text and the meta-text as there are subjects, critics and interpreters of meaning. Dev Sen and Bersianik unveil the body of women and her speech, long contorted by text, ideology, history. They re-incarnate and re-weave the lives of women past, depositories of another 'cultural capital', legitimizing woman's speech, her multiple forms of perception and creation.

Notes

1. Champagne Patrick et Olivier Christin, *Mouvements d'une pensée Pierre Bourdieu* (Paris, Bordas, 2004), p. 224–225.
2. Je veux retourner aux sources du patriarcat. Ré ouvrir le procès d'Oreste .... On n'est pas conscient que la réalité part des mythologies. Si on ne comprend pas cela, il y a beaucoup de choses qu'on ne saisit pas. Il faut absolument sortir des catégories mentales issues du patriarcat et dans lesquelles se meuvent tous nos raisonnements. The English translation is by the author of the article.
3. Hors du Phallus, point de salut ...'. L'individu qui naît sans phallus est handicapé ... [I] l devra construire sa vie autour d'un manque.
4. L'homme peut exister parce que Dieu l'aide à définir son genre, à se situer comme fini par rapport à l'infini...Pour poser un genre, il faut un Dieu: caution de l'infini. [...] Pour devenir il est nécessaire d'avoir un genre ou une essence (dès lors sexuée) comme horizon. Sinon, le devenir reste partiel et assujetti .... Devenir signifie accomplir la plénitude de ce que nous pouvons être. The original version is in French.
5. Voilà ce qui s'est d'abord gravé dans chaque inconscient issu d'un utérus: le Corps maternel, seul mémorable et signifiant fondamental pour tout être-au-monde quand il arrive au bout de son voyage au *centre de la terre*, quand il refait surface après une longue immersion *vingt mille lieues sous les mers*. The original French version has been translated into English within the text by the author of the article.

References

Beauvoir, Simone de (1953), *The Second Sex* (translated and edited by H.M. Parshley), Knopf, New York.

Benveniste, Emile (1996), *Problèmes de linguistique générale-1*, Gallimard, Paris.

Bersianik, Louky (1976), *L'Euguélionne*, La Presse, Montreal.

Bersianik, Louky (1980), *Maternative. Les Pré-Ancyl*, VLB Editeur, Montreal.

Bersianik, Louky (1992), *Le Pique Nique Sur L'Acropole*, l'Hexagone Typo, Montreal.

Bourdieu, Pierre (1998), *La Domination Masculine*, Seuil, Paris.

Campbell, Joseph (2001), *Creative Mythology*, Souvenir Press, London.

Champagne Patrick et Olivier Christin (2004), *Mouvements d'une pensée Pierre Bourdieu*, Paris, Bordas.

Chaudhuri, Maitrayee (Ed.) (2004), *Feminism in India*, Kali for Women, New Delhi.

Daly, Mary (1976), *Gyn/ecology*, Beacon Press, New York.

Dev Sen, Nabaneeta (1996), *Sita Theke Shuru*, Ananda Publishers, Kolkata.

Gilbert Lewis, Paula (ed.) (1985), *Traditionalism, Nationalism and Feminism*, Women Writers of Quebec, Greenwood Press, Connecticut, London.

Gould, Karen (1990), *Writing in the Feminine, Feminism and Experimental Writing in Quebec*, Southern University Illinois Press, Carbondale and Edwardsville.

Irigaray, Luce (1987), *Sexes et parentés* (trans. As *Sexes and Genealogies*), Editions de Minuit, Paris.

Lamy, Suzanne (1979), *D'elles*, L'Hexagone, Montreal.

Moi, Toril (1987), *French Feminist Thought*, Blackwell, Oxford.

Articles

Dupré, Louise (Autumn 1991), 'Le tremblement de la conscience, Entretien avec Louky Bersianik', *Voix et Images : Littérature Québécoise*, Vol XVII, No. 1, pp. 11–21.

Gervais, André (Autumn 1991), 'D'un nom et d'une parenthèse', *Voix et Images: Littérature Québécoise*, Autumn 1991, Vol XVII, No. 1, pp. 48–63.

Gould, Karen (Autumn 1991), 'Vers une maternité qui se crée: l'œuvre de LoukyBersianik', *Voix et Images: Littérature Québécoise*, Vol XVII, No. 1, pp. 35–47.

Hajdoukowski-Ahmad, Maroussia (1985), 'Louky Bersianik: Feminist Dialogisms', in Paula Gilbert Lewis Ed. *Traditionalism, Nationalism and Feminism*, Women Writers of Quebec, Greenwood Press, Connecticut, London, pp. 205–225.

Kaul Dhar, Aarttee, http://kriticulture.blogspot.in/2010/02/new-age-avatars. Accessed on 12/06/2013.

Kishwar, Madhu (2004), 'A horror of isms, why I do not call myself a feminist', in Maitrayee Chaudhuri (ed.) *Feminism in India*, Kali for Women, New Delhi, pp. 26–51.

Potvin, Claudine (Autumn 1991), 'Féminisme et postmodernisme: la main tranchante du symbole', Voix et Images: Littérature Québécoise, Vol XVII, No 1, pp. 66–74.

Smart, Patricia (Autumn 1991), 'Rendre visible l'invisible: l'univers imaginaire de Louky Bersianik', *Voix et Images: Littérature Québécoise*, Vol XVII, No. 1, pp. 22–34.

Web References

http://kriticulture.blogspot.in/2010/02/new-age-avatars-seeta-up-close-by.html. Accessed on 12 June 2013.

http://timesofindia.indiatimes.com/home/sunday-toi/True-feminism-does-not-mean-raising-slogans/articleshow/37758546.cms. Accessed on 12 June 2013.

http://www.calcuttaweb.com/bangla/nabanita1.shtml. Accessed on 12 June 2013.

10

Gender and Caste Politics in Shauna Singh Baldwin's *We Are So Different Now*

Soham Pain

While sharing her diasporic experience with the readers, Vasudha Dalmia says: 'On the one hand, I think we all agreed that knowledge was a continuum which refused to be compartmentalized. What was old, clearly reached into the present and what was new stretched into the past. There was no real cut-off point between classical and modern, between East and West. On the other hand, as I saw it, it had to be acknowledged that there were no utopias and no encounters innocent of the notion of power. Then as now, there have always been keepers of knowledge, sometimes self-appointed, from whom it had to be wrested and this itself was a never-ending exercise.'[1] In these lines, Dalmia problematizes not only the notion of the compartmentalization of history and subjective experience, but also draws a connection between time and space. For the diasporic subject, the ideas of *home* and *host* are identified respectively with a 'classical' past and a 'modern' present, but the exact points of departure from the first and entry into the latter are blurred.

In Shauna Singh Baldwin's play, *We Are So Different Now*, the theme of time-and-space transgression reigns supreme. The play dramatizes the complexities and discriminations faced by Indian women, using the subtext of *The Mahabharata*. With just two women characters, Sheetal (the protagonist), and Draupadi, who claims to be none other than the heroine of *The Mahabharata*, the play is at times reminiscent of the South African playwright Matsemela Manaka's *Goree*, for in both plays, the predicament of the modern postcolonial woman is analysed with respect to the archetypal victim of gender discrimination in the respective cultural traditions. Neatly divided into three acts, the action of the play covers Sheetal's suicide attempt due to her being under the impression of the death of her 'would-be' husband, the unveiling of the truth, her marriage and her subsequent victimization by her cousins-in-law, court cases which initially lead her family through a financial setback, and her final victory.

Throughout the play, the character of Draupadi not only appears in the role of *deus ex machina*, but also as Sheetal's 'Other'. As the realizations dawn one by one on Sheetal, it is revealed that her mentor Draupadi herself is in an almost equally precarious situation, hung between the worlds of the dead and the living. To quote from the play, Draupadi says: 'Vyasa ... just wasn't too sure how to end it, so in several versions he left me, well-hanging between earth and sky.'[2] In another place, she laments: 'I've been here since. One foot in this world, one foot in the other.'[3] Thus the politics involved in the discursive construction of 'the feminine' are problematized in the play with reference to the predicament of the diasporic subject. Draupadi's liminal, 'in-between' position likens her to the latter, and her eagerness to help out the contemporary woman Sheetal in lieu of her own final salvation and permanent departure to the other world, reveals how she struggles to identify with the spaces of both the *home* and the *host*. This point is revealed strongly when Sheetal says that in order to attain her required salvation, either the required religious rites should be performed on Draupadi's behalf in Badrinath, the place where Draupadi died, or there has to be another war started in Kurukshetra, either of which is impossible due to financial constraints and modern urbanization of the battle-field.[4] Thus it may be possible to 'visit' the geographical place of 'origin' physically, but it is impossible, to 'reclaim precisely the thing that was lost'.[5]

However, it is important to note that Sheetal would have been successful in taking her own life, had not Draupadi intervened. It is also through the constant support of this lady from the 'Other' world, that Sheetal is restored to her self-esteem at the end of the play. This may possibly go on to attest to Makarand Paranjape's argument that 'a nation needs a diaspora to reaffirm its own sense of rootedness'.[6] In this context, Paranjape also classifies the authors from the South Asian diaspora in Canada into four groups, and argues that the third group which consists mainly of post-1960 migrants from South Asia, generally construct plots located in India, but rarely with a nostalgic tone. In order to substantiate his argument, Paranjape draws our attention to Rohinton Mistry's *Such a Long Journey* and *A Fine Balance*, and points out that they 'do not celebrate the homeland but mourn its relentless and innumerable atrocities and tragedies'.[7] Such a tendency applies to Baldwin as well, and metaphorically to Draupadi in the play. In her case, the homeland is all the more bleak, because it is identified with a memory of patriarchal dehumanization. It is important to note that Draupadi does not glorify the Indian past at any place in the play; nor does she want to identify with the geographical space where she had once belonged. Unlike the nationalist glorification of the mythical past of one's own land, we find here a scathing criticism of both the past and the present of the so-called 'homeland'. This endorses the following remark by Singh, Skerret and Hogen that 'the good old days when the grass was greener and young people knew their place was also the time when women knew their place, and it is not a place to which most women want to return'.[8]

This introduces the question of 'memory', which has been considered by critics like Anh Hua to be integral to the issue of diasporic identity-formation, especially when the diasporic subject is feminine. Hua describes memory as a 'faculty that is gendered, appropriated, politicized, nationalized, medicalized, and aestheticized', and while 'studying memory, one should pay attention to absence, distance, witness, testimony, tradition, nostalgia, and forgetting'. Hua concludes that 'both memory and history are forms of partial epistemology'.[9] Thus, within diaspora studies, memory is conceived of as an essentially 'fractured' element, to borrow S. Vertovec's term, which may be more clearly defined to be 'a multiplicity of histories, 'communities' and selves'.[10] In *We Are So Different Now*, these fractured memories are resurrected through the flashback-sequences. The first flashback in the play is that of Draupadi's *svayamvara*,* wherein the scene of Arjuna's victory in the shooting contest is re-enacted, but the veiled politics behind this apparently feminist custom of allowing the bride to select a groom for herself, is brought out as Lord Krishna is made to register

* *Svayamvara*: The name of the ancient Indian practice where a princess was allowed to select her husband from among the invited princes in the court.

apparent grief at the victory of Arjuna. The strategy of Drupada behind the arrangement of this ceremony is also brought out by Sheetal who mockingly says to Draupadi: 'You didn't have a choice, Draupadi-ji! Everyone knows your father stage-managed that *swayamvar* so that only Arjun could pass his test.'[11] Baldwin also reveals that the example of Draupadi's polyandry cannot be securely tagged as a case of women's freedom, for the multiple marriages did not take place because she wanted them, but because her 'mother-in-law said they must share everything equally'.[12] Again, when Draupadi is prompted to share her conjugal experience by the insulting remarks of Sheetal about her polyandry, she reveals that the commodified woman is actually the victim of the supposedly empowering act of polyandry. She 'pauses, remembering pain', as she remembers how her body had been the site of torture and patriarchal domination.[13] This domination is a part of Sheetal's memory as well, whose past history is also represented before the audience in two fragmented flashbacks. In the first one, in a comic re-enactment of Arjuna's test, Sheetal's father is seen darting at the picture of one of the suitors, and handing it over to Lord Krishna, who, in turn, hands it over to Sheetal, with a deceptive smile. Sheetal's docile acceptance of her father's decision is criticized by Draupadi, but Sheetal defends her own behaviour: 'Then how does it matter? All I needed was one man to be my husband ...'[14] Her mental state is perhaps best explained with reference to Althusser's concept of 'interpellation', by which he means that ideology 'recruits' subjects among the individuals' so much so that 'those who are *in* ideology believe themselves by definition *outside* ideology'.[15]

It is important to note that Draupadi says that Vyasa had 'reincarnated several times' in order to have the same story 'retold' every time, and she had consulted the different versions of the *Mahabharata* in the libraries in order to know for certain her ultimate destiny.[16] Barring the poststructualist assertion that history is politicized and incomplete, and no one version can be securely termed authentic, the other point to be noted here is that the role of the woman is *always already written* by the patriarchal society which works through the ideology of domination. It is ironical that Draupadi has not only to seek guidance in the discourse, but that she actually fails to remember her role which is absent from the discourse. 'Sheetal', she asks, 'do you know where I was when my Pandav husbands were fighting with their Kaurav cousins at Kurukshetra?'[17] To return to one of the observations made above, here we once again encounter the problem of 'memory' and its relevance in feminist discourse. Draupadi's 'act' of forgetting, to borrow Anh Hua's words, 'is more active than we think ... a creative invention, a performance, a selective loss.'[18] This 'selective' loss on the part of Draupadi, is, however, ordained by the patriarchal social order, who prefer to depict the 'subaltern' as defined essentially through silence and absence. Moreover, it appears that the uncertainty involved in the assigning of gender-specific roles to women, is mired in a kind of 'ambivalence', a term used by Homi Bhabha in defining the invariable contradiction involved in the construction of the colonized as its 'Other' by the colonized. In this case, too, the construction of 'the feminine' as the 'other' of the masculine, is not final. The stereotypes have to be frequently repeated in imperfect, anxious attempt to *secure* the 'woman' in the discourse of patriarchy.[19] This concept of repetition has been introduced in the specific analysis of feminist subjectivity by Judith Butler, who defines gender as 'a set of repeated acts within a highly rigid regulatory frame'.[20]

The irony lies in the fact that while Sheetal gains her final victory at the end of the play, Draupadi's wish is not granted. She remains trapped in a 'border life'. However, it is important to note that Draupadi willingly accepts staying in this world and is happy to go on helping distressed women. This may be an example of what Homi Bhabha calls the 'art of the present', which involves on the part of the diasporic subject an act of embracing the contrary logic of the border, whereby the contemplative subject produces 'complex figures of difference and identity, past and present, inside and outside, inclusion and exclusion'.[21] The generational difference within the diasporic community is also highlighted in the play, as Draupadi explains that her grandson Parikshit has been reborn as a rockstar in Chile, and has her figure tattooed on his arm, though he does not know her name.[22] This is the generation which has not *experienced* migration, but the past migration history remains dormant in their psyche, in an unconscious way.

The gender issues dealt with in the play are diverse. They range from arranged marriage and the financial dependence of women to domestic violence and female foeticide. As observed earlier, Sheetal accepts the person whom her father chooses as her groom, thus unconsciously entrapping herself into the 'interpellative' strategy of patriarchal society. Her apparently unquestioning dependence on her husband for financial support and her initial pride in her marriage and children reveal how power acts from within and not by forced imposition. The respect which she extracts from the society is derivative of her husband's, and even after her apparent molestation, she is anxious concerning her husband's reputation rather than her own.

The derivative nature of Sheetal's respect brings in another important and debated concept into the feminist discourse of the play. This is the question of 'caste', which is a typical problem in almost any analysis of power politics in the Indian context, but is absent in social theorization outside India. The passage which demands our special attention in this context, is the dialogue between Sheetal and Draupadi in Act II, Sc. I, where the former says that after her molestation by her cousins-in-law, she was not only asked to maintain a silence about the incident by her husband, but also made to believe by her mother-in-law that the incident was nothing but a deluding image created by her feminine fantasy. Sheetal quotes her mother-in-law: 'these things only happen in other people's families ... Not ours.'[23] The order comes even from her father: 'He said I mustn't shame him by leaving my husband, for what will people say?'[24] These remarks not only reveal the patriarchal society's male gaze that a woman is expected to live up to, but unveils the problematic caste affiliation of Sheetal as well. This point is finely elucidated by Uma Chakravarti in her analysis of the diversity of patriarchal practices among the different castes in India. 'Upper caste women's own respect', Chakravarti writes, 'is derived from the respectability of their men, whereas Dalit women have less of a derivative position. Codes of izzat-honour, respect and shame-imply further that upper caste women cannot really reveal the experiences of oppression that they may have to live with. Such codes of maintaining a discreet silence, no matter what is happening inside the family, do not have the same bearing among Dalit women.'[25]

However, Dalit scholars have also pointed out that the upper caste woman, though herself a victim of patriarchal power politics in her own household, is in an empowered position with respect to the Dalits. Sheetal, once forced into financial difficulties, resents cleaning toilets, cooking and washing,[26] which reinforces the notion that like the gender-roles, the caste-roles are also 'given' and fixed. Critics like Surendra Jondhale have complained about the absence of the Dalit woman in the emancipation movement for women in India, and Vidyut Bhagwat has drawn our attention to the active participation of upper caste women like Sadhvi Ritambhara in the casteist violence in recent years.[27] In fact, the play begins with a modern repetition of the epic episode of the 'House of Lac', wherein the Pandavas along with their queen-mother Kunti allowed a Nishadini and her five sons to die in order to get their charred bodies passed for their own corpses. In the play, the newly erected Wax Museum in Mumbai is burnt to ashes, and it is revealed after initial tension and trauma that the people dead were not the would-be in-laws of Sheetal.[28] Later in the play, Sheetal says that the site was originally the location of a Draupadi temple, and the fire was started by vengeful Dalit men.[29] This act is perhaps best explained with the help of B.R. Ambedkar's observation that the symbolic 'emasculation' imposed on the Dalits by the upper caste men amounts to the latter's entitlement to the body of the Dalit women, thereby instilling in the Dalit men an innate urge to express their vengeance through a violent process which 'fails to transcend the limits imposed on it by the masculine identity'.[30] Thus we find that the icon of upper-caste Hindu womanhood is dubbed by the Dalits as an agent of domination and oppression as much as her male counterparts. In this context, it would perhaps not be out of place to mention that two other modern retellings of *The Mahabharata* also question the justification of the episode. Though removed from Baldwin's work generically, Mahasweta Devi's short story, 'Kunti O Nishadini', and Chitra Banerjee Divakaruni's novel, *The Palace of Illusions*, also draw their material from the same source, and beg comparison due to the proximity of their approach to the social issues of caste and gender. In *We Are So Different Now*, the moral conscience of Sheetal is subdued by her overwhelming joy at her discovery that her suitor is alive, and is not boosted even by Draupadi's appeal for condolence: 'Other men died, though, and their families must be grieving.'[31] But in Mahasweta Devi's story, the widow of one of the five brothers reminds Kunti of her now forgotten misdeed, thereby making her repentant so much so that she does not try to save herself from the forest fire.[32] Chitra Banerjee makes her Kunti willingly shoulder the responsibility of and accept the retribution for the sin involved in the act, thereby 'invoking the concept of transfer of *karma* ... This move redeems Kunti, turning her act of murder into an act of maternal love and sacrifice'.[33] The three different responses to the same episode by three feminist writers, two from the Indian diaspora and Anglophone, and one rooted in Bengali life and culture, and with first-hand experience of the predicament of the tribal population of India, possibly attest to the fact that while caste is not a serious problem among the diasporic Indians, it continues to be a major issue in the country itself. It is important to note that in the play, it is Sheetal, and not Draupadi, who resents any change in her social and economic predicament. While Draupadi still takes pride in her royal lineage, she has adjusted to the modern circumstances, and started taking computer classes and bought a residence for herself. This may possibly reflect the predicament of the diasporic Indian woman whose original social and economic position may undergo drastic changes with respect to her crossing of spatial (and temporal) boundaries.

Notes

1. Vasudha Dalmia, 'Crossing Borders and Boundaries', in Jackie Assayag and Veronique Benei (eds), *At Home in Diaspora: South Asian Scholars and the West*, New Delhi: Orient Longman, 2006, p. 75.
2. S.S. Baldwin, *We Are So Different Now*, http://www.shaunasinghbaldwin.com/SSB-WeAreSoDifferentNowJune1-2009.pdf, accessed on 24 March 2012, Act II, Sc. I.
3. *We Are So Different Now*, Act I, Sc. II.
4. *We Are So Different Now*, Act II, Sc. I.
5. Salman Rushdie, *Imaginary Homelands*, London: Granta Books, 1992, p. 10.
6. Makarand Paranjape, 'One Foot in Canada and a Couple of Toes in India: Diasporas and Homelands in South Asian Canadian Experience', http://www.makarand.com, accessed on 24 March 2012.
7. Ibid.
8. Amritjit Singh, Joseph T. Skerrett and Robert E. Hogan, *Memory and Cultural Politics*, New England: Northeastern University, 1996, p. 10.
9. Anh Hua, 'Diaspora and Cultural Memory', in Vijay Agnew (ed.), *Diaspora, Memory, and Identity: A Search for Home*, Toronto: University of Toronto Press, 2005, p. 195.
10. Quoted in Sam Naidu, 'Women Writers of the South Asian Diaspora: Towards a Transnational Feminist Aesthetic?', in Parvati Raghuram (ed.), *Tracing an Indian Diaspora: Contexts, Memories, Representations*, New Delhi: Sage, 2008, p. 375.
11. *We Are So Different Now*, Act I, Sc. II.
12. Ibid.
13. Ibid.
14. Ibid.
15. Louis Althusser, 'Ideology and Ideological State Apparatuses: Notes towards an Investigation', in Saugata Bhaduri and Simi Malhotra (eds),

Literary Theory: An Introductory Reader, New Delhi: Anthem Press, 2010, p. 57.

16. *We Are So Different Now*, Act II, Sc. I.
17. Ibid.
18. Hua, op. cit., p. 198.
19. John Mcleod, *Beginning Postcolonialism*, Manchester, New York: Manchester University Press, 2007, pp. 52–54.
20. Quoted in Sarah Salih, *Judith Butler*, London: Routledge, 2002, p. 55.
21. Ibid., p. 217.
22. *We Are So Different Now*, Act II, Sc. I.
23. Ibid.
24. Ibid.
25. Uma Chakravarti, *Gendering Caste: Through a Feminist Lens*, Kolkata: Stree, 2003, p. 87.
26. *We Are So Different Now*, Act II, Sc. II.
27. Surendra Jondhale, 'Theoretical Underpinning of Emancipation of Dalit Women' and Vidyut Bhagwat, 'Dalit Women: Issues and Perspectives: Some Critical Reflections', in P.G. Jogdand (ed.), *Dalit Women in India: Issues and Perspectives*, New Delhi: Gyan Publishing House, 1995, p. 107.
28. *Vide* Act I, Sc. I and II.
29. Ibid., Act II, Sc. I.
30. Quoted in V. Geetha, *Patriarchy*, Kolkata: Stree, 2007, p. 109.
31. Ibid., Act I, Sc. II.
32. Wendy Doniger, *The Implied Spider: Politics and Theology in Myth*, New York: Columbia University Press, 2011, p. 130.
33. Ibid., p. 131.

11

Mnemonic Body of the Female Subject

'Personal' in History in *What the Body Remembers*

Shweta Kushal

A study of the Punjabi community, both within and outside India, is incomplete without due accounting of the bereavement and loss that the Partition of India brought to the people of the community. The reality of Partition in the past of the community has had an ineffaceable impact on the psyche of the Punjabi people. The community experienced unprecedented violence, which lives in its collective memory to this date in both Indian and migrant populations. As the borders between India and Pakistan were drawn through the heart of the land that was Punjab, the division was not effected merely in terms of territory but also in terms of communities, families, individuals, emotions and hearts. Populations that had never known any other place as home were required to move not just to a new place but a new country with, as it turned out later, no hope of return or retrieval of what they had left behind in terms of lands, fortunes, belonging, identities or even self. The requirement to move across an imaginary line that neither existed on the maps nor in the psyche of the people just to be on the 'right side' of the border baffled and confused many. The protagonist of Shauna Singh Baldwin's *What the Body Remembers* (1999), Roop notes that 'since they know not where the border will be,

---

This paper is a part of Shweta Kushal's doctoral research which was conducted at the Indian Institute of Technology, Madras, under the guidance of Prof. Evangeline Manickam.

they know not where to stop' (395). In the documentary *Partition: The Day India Burned*, there are accounts of Hindu families who were unwilling to leave Lahore as they did not know on which side of the border it would fall and were loath to let go of their homes, their heritage and their lineage. The sudden announcement of the boundary line after the Independence resulted in the mad rush to the border from both sides. Gyanendra Pandey in *Remembering Partition* (2004) recalls the pre-Partition environment very succinctly:

> The partition of the subcontinent, and the establishment of the two independent states of India and Pakistan, occurred with remarkable suddenness and in a manner that belied most anticipations of the immediate future. There was a very short time – a mere seven years – between the first formal articulation of the demand for a separate state for the Muslims of the subcontinent and the establishment of Pakistan. The boundaries between the two new states were not officially known until two days *after* they had formally become independent. And, astonishingly, few had foreseen that this division of territories and power would be accompanied by anything like the bloodbath that actually eventuated. (2)

Kavita Daiya in her *Violent Belongings* (2008) discusses the simultaneous Partition and Independence of India and states that the 'large scale ethnic violence and mass migration that accompanied it' made this event 'singular' (6) in nature. She describes the Partition of India thus, 'In the nine months between August 1947 and the spring of the following year, by unofficial counts, at least sixteen million people – Hindus, Sikhs and Muslims – were forced to flee their homes and become refugees; at least two million were killed in ethnic violence' (6). The belief or hope that Hindu, Muslim, Sikh communities could live peacefully with each other in the wake of the Partition was summarily shattered as with the blame game came hatred and the consequent indiscriminate massacre of human beings. The partition of India with the formation of Pakistan – the actual drawing of the border line – was carried out by Sir Cyril Radcliffe, an Englishman who had never set foot in the Punjab region of India. As he drew lines on the map, the land that gained independence through non-violent means imploded with unprecedented violence, bloodshed and rampage. The division of the land on maps was done through 'tortuous lines drawn on small, often out-of-date maps – pen lines that are incisions, flooding the map with blood. The world's greatest exodus had begun, and a holocaust had commenced its carrion work. Thirteen million people were uprooted and millions killed' (Randhawa 2001: 235). The movement towards the border began with millions of human beings crossing each other in caravans along the same road to be on the side of the border they would belong to – Muslims to Pakistan, Hindus and Sikhs to India. In the documentary *The Day India Burned*, this movement is described thus, 'This huge mass of humanity is moving along, barefooted, no food, thirsty, it was a terrible sight' (1:00 to 1:10). What followed was the 'worst communal massacre of the twentieth century' (*The Day India Burned,* 1: 17).

Official histories of Partition account mostly for drawing of lines through which two nations were born out of a single entity, with allowances made for deaths in terms of statistics. Seen largely as an aberration in the history of modern India that attained freedom through non-violent means, the nation-state has built no memorials for the event or for those affected by it. Urvashi Butalia comments on this official silence on Partition in *The Other Side of Silence* (1998), 'In India, there is no institutional memory of Partition: the State has not seen fit to construct any memorials, to mark any particular places – as has been done, say, in the case of holocaust memorials or memorials for the Vietnam war' (272). However, memories of people are not always clinical and sterilized. They cannot be erased by the absence of recognition in the public space. Gyanendra Pandey makes the distinction between official histories and lived experience of Partition very apparent. He argues that Partition historiography is very different from the literature of the Jewish holocaust as its main aim is not to place blame, create or consolidate different ethnic identities. Instead, it focusses on 'justifying, or eliding, what is seen in the main as being an illegitimate outbreak of violence, and at making a case about how this goes against the fundamentals of Indian (or Pakistani) tradition and history: how it is, to that extent, not *our* history at all' (3). He further argues that even when the history is written as that of struggle, it excludes 'force, uncertainty, domination and disdain, loss and confusion, by normalizing the struggle, evacuating it of its messiness and making it part of a narrative of assured advance towards specified (or specifiable) resolutions' (4–5). As a result, there exists 'a wide chasm between the historians' apprehension of 1947 and what we might call a more popular, survivors' account of it – between history and memory, as it were' (6). In nationalist historiography, there is an all too facile separation between the Partition and violence. Pandey further argues that the official historians' history suggests that the Partition was mainly a constitutional/political rearrangement without any deep, long-lasting effect on the central structures of Indian society or the broad contours of its history. However, for the survivors, this distinction does not exist, for them 'Partition *was* violence, a cataclysm, a world (or worlds) torn apart' (7). As a result, the survivors' accounts say that Partition was a 'sundering, a whole new beginning and, thus, a radical reconstitution of community and history' (7).

The feminine retelling of Partition by Shauna Singh Baldwin in *What the Body Remembers* creates a space in which the sundering and reconstitution of life is documented in terms of memory and oral traditions that capture the experiences of women during the Partition. Discussing her engagement with the novel in an interview with the editor of *Borders.com*, Rich Rennicks, Shauna Singh Baldwin (2008) says:

> My writing seems to rise from a sense that there is something missing, a subject, a story or an area that has received too little attention, and *What the Body Remembers* rose from that same dissatisfaction. The Partition of India in 1947 into India, East Pakistan and West Pakistan has received academic attention, but you can count the number of novels in English about it on the fingers of one hand.

Shauna Singh Baldwin points out the dearth of Sikh women's narratives in Partition literature even though they were one of the most affected sections of society. She says 'so far, we haven't read novels in English that put Sikh women front stage centre and certainly none that are about the experience of these women during Partition' (Baldwin, 2008). In her address on *What the Body Remembers*, she tells her readers:

> My challenge to myself was not to tell the story of the Sikhs from the standpoint of the men – there are a few non-fiction books that cover their story – but from the perspective of the Sikh women. This quickly became very frustrating because books on Sikh history are usually written by men. They contain on average a single index entry under 'women' or mention a maximum of two Sikh women by name. As a member of one of the few religions in the world that actually says women and men are equal, and demands that a Sikh woman be called 'princess' to show how valuable she is, I found my research running up against the difference between theory and practice. My solution was to resort to oral histories and imagination. (Baldwin 2)

In this paper, there is an endeavour to study Shauna Singh Baldwin's *What the Body Remembers* with a focus on the orality of the horrific memory, as related from one member of the community to another thereby differentiating it from the official history of the Partition. This recounting of a traumatic event, as pointed out by Marianne Hirsch, holds the unique space of 'postmemory' in the second generation of a particular community. In 'The Generation of Postmemory'(2008), Hirsch describes it thus:

> Postmemory describes the relationship that the generation after those who witnessed cultural or collective trauma bears to the experiences of those who came before, experiences that they 'remember' only by means of the stories, images, and behaviors among which they grew up. But these experiences were transmitted to them so deeply and affectively as to seem to constitute memories in their own right. Postmemory's connection to the past is thus not actually mediated by recall but by imaginative investment, projection, and creation. To grow up with such overwhelming inherited memories, to be dominated by narratives that preceded one's birth or one's consciousness, is to risk having one's own stories and experiences displaced, even evacuated, by those of a previous generation. It is to be shaped, however indirectly, by traumatic events that still defy narrative reconstruction and exceed comprehension. These events happened in the past, but their effects continue into the present. This is, I believe, the experience of postmemory and the process of its generation. (106–107)

Shauna Singh Baldwin's *What the Body Remembers* has a narrative that treats the Partition as a living presence. Set with the Partition of India as the major event, the text covers the time period from 1937 to September 1947 in its telling, moving from before to during to a little after Partition. This momentous event in India's history is presented through the perspective of Roop, one of the protagonists of the text. Roop is a motherless Sikh girl with two siblings, Jeevan and Madani. Their father Bachan Singh and his watchful and overprotective eyes keep them close in the village with the evocative name of Pari Darvaza, 'Doorway of the Fairies', in which both Muslim and Sikh households co-existed. Roop is educated in feminine graces and mannerisms by the array of female relatives that are resident in her household: Nani, her maternal grandmother, Revathi Bhua,[1] her father's sister, and Gujri, the domestic caretaker and surrogate mother in one. Roop is further instructed by her aunt, Lajo Bhua, who imparts to her the rules of acceptable feminine behaviour – agreeing with her elders, speaking softly, and never feeling angry – lessons that she internalizes and carries into adulthood. At the age of 16 in 1937, Roop becomes a second wife to Sardarji, to pay off debts incurred at her older sister's marriage. She meets his first spouse, Satya, who is barren. The narrative moves back and forth through Roop's early life and her wedding, and follows her as her children are given to Satya. The dynamics of the narrative change in the year 1947 with independence from the British, and the Partition of India into India, West Pakistan, and East Pakistan.

What the Body Remembers is a heart wrenching, painful as well as powerful account of the Partition and the madness of the time. Delving into deep-seated animosities and prejudices, along with the manner of withdrawal of the colonial power, it paints a vivid picture of the insecurities, dangers and ghastliness of the time. It traces the beginnings of the act of 'other'ing and the consequent definition of self as opposed to the other community, with the 'other' gradually converted into the enemy through the interactions of Roop and Sardarji, both Sikhs, with their fellow Muslims. It follows the path of changing locations of identity from space, neighbourhood and lineage to religion and, more importantly, nation as defined by communal associations. From an atmosphere of collective existence with instances of mild discrimination, the text moves to a more aware distinction between 'us' and 'you' towards the end as the time moves closer to the Partition. The chapter titled 'Simla, May 1944', begins with the discussion of the potential Pakistan between Sardarji and Rai Alam Khan which leads to these demarcations and distinctions being voiced. In this conversation Sardarji asks Rai Alam Khan:

> 'My dear sir, you *can't* be serious. Surely you don't ... you can't possibly want this Pakistan of Jinnah's?'
>
> 'Why not?' says Rai Alam Khan. 'It will take us further than we are at present.'
>
> *'Who is 'us'?'* The expression on Sardarji's face frames the mute question.
>
> 'Muslims,' Rai Alam Khan says impatiently. Sardarji's thick black eyebrows rise towards the line of his turban. (*What the Body Remembers* 341)[2]

The surprise and the incredulity that Sardarji feels arise from the fact that with one word Rai Alam Khan has effected a separation between the two. This is the moment of establishing difference. It further demonstrates that the desire for a land that belongs only to 'us' is not a fancy of the poor but also of the educated like Rai Alam Khan. 'If Rai Alam Khan, a gentleman landlord like himself, well travelled and well schooled, wants Pakistan, it is not merely the malcontents and the poor that Jinnah and the Muslim pirs, maulvis and mullahs have stirred into protest' (*Body* 344–345). This is the appeal and reach of the ideal of *Pak*istan – the pure (*pak*) land as well as the land of the pure which in turn implies the purity of Islam so that there is no space for a non-Muslim in this land. While the men engage in these exchanges, for the women the reality of Pakistan is realized differently as is demonstrated by the conversation between Roop and Huma, a childhood friend of Roop's who is now the wife of Rai Alam Khan. For Roop, Huma is her childhood friend and still 'the girl who once played Kikli[3] in the tunnel at Pari Darvaza' (*Body* 348). However, the moment of reunion between two friends turns into an interaction that makes Roop realize her and her kind's unwantedness in the world view that Huma holds now. Roop is shocked to learn that for Huma she and her family symbolize 'the other' when Huma calls her 'tum-log'. 'Tum-log. You people. A shudder passes through Roop; with one word, Huma has excluded her, Papaji, Jeevan, Revati Bhua, Gujri, Shyam Chacha and his family and all the other Hindus and Sikhs in Pari Darvaza neatly, so neatly' (*Body* 350). In a single stroke, both exclusion and excommunication occur. People like Huma, people who have been part of Roop's life are suddenly relegating her to the realm of the other. The idea of a separate province free of the other exists even in the mind of the friendly and homely Huma. Self is defined in terms of Muslim and Pakistani where the other can go live in Hindustan, made evident by Huma's remark, 'You can go to Hindustan', says Huma, as if it is all resolved. 'But you can't stay in Pakistan. We don't like Hindus here" (*Body* 350) as they are all 'Kafirs' (*Body* 351). The idea of faith and separation is deep-seated so that Roop, Huma's childhood friend, is also branded by the same label of Kafir – the non-believer, the heathen – which in turn makes her impure and unwanted in Pakistan.

The text then moves from the particular to the general with a clear and succinct account of the massacre in Bengal and the call for Pakistan. 'Comes the heat of August and Mr Jinnah turns away from words, calling for Muslim followers to wreak violence upon Hindus, to break the stalemate on 'Direct Action Day'' (*Body* 358–359). The text gives a vivid description of the British contribution in the chaos preceding the Partition in the years 1945 and 1946. This is the legacy that the British have created through two centuries of colonial policy. *'Divide et impera ... That was the policy, divide and rule. Separate electorates for Hindus, Muslims and Sikhs, remember? The Hindu and Muslim faiths were tools, the instruments by which you British divided us, then stood back complaining how we Indians fight, never giving you any peace'* (*Body* 378). The division rooted in the people over the years enables them to create these identities and selves that are opposed to and unrelated to one another. The narrator describes it thus, 'In the chaos the British have created and are leaving behind, a man will no longer be measured by his achievement or contribution, but by his father's blood, whether he wears a round cap, a Gandhi cap or a turban, whether he is circumcised Muslim, or an uncircumcised Hindu or Sikh' (*Body* 378). Moreover, the British added fuel to the fire by advancing the date of independence and their imminent departure by almost a year from June 1948 to 15 August 1947 without much thought for the consequences that this decision might have. All objections about the time being too short to negotiate the division of the two states amicably and judiciously were rendered void as the new date made it even shorter:

> 'August 15th!'Sardarji's eyes fall to the calendar on his desk. A date chosen arbitrarily, pulled out of that showman Lord Mountbatten's hat. With little consultation with the Indian National Congress or the Muslim League or the Akali Party, or even Prime Minister Attlee, Lord Mountbatten hastened the date. Brought it from its future greyness to overshadow the present ...
>
> *Seventy-three days!*
>
> Seventy-three days to cut a land in three, West Pakistan, India, and East Pakistan, like cutting arms from a body. (*Body* 387)

This cutting of the land into three was never an easy task, and now this severance will be effected by Sir Cyril Radcliffe without any experience of the lived reality of the domain he is about to divide. The only things he has to go by are maps, objects of cartography that are in no way tuned to the lived experience of what they represent. They are the pedagogic realm of the land which breathes and lives and can never depict the performative reality, hence they lie:

> ... for their colours can show nothing of what a man feels when he says 'I come home.' They say nothing of the distance a man will ride to avoid passing through areas inhabited by another's caste or quom,[4] or the direction a man turns when he bows his head to pray. Maps lie, their scrupulous lines diminishing height to hair's breadth, contracting the realms of the material to fit in the mind. Maps lie, the artful cartographer separating earth from sea with a simple line that refuses to tell that one does not end where the other begins, but continues, undergirding the sea. (*Body* 385)

However, the text refuses to be an example of the pedagogic and gives an account of Partition as experience rather than the detached history with no emotion, loss or rootlessness. In his article 'The Rebirth of Inherited Memories' (2009), Richard Lee observes, 'In *What the Body Remembers*, Baldwin undermines revisionist histories that underplay the horrors of 1947, and depicts how horrific memories can be as much embodied as, as it were, embrained' (18). Baldwin's narrative refuses to 'underplay the horror' and highlights the meaninglessness of this movement for the people who had to cross borders only to be on the right side even when it held nothing for them – no home, no neighbourhood, no belonging. They were all refugees in the land that should have been their own but for the formation of two new nations, but for Partition. 'Roop, with Sardarji's children, has turned her back to the Indus; she travels east from the Club Road bungalow in Lahore to 'India' – word, name, label, all shorn of meaning.' The Partition has created 'the Dominion of 'India', 'East Pakistan' and 'West Pakistan', empty names with no history' (*Body* 394). This is not her homeland, she is an outsider in this 'India' and it is alien to her. She has not been given a choice in the matter of moving to India because she has to follow her husband's orders and also because there is no possibility of a peaceful survival for Sikhs in Pakistan. She is forced to leave all that she has known and held dear throughout her life and move with the few valuables and her children from a country that did not exist earlier, to another that she has no desire to live in.

The narrative gives a harrowing account of the movement of people across borders through trains as well as on foot on the Grand Trunk Road by separating Roop's family so that they may travel by two separate routes. While Sardarji takes the train, he sends Roop and his children with Jorimon, Narain Singh and Dehna Singh in his car to cross the border using the Grand Trunk Road – the road with the horrible caravan of hungry, thirsty, barefooted people travelling in the Indian summer heat to the other side so that they may not be the 'other' any longer. The horrors of the train journey and the massacres on the road are both depicted with the use of this clever narrative turn. The sheer panic and the huge numbers of people waiting on the platform to board the trains that will carry them to the right destination, trains filled more than to the brim with people sitting on the coupling between carriages and on the top of the train, and yet the swarming mass that is trying to get a foothold on to this train of hope in order to avoid what might be in store for them if they are left behind makes the terror and desperation of the time palpable. Sardarji and Atma Singh's boarding of the train through windows with the press of bodies and the pull of hands on them is just one of many such tales of despondency and last resorts. Though there is so much loss and sacrifice for those who have left everything behind, the future remains indeterminate. 'Let's see what India brings – let's see if India will be grateful for our sacrifice' (*Body* 415). The idea that a nation needs to be grateful for the sufferings that its people have endured is introduced here and left hanging as there are no real answers possible for the same. It is as if Shauna Singh Baldwin is asking for accountability on the part of the two nations that were created through Partition. The labels of India and Pakistan do not mean anything to the people who feel bereft and aggrieved by the loss of their homes, their lives and their certainties. Their suffering is insurmountable and Sardarji's statement comments on the desperate nature of the situation.

Roop's journey on the Grand Trunk Road brings the suffering and terror of that caravan across borders home with shocking clarity and vividness. Hopelessness, desperation and danger, blood and terror are all mixed into a hellish amalgam where there is no respite. In the midst of defeated and zombie-like refugees, there is always the threat of death, rape, pillage that might be unleashed on one by the other. The result is death and destruction in which there is no value for human life, all will die by the hands of the other and will be reduced to the despicable state of carrion. '*Vultures, feeding on the bodies from a Hindu or a Sikh village! Hai Ram!* Bodies, purple-black and bloated, show in patches where the satiated vultures cannot eat any more. Clawed feet tear and rip, featherless heads delve into flesh, strong beaks peck away eyes' (*Body* 429). This is the ghastly picture of the freedom that was purchased at such dear costs. In this senseless massacre, people of different religions and castes suffer the same atrocities. Pain is the common denominator:

> Is this India we fought for God-chosen or Godforsaken? She is like a woman raped so many times she has lost all count of the trespassers across her body. Who will rescue and pyre the bodies of my quom? What use now to be Hindu, Sikh, Muslim or Christian, what use the quom, the biradari,[5] the caste, the compartments that order our lives? What do they do for us now in time of chaos when person meets person and the question between us is only this: Can you feel as I feel? Do you agree to let me live if I let you live? And will you keep that promise even when no one watches, under cover of sandstorms, when the veil is snatched away, will you be kind? (*Body* 429)

The dream of independence has turned into a nightmare. India is like a woman who is the victim of abuse and rapes to such an extent that she lies wasted and abandoned by it. She has no control over what is being done to her much like the women in Partition – the most vulnerable of all. The paradigm of religion used for ordering life has led to utter and complete chaos and no help or meaning is possible in belonging to one or the other as there is destruction everywhere and for everyone. The only thing to bond on is pain and suffering. At the same time, there is a constant fear that this bond of pain signed between two will not hold the test of loneliness and darkness.

Shauna Singh Baldwin in *What the Body Remembers* uses the body itself as a mnemonic device, something that can be marked and in turn recall the memory. This is memory that lives in the flesh rather than the mind. The title of the text *What the Body Remembers* highlights this function of remembrance that the body fulfils in this narrative. The most significant vessel of this memory in the text is a woman's body because of its vulnerability and the fact that it can be used to mark and imprint upon. Ritu Menon and Kamla Bhasin in their *Borders and Boundaries* (1998) delineate that women's bodies and violence become interminably linked in stressful times such as the Partition. They highlight that during the Partition women suffered violence both 'at the hands of men of the other community and within their own families', and demonstrate 'how these diverse, yet linked, kinds of violence formed part of a continuum of violence that began pre-partition and continued into the early Fifties' (40). They discuss the specific acts of violence perpetrated against women and point out that its most predictable form is when the women of one community are sexually assaulted by the men of another in 'an overt assertion of their identity and a simultaneous humiliation of the Other by 'dishonouring' their women' (40). This violence that is unleashed upon the women systematically lives within their bodies as memory even when one has not experienced it directly so that one woman is incapable of rescuing another for fear of what might happen to her. 'Because they 'retained the memory of loot, rape and plunder' in their bodies they remember it differently' (55). The text beautifully illustrates this remembrance. In her journey from Lahore to India, Roop believes that she sees Huma being attacked by Sikh soldiers. Roop's compassion threatens to overtake her. 'What was she doing in the street, so far from home? The woman's face was dust-stained, tear drops channelled their way to her chin, too many to make wiping them worthwhile.' In that instant, Roop wishes to save her old friend but is reminded of all the injunctions on her to safeguard her own person from anything untoward that might happen. *'Beware of pity. Pity charmed Sita, pity for an old beggar lured her out of her circle so Ravan could steal her away from Ram'*[6] (*Body* 403). She remembers the tale of Sita being rejected by her husband for this unwitting abduction in spite of being the ideal and chaste wife, even though her husband was the epitome of mercy and goodness. This fate of the ideal woman in Indian mythology leaves no hope for someone like Roop if she steps out of the line of protection. As Huma is hauled up into the soldier's truck, Roop looks on fearful for her own self because she is aware of the terror and violation that resides in that truck even though the men belong to her own community. The question in a woman's mind is always, *'How can I know my own Sikh people's intention?'* (*Body* 404). Roop has no illusions of goodness of her own people as her body is aware of the atrocities that any man can bring upon it. She is aware that the Sikh men are as savage as any other and women are the real sufferers in this insanity. The attack on Jorimon, one of Roop's servants who is travelling with them to finally reach East Bengal to be with her family, by men of her own community only highlights this fear. The fact that they try to gang rape a woman who belongs to their own community shocks Roop into believing the worst of mankind. *'If men treat a woman they know to be of their own quom in this cruel way, can any woman be safe?'* In this world where there are no checks on the beast within, there is no safety for women. 'In these few minutes of recent terror, Roop has learned, like simmer coming to boil, that there are so many things men can do to girls and women that are much worse than death' (*Body* 425–426).

The acts of violence on women belonging to another community was an effective way during Partition of establishing ascendancy over the other as women are used to construct the honour ideal of a community. Menon and Bhasin (1998) argue:

> The range of sexual violence ... stripping; parading naked; mutilating and disfiguring; tattooing or branding the breasts and genitalia with triumphal slogans; amputating breasts; knifing open the womb; raping, of course; killing foetuses – is shocking not only for its savagery, but for what it tells us about women as objects in male constructions of their own honour. Women's sexuality symbolises 'manhood'; its desecration is a matter of such shame and dishonour that *it has to be avenged*. Yet with a cruel logic of all such violence, it is women ultimately who are most violently dealt with as a consequence. (43)

Since this desecration has to be avenged because of its symbolism, there is no way that it can be forgotten by the community let alone the woman. In this manner, the body becomes the seat of violence and the consequent memory of the same which is then passed on to generations. Menon and Bhasin discuss one of the violent acts and remark, 'Tattooing and branding ... not only mark the woman for life, they never allow her (or her family and community) the possibility of forgetting her humiliation. In the deep horror of its continuous and forever present recall of brutality, this particular violation has few parallels' (43). However, the other forms of violation can also not be ignored as they not only affect the woman but defile an ideal that is built around her – honour. Kusum's violent death by dismembering her body and ripping out her womb discussed in the last subsection of the text is horrific and appalling. It is described as an eyewitness account as Roop's brother, Jeevan, recounts the memory of the mutilated body of his wife, Kusum. As he enters his house, frantically searching for his wife, he notices, 'A woman's body lay beneath, each limb severed at the joint. This body was sliced into six parts, then arranged to look as if she were whole again' (*Body* 449). This is the partitioning of women in the wake of the Partition of India. Jeevan, however is unsettled not only because of this but because, 'She looked accepting ... Her hand was ... unclenched. Her feet were ... not poised to run. Her legs cut neatly at the thigh, why they must have surely used a sword or more than one! Why were her legs not bloody? To cut a woman apart without first raping – a waste, surely. Rape is one man's message to another: 'I took your pawn. Your move' (*Body* 450). It is a waste to not rape her before dismembering her as there is no message to be given out by that. However, Jeevan learns the message soon enough as her womb has been ripped out to symbolize the annihilation of the entire race. 'We will stamp your kind, your very species from existence. This is no longer merely about izzat or land. This is a war against your quom, for all time. Leave. We take the womb so there can be no Sikhs from it, we take the womb, we leave you the shell' (*Body* 450). In this view, the woman is important only as a mother of the species and as a repository of honour, else she is but a shell. Without the womb her purpose in life is lost, as a woman is meant for giving birth to children for her husband – the only reason for Roop's existence in this narrative and for Satya being rejected for her barrenness. Her body is not important except as a pawn in this game between men. The story of Kusum's death becomes a part of Roop, 'Jeevan continues and his story enters Roop's body. This telling is not for Roop, this telling is for Roop to tell his sons, and her sons' (*Body* 448). She becomes a living embodiment of Kusum's memory, which in turn imprints itself on her for her to carry forward as body-memory. However, she learns the complete truth of Kusum's death only later through her father's recounting of his journey from Pari Darvaza to India. The fact that her father has killed Kusum to protect her is horrifying for Roop. 'Kusum was entrusted to me by Jeevan, she is young, still of childbearing age. I cannot endure even the possibility that some Muslim might put his hands upon her. Every day I had been hearing that the seeds of that foreign religion were being planted in Sikh women's wombs. No, I said: I must do my duty' (*Body* 458). Roop's father continues, 'I raised my kirpan[7] high above her head. Vaheguru[8] did not stop it; it came down. Her lips still moved, as mine did, murmuring 'Vaheguru, Vaheguru', as her head rolled from my stroke' (*Body* 459). At this moment, Roop realizes what Revati Bhua used to say was right, *'Papaji thinks that for good-good women, death should be preferable to dishonour'.* Moreover, Kusum decides to align herself to her father-in-law's wish of death before dishonour and she goes to her death without refusing even once as it has been ingrained in her that good girls never say 'nahinji' or 'no-ji'. 'Those words could not get past her lips because she had no practice in speaking them, because those words drowned before they took shape or sound, in the blood she bore within. Blood of the quom' (*Body* 459–460). This blood of the quom demands silence and obedience from its women, even when that silence could lead to their own annihilation. Menon and Bhasin (1998) comment on this violence against once own kin and family, 'So powerful and general was the belief that safeguarding a woman's honour is *essential* to upholding male and community honour that a whole new order of violence came into play, by men against their own kinswomen' (44–45). Urvashi Butalia argues that the phenomenon of Partition provided the reason for the construction of women as symbols of honour. She observes, 'If colonialism provided Indian men the rationale for constructing and reconstructing the identity of the Hindu woman as a 'bhadramahila', the good, middle class Hindu wife and mother, supporter of her men, [then] Independence, and its dark 'other', partition, provided the rationale for making women into symbols of national honour' (Butalia, 1998: 145). The construction of women as ideals and repositories of honour leads to many crimes and atrocities that are justified in the name of the community and its practices.

This feminine retelling of the Partition, undertaken by Shauna Singh Baldwin, exhibits the 'recalcitrantly ambiguous character of lived experience' (Daniel in Menon and Bhasin, 1998: 56), which in turn challenges the dominant normalizing discourse of the patriarchal state as well as their community. While women's voices are dissonant and ordinarily, 'deflected, ignored, subordinated, excluded or destroyed' (56) this retelling not only makes them audible but also offers a gendered history of Partition that provides a counter-narrative to the hegemonizing histories of communities and nations, ensuring that traumatic events are not subsumed by these meta-narratives. The concept of body-memory, as represented by Baldwin, highlights the manner in which women's experiences are reimagined. It further underlines that 'Passing on memories within families or social groups, either through storytelling or via more elusive mind-body connections, acts to ensure that traumatic events are not glossed over in the histories of communities or nations' (Lee, 2009: 24). The retellings that are individual in nature grant immediacy and pathos to a historical event that can be subsumed under the rhetoric of statistics and numeric representation of this lived reality. They provide a phenomenological reality, which is anchored in difference and cannot be homogenized into the mainstream historical narrative as they 'expose and counter the representational violations of patriarchal memory' (Misri, 2011: 20).

Notes

1. *Bhua* is a relationship term used to refer to the sister of the father.
2. Referred to as *Body* in all subsequent parenthetical references.
3. *Kikli* is a sport that is generally popular with young girls and is usually played in pairs. It can be played by any even number of participants. The two participants stand face to face with their feet close to each other's and their bodies inclined back. Standing in this pose with their hands interlocked firmly and arms crossed they are able to stretch their arms fully and arch their backs to the maximum limit. The pairs maintain this pose and wheel round and round in a fast movement at the same spot with their feet serving as pivotal points.
4. *Quom* or *Qaum* is an Arabic term used to refer to a people, nation or community.
5. Parvez A. Wakil points out that *Biradari* or *Biraderi* 'literally means a brotherhood. It is a bilateral system and consists of consanguineal and affinal relatives among whom a brotherly sentiment or system of relationship is supposed to prevail' (700). In a footnote on the same, he further adds that the term need not necessarily apply to ecological or geographical groups, or patrilineages, or even to blood relatives alone. It is true that members of a *biraderi* 'regard themselves as related to each other through blood and sometimes, overlappingly, through marriage but in effect whether they are related exclusively through blood is not evident. Certainly there is evidence of fictive relations and outright 'assimilation' through marriage' (700).
6. In the *Ramayana*, Rama goes after a golden deer and does not return for a long time. On Sita's coercion, Lakshmana agrees to leave in search of his brother, but draws a protective line, Lakshmana Rekha, that Sita should not cross. Anybody other than Rama, Sita and Lakshmana attempting to cross the line would be singed by flames erupting from the line. After Lakshmana leaves, the Rakshasa king Ravana comes in the form of a mendicant and asks Sita for alms. Not expecting a trick, she unsuspectingly crosses the Lakshman Rekha to provide alms to him and Ravana kidnaps her.
7. *Kirpan* is a ceremonial sword or dagger carried by Sikhs who have gone through a holy religious ceremony. These are known as baptized Sikhs and are members of *Khalsa*.
8. *Vaheguru* or *Waheguru* is a term most often used in Sikhism to refer to God, the Supreme Being or the creator of all. It means 'The Good/Best Teacher' in the Punjabi language. Wahi means good (a Middle Persian borrowing) and 'Guru' means teacher.

References

Baldwin, Shauna Singh, *What the Body Remembers*, New Delhi: HarperCollins, 1999.

——, Author essay on *What the Body Remembers*, http://www.shaunasinghbaldwin.com/wtbressayo99.pdf., accessed on 11 January 2011.

——, 'Talking with Shauna Singh Baldwin', Interview by Rich Rennicks, *Sawnet*, http://www.sawnet.org/books/ writing/SSBBordersInterview.html, accessed on 9 September 2008.

Butalia, Urvashi, *The Other Side of Silence: Voices from the Partition of India*, New Delhi: Viking, 1998.

Daiya, Kavita, *Violent Belongings: Partition, Gender, and Postcolonial Nationalism in India*, Philadelphia: Temple University Press, 2008.

Hirsch, Marianne, 'The Generation of Postmemory', *Poetics Today* 29.1 (2008): 103–128.

Lee, Richard, 'The Rebirth of Inherited Memories', *MHRA Working Papers in the Humanities* 4 (2009): 18–24, http://www. scribd.com/doc/85835621/WTBR-Article-Inheritance-of-Memories-RLee, accessed on 11 January 2011.

Menon, Ritu and Kamla Bhasin, *Borders and Boundaries: Women in India's Partition*, New Delhi: Kali for Women, 1998.

Misri, Deepti, 'The Violence of Memory: Renarrating Partition Violence in Shauna Singh Baldwin's *What the Body Remembers*', *Meridians: Feminism, Race, Transnationalism* 11.1 (2011): 1–25.

Pandey, Gyanendra, *Remembering Partition: Violence, Nationalism and History in India*, Cambridge: Cambridge University Press, 2004.

Randhawa, Ravinder, *The Coral Strand*, London: House of Stratus, 2001.

The Day India Burned: Partition. Produced and Directed by Ricardo Pollack, Birmingham: BBC, 2007.

Windelband, Wilhelm, *Geschichte und Naturwissenschaft*, 3rd edition, Strasburg: Heitz, 1904.

III

Life-Story / Her Story

12

Translating Life Writing Across Cultures

Narratives of Select Indian and Canadian Women Writers

Jameela Begum A.

The field of autobiography studies has expanded to accommodate it as a cultural practice and as an institutionalized arena of intellectual and pedagogical work which brings new generic and cultural complexities to it. Life writing opens up ways of understanding experience based narratives of geographical, social and historical contexts as much as concepts of selfhood and identity, as individuals are swept along struggling to find expression of their experience through great historical or personal traumatic psychological moments. The new speaking position of the critic necessitates a transcultural, transnational, transhistorical, and sometimes translingual communication between auto/biographer and critic.

Modern criticism no longer believes that autobiography can offer a faithful and unmediated reconstruction of a historically verifiable past: instead, it expresses a play of autobiographical act itself in which the materials of the past are shaped by memory and imagination to serve the needs of the present consciousness. The autobiographical act tells us less about the past than it tells us of the present at the moment of creation. As the scriptor of the text, the writer occupies a space that is multidimensional in which the monological gets displaced and is substituted by a polyphony of voices of the past and the present. This relationship is further heightened when the text is constructed by a doubling of scriptors who belong to two different cultures and reach out to a mutual understanding of one another through sharing life narratives.

Autobiography in the Western tradition had always been associated with an ego-centric individualism and the process of individuation, the cultivation of originality and difference, and the notion of linear history in written discourse. It was a means of exploring the inner self and bringing an ordering and intelligibility to an otherwise chaotic inner text. To write a text of the self was often an attempt to project a self-centred vision of the reality of the experience. In other words, the self became the subject of the text and the writing of it a subjective account of self experience. However, today the symbolic use of language to recreate the past experiences of trauma has become a popular form for the marginal sex and minority race especially since they lend themselves to writing the self and the cultural communal experience. Life writing is a resistance text that extols freedom and lays the foundation for a possible convergence between aesthetics and cultural history more than self projection.

Writing from different/silent positions, women writers have paved the way for the collapse of boundaries, the divide that separate women from women. Even as we talk of different feminisms, understanding and translating them into collaborative experiences alone can build up the bonding of sisterhood. Life writing is only the beginning of a sharing of with the reader, for the scriptor is both the experiencing self and the narrator of a cultural and geographical space. Kamala Das, Kerala's feminist voice hailing from an established South Indian Nayar tharavad with its traditions and beliefs and an unique literary phenomenon in India and Maria Campbell, Canada's feminist voice of the Metis community, tread unexplored terrains and journey into the interior through life writing to expiate the hurt, and the agony of past experiences as much as to come to terms with society. Seen critically, both writers transcend the self to engage in a moment in history that has possessed them. The traumatic experience of marriage in Das and of childhood in Campbell problematizes the relation between experience and event. It carries the force of a literality which renders it resistant to narrative structures and linear temporalities. Insufficiently grasped at the time of its occurrence, trauma does not lie in the hand of the individual, to be recounted at will, but rather acts as a haunting or possessive influence which not only insistently and intrusively returns but is, moreover, experienced for the first time in its belated repetition. Cathy Caruth's emphasis on trauma's disruption of time or history draws on Freud's concept of 'Nachtraglichkeit' which has been translated as 'deferred action' or 'afterwardness'. For Freud, the concept refers to the ways in which certain experiences, impressions and memory are revised at a later date in order to correspond with fresh experiences or with the attainment of a new stage of development. Freud's conception involves a radical rethinking of causality and temporality of memory. The traumatic incident is not fully acknowledged at the time that it occurs and only becomes an event at some later point of intense emotional crisis.

Memory and translation of experience within different spatial contours marks the writing of the text as an act of re/creation in collaborative writing of the self. Maria Campbell's *Halfbreed* (1973) and Linda Griffiths and Maria Campbell's *The Book of Jessica: A Theatrical Transformation* (1989) is a doubling of the story of the mind/nativescape. Campbell calls *Halfbreed* an autobiography, a powerful life story of a woman whose courage and strength you will never forget. The text was written when she was 32 years old. For Campbell writing is a way of educating her community caught in similar situations as her own. Writing, for her, is a process of healing and the experiences engendering a curative and recuperative power. The link she establishes with her Cree great grandmother Cheechum displaces time frames and projects the memory of the spirituality and joy that can regenerate the mangled spirit of a defeated people.

The text foregrounds the historical strength of a group of people who are neither whites nor Indians but who were the only race indigenous to Canada having established a civilization at least a century before the confederation and as equal to the French and English. Seen in this context *Halfbreed* is a tale that draws on the strength of the past to locate within the present. The memory of the Cree great grandmother is the text on which the writer scripts her own text.

Locating oneself in place is as much a need of life writing as personal cultural/communal experiences. Campbell writes:

> My people fled to Spring River which is fifty miles North west of Prince Albert. Half breed families with names like Chartrand, Campbell and Vandal came here after the Riel Rebellion where the men had been actively involved. (4)

However, during the 1920s when the Metis were overrun by immigrants they were on the road once again and from then on they were known as the Road Allowance People. Maria Campbell sees this as the beginning of poverty and hardship, social evils like prostitution, drugs and drinks, and humiliation which reduced a whole community to a dehumanized state of existence. The story recalls what it is to be a half breed. She writes, 'I want to tell you about the joys and sorrows, the oppressing poverty, frustrations and dreams' (1). The history recorded here is the agonizing cry of a community deprived of a place and haunted by the Mounties for poaching on State preserves. This traumatic experience that is not her own but intensely felt as the trauma that haunted her community is relived again and again through Campbell's self writing. The geographical displacement that shattered the cultural strength of the community is the context in which she writes.

Years later in Campbell's retelling of the tale along with white Canadian Linda Griffiths in *The Book of Jessica: A Theatrical Transformation,* the therapy of purging is extended to a theatrical transformation and the process of arriving at an understanding of cross-cultural nuances.

The book is a collective effort of the actress/playwright Linda and Metis activist/author Campbell and Paul Thomson, artistic director of theatre Passe Muraille. The composition of the text was spread over a number of years (1974–1981). During these seven years, a period during which the writers reached across trying to relate to one another and live through a process of initiation. Divided into four parts, 'History', ' Spiritual Things', 'Red Cloth" and ' Jessica' the text recreates an ambience between two cultures, with the understanding that cultures and histories are dependent on one another. The process of rewriting the earlier text becomes as significant as the thrashing out of the bitterness and anger and the Other's understanding of the same through an initiation into the rituals and spirituality of a community that had been wronged.

The natives' right to their own stories is challenged here. Campbell at the beginning of the writing of the play, paradoxically makes a statement:

> I couldn't tell your people's story. And I don't need you to tell the story of our people to other white people. How can somebody interpret or tell? How can a white person tell you, another white person about my community and my people, when he is only coming

> from half a place? He has to believe the other half, too. He has to believe it's there ... . The bear doesn't try to tell the deer's story.(Quoted in Grant, 1992: 43)

Agnes Grant observes that 'Griffiths and Campbell wrote a mythical dramatization of Campbell's autobiography – *Halfbreed* and the difficulty of the collaboration was later documented by the writers in the first part of *The Book of Jessica*'(43). The prefatory discussion of this collaboration addresses the issue of cultural appropriation and how two artists can negotiate the dialectics of this binary. If Campbell sees writing as a healing process Griffith translates the trauma through identifying with the spiritual world that has been alien to her until then. The process of writing is a therapy and a revelation for the scriptors. Through this interdependency Campbell reinstates a past strength in the conflict of cultural binaries. Campbell remarks:

> This was not supposed to be a play about spiritual worlds, it was supposed to be a play about a woman struggling with two cultures and how she got them balanced: because when she leaned into one, a part of her got lost, so she had to lean into the other one and try to understand and find a balance .... (80)

Campbell is forced to accept that here is a play that got away from the proposed agenda of writing a purely subjective experience. The spiritual world in which characters play more than one part, the symbols of a native tradition, the coyote, the bear, wolverine and the crow coexists with the unicorn, assume various human forms and merge with one another. The theatrical transformation of the Metis experience moves to another plane of the fantastic and mystic. The doubling of self leads Campbell to say: 'I still feel like some Siamese twin with her (Linda). I want her to go away ... but I hear myself saying, 'Lets tell the whole story of what happened ... then maybe we will be free of the whole thing, heal everything and I kick myself ...' (40). Griffith in her turn sees the writing as a merging with the Metis race:

> We began Jessica and I started to feel the stuff again. When the native world got opened up to me, it was like coming home. Here were people that believed the air was thick with things, like I did, that you could listen and hear voices .... Then I saw your culture and it was like a treasure chest opening up and the maniac romantic in me just dived in up to my elbow. These images and stories were fresh, still alive, people still believed in them, they had real power .... (84)

It is from this power and belief that the play Jessica came into being – a bonding between the White and the Metis. Experiences get relived through the binding of subjectivities that seek to demolish the notions of binaries. The many instances that Campbell turned away in anger and bitterness, because she felt that the collaborative writing was moving towards the logic of dominant thinking, reveal the long and problematic journey which teaches the Other to enter the spirit of the experiences within the context of the native tradition rooted in the essence of the ritual and mythical where the real and the surreal are the same. The guy sitting in the middle in the play remarks:

> ... the frustration and the potential for mistrust fuelled the future work on the work, underscoring its themes of racial tension as well as emphasizing the problems of male-female relations. It also propelled Maria and Linda into the transcontinental dance of understanding/misunderstanding which is at the core of their understanding. The final version of Jessica is richer for all our experiences and the story of Linda's and Maria's journey has become a fabulous tale of its own.(24)

In fact the pathetic cry of Jessica echoes the vulnerability of the Metis community which seeks an affirmation of its existence.

> I'm not Indian, I 'm not white, I'm a Halfbreed.I live in a white world full of filing cabinets and common sense. The years go by and everyone round me is making decisions and calming down, and my life just gets weirder – no it is worse than that – waves and waves and waves of fear. I'm drowning and I'm cracking apart. (121)

Campbell's own narrative leads to another dramatic representation which is sparked off by her experiencing another theatrical production, another ritual. She remarks, 'In that production of Almighty Voice, I saw something really powerful happen, something that educated, that healed, that empowered people: it was fun and it was magical'(16). The repeated invocations, and the multiplication of the spirit of the grand mothers lineage facilitates the affirmation of identity. The challenge before the story tellers is to empower cultures and communities through the ritualistic representation of the experience. True art steals from the people all their stuff and then gives it back to them and heals them, empowers them, and its beautiful, said Campbell. Art is a collective, collaborative effort and Jessica is a dialogue between native and non-native cultures.

Jessica began to take on new contours of meaning for me, when as a reader, I came across another collaborative text, this time by a Keralite, a Malayalee and a French Canadian. The recent publication of Merrily Weisbord's *The Love Queen of Malabar: Memoir of a Friendship with Kamala Das* (2010) suggests the possible ramifications that texts such as these can have in cementing cultural platforms in understanding one another. Merrily Weisbord found Kamala Das's work so compelling that she flew to Kerala to meet Kerala's most revered artist who has been both hailed and reviled as the first Indian woman to write an autobiographical cult classic about love and lust. Das' autobiography, *My Story* (1988), earned for her the dubious distinction of being the first emotional revolutionary of our times.

Merrily Weisbord had never dared to publish a memoir as personal as *My Story* but had written intimately about her life and believed that 'if she and I were in each other's countries and in each other's lives, we could travel beyond cultural stereotypes, perhaps into friendship. I could go to Kerala and see Kamala's world through her eyes and she could come to Canada and do the same with mine' (5).

Cultural stereotypes divide people and set up diversities that challenge the existence of one another. Collaborative life writing looks for an understanding of each others life and society, the circumstances that have triggered the urge to write the self into existence. This text is a life writing of two women, drawn together by a fascination to know more about the other. The particularity of the text is that it is a recording of conversations between them as well as of people and their lives around them. It is a sharing of social, familial life as much as an exploration of the intimate moments in their lives. Weisbord remarks '... when I read her autobiography, *My Story*, I saw that Kamala Das was also writing to comprehend, remember, reinvent and transcend her life ...'(5). What followed was a relationship that opened up a dialogue of the selves, with Merrily assiduously recording her words through a period of over ten years, until Kamala Suraiya's death. During these 10 years Merrily came to India over half a dozen times and stayed with Kamala in Cochin, travelled with her to the North of Kerala and to her childhood home in Punnayoorkulam. Kamala in her turn visited Merrily's home in Montreal twice, lectured at universities, wrote poems, painted profusely in the new freedom of a country that received her without prejudices and lived with Merrily's Jewish family of aunts and parents. The trust that evolved in the relationship made Kamala open up more emotionally and imaginatively to draw out a life that constantly denied her longing to experience a love that was spiritually and sexually satisfying.

When Kamala wrote *My Story*, in 1988, she believed that she was on her death bed with heart disease and she would not live to hear her social critics tear her to pieces for her openness about sex and her relationship with her husband and other men. In her Preface she wrote, 'My recovery was such an anticlimax! ... This book has cost me many things I held dear, but I do not for a moment regret having written it.'

I prefer to read the book as a memoir that highlights the innocence and joy of childhood, the close relationship she had with her great grandmother, her grandmother and her weak mother who lived in a world of soft feelings and aesthetics. The pain of uprooting, unfamiliar faces, pushed into the responsibilities of a wife at the age of 15 when she was not mature enough to understand what was happening to her and the heart disease which made her fear for her life as much as the financial need to meet the expenses of her treatment, all have contributed to the making of the text. The times she ran away to the shelter of her Nalapat home, to escape the harshness of the world outside convinces a perceptive reader of what Weisbord sees in her text.

The text is a recapturing of memories of the past in distant time which is antithetical to the joys of childhood. So, when Kamala Das portrays these, she both idealizes the very past and comes to terms with the present. She says: 'During the long weeks of my convalescence I was obsessed with the recollections of my childhood days spent at Nalapat'(208). Divided into 50 sections, the first 19 sections recapture early childhood culminating in section 20 with a reference to the unwanted sexual overtures she is forced to endure from a lesbian girl and the man who is eventually to marry her. Section 20 to 50 is a wild narration of sexual fear and hate, drawing gory scenes of lust that drive her into herself. Section 41 is titled 'I withdrew into the cave I had made for myself.' Her devotion to Lord Krishna and her search for spiritual love culminates in her yearning for an emotional anchoring in human love that could embalm and cleanse her. This journey of expiation and spiritual rejuvenation is located in place and time. The text moves from Calcutta to Malabar, from Malabar to Calcutta and back again from Bombay to Malabar. It draws for the reader a cross-section of south Indian society, the traditions of the nayar tharavad, the city life of Calcutta and Bombay, thus rendering a microcosmic image of India of the 1970s and 1980s. Living through a period of colonization, Das has asserted her subjectivity rooted in tradition and ritual as much as her resistance against a conventional society that had no place for the woman's voice. Years later talking to Merrily about her writing, she was to say, 'I fling arrows at the uncivilized brutal norms of life for women in Kerala … . I tweak the noses of puritans.' Born to one of Kerala's most romantic and mythical poetess, Balamaniamma, who was a very conventional Hindu woman, Kamala broke the accepted social patterns of a woman's life and made her critics sit up in disbelief. Her forthrightness about sex has been much reviled and yet much read. It is interesting to note that the magazine which serialized her autobiography in 1971–1972 was instantly sold out. Before the serialization the weekly was below 40,000. With the story on, the distribution went up to 55,000 and the full text ran through six editions and is reported to have sold 36,000 copies in 11 months. What does this point to? This should alert us to the male voyeurism in society and the publisher's eye on the market value. It would not be off the mark to conclude that the 'sexual play' within the text was crafted to meet the demand. The force that operated behind her writings she attributes to her husband. 'Forty-three years of married life with a man I married at fifteen. So, you see it grows on you. I don't resent, I don't regret. All the grief inflicted upon me by my husband paid dividends … . Poetry came oozing out like blood out of injuries'(16). She recalls in a letter to her sister in 1958: 'I was persuaded to marry and I had no courage to refuse, to do whatever my father wanted to do. I have not shown by a word or a sign that I felt trapped. Let down and disillusioned … .' The image of the father figure and the husband portray the conventional male figures for whom the sentiments and wishes of women do not matter. Her poems and short stories expose the struggle of women against a male oriented society even within a so called matriarchal society.

In *My Story* she says, 'I had used them (words) like swords in what was meant to be a purification dance, but blood was unwittingly shed'(202). But calls these words that exposed her nudity 'on sheets of weeklies and monthlies/Quarterlies a sad sacrifice'. Yet at the same time the incompleteness of life and growing up, changing and altering, form the foundation of her life writing. Her search for spiritual love within the bonds of human relationships, underlie her aversion and fascination for physical sexual life.

It is this that drew, the Jewish French Canadian, Merrily Weisbord to her. She writes , 'I was intensely drawn to her as millions of others, to her vulnerable longing for someone to love, 'like alms looking for a begging bowl', and to her great wild hunger 'to take in with greed like a forest fire that consumes all that comes my way ... a fire I could feel igniting in me. Even though Kamala was a grand celebrity, short-listed for a Nobel Prize, her confessional tone encouraged me to think I could know her. I wanted to smell the wind from the Arabian Sea as she described it. Walk the Malabar coast, taste a Nayar feast, see the poet whose sensual poems stirred the heart of modern India ...' (5). What followed was a long association that took them to each others country and to an exchange of confidences and a laying bare of personal and the political. The book is a faithful recording of conversations, events, public discussions and appearances. More than that the text is a sharing across boundaries, and in Weisbord we get a very involved and sympathetic recorder of the whims, moods, and events that shaped Kamala's life which made Kamala say, 'I knew that we belonged to the same tribe, although we came from different cultures, different backgrounds ...' (54).

The Queen of Malabar finds in Canada's sparse population and the quietness of the forests of Montreal, the Panchgani Hill station near Bombay. She is reminded of India, 60 years back when her ancestors went to Benares on bullock carts and some of them died on the way because of exhaustion. She has made a longer journey to Canada to find her peace in the autumn of her life. Her stream of consciousness narration of the there and the here makes interesting comparisons. The joy and peace she finds in Montreal on her two visits in the company of a Jewish family with its many close relationships is for her a homecoming. She says, 'Totally different cultures. That makes a difference. And me coming from an orthodox Hindu household. We'll have to be honest because there is no compromise, otherwise the book will be fake.' What begins as a Johnson-Boswell relationship, when Kamala is passing through what she calls, 'the healing simplicity of life' the bonding becomes stronger as they pass through tortuous streams of conflict and suffering. The writer Kamala Das sees her own writing in retrospect and many of the fears that had ridden her life getting reinterpreted through her narration to Weisbord. Merrily's father cannot understand how a father would marry off his own daughter at the age of 15, for him it is a grave betrayal. Merrily, in turn, realizes her own strong attachment to her father. The juxtaposition of the two father figures offers an interesting platform for comparison. Merrily tells her father that despite Kamala's father she had as blessed a childhood as her own. For Merrily as for Kamala, the presence of the women figures ... great grandmothers, grandmothers and mothers who handed down a lineage of love and caring is the strength that roots them in their culture. Merrily tells her father what Kamala has told her, 'Ammamma opened up the portals of mythology for young Kamala, taught her to pick medicinal herbs, light the sacred oil lamps, apply vermilion, sandal wood paste and oils. Ammamma bought modest long skirt to cover her granddaughters legs, gave her oil baths and washed, untangled, oiled and braided her long curly hair.' This translation of the cultural rituals through the voice of a Jewish Canadian and her family's understanding of Kamala leads to a further exploration of the cultural self. The geography of the land to which they belong and their bonding is felt in these words of Merrily: 'I think of the freedom I took for granted as I roamed our family land and wonder how much greater Kamala's sense of entitlement must have been at Nalapat in the 1930s when her family was one of her village's five rich landowners, with over two hundred families to serve them. I think Nalapat is Kamala's emotional centre as this place is for me. I store images of the land I love ...' (78).

Kamala's reminiscences of her childhood are much more evocative and her sexual life with Das much more graphically described here as she narrates them to a Westerner whom she feels will be able to understand her better than the conservative society in Kerala. Citing the hypocrisy of the Indian society she recalls a letter that she had received from a young man who said that his father had caught him reading *My Story*, snatched the book from him and said that he was going to burn it. But weeks later the young man found his father reading the book while his mother was asleep. The father committed suicide because he could not face his son after he had caught him reading the book. Merrily's reaction to this is instant ' You live in such a censorious culture ... . They pick at you like vultures.' And Kamala retorts, 'Yes, I see them as if they have sores all over their bodies, pus coming out, stinking. They are horrible'(123). As Kamala graphically narrates her gruesome experiences of going to men to further her husband's professional standing at his demand, she relives them as though she was living through them over again. She repeats, 'No one knows how much I suffered, being the wife of a homosexual, ... and the rape that went on and on ...' Kamala's revelations throughout the writing of this memoir, makes one interrogate her positioning in the tale. The trauma is distanced and the narrator of these is as much an observer as Merrily. 'One suffered, one watched and wrote'(131). One wonders where the fantasy ends and the reality takes over. As a devotee of Krishna and her belief in destiny, she tries to unequivocally forgive and love her husband, but the wounds are too deep. Kamala has always through her writing sought sympathy and love from her readers. Such self writing makes her expiate her pain and she can say, 'It's not enough romanticizing things, romanticizing even hurts and slights. You've got to continue to live, accept your enemies as attackers, but still serve them a cup of tea'(131). These unresolved ambivalences continue to be a part of her life.

The aristocratic, upper caste Hindu, and Krishna devotee, Kamala, decides to convert to Islam and on 16 December 1999, amidst a storm of controversy she converts. Her insatiable thirst for love drives her to a man who promises marriage and sees her through a conversion to Islam and then absconds, leaving her to face the wrath of the Hindus and the fanatic zeal of the Muslims. Newspaper clippings proclaim the reason for her conversion an act of convenience to marry her so called lover Sadiq Ali, a 38-year-old man. Her conversion is reviled by Hindu fanatics who threaten death while it is welcomed by the Muslim's for whom she has become a cult figure all dressed in black purdah and learning Arabic, calling Islam the religion of love and changing her name to Suraiya. The communal divide in society and her life once again is under the ethical surveillance of social traditions. The conversion can be seen as yet another resentment of social values. She writes, 'Hindus have abused and hurt me. They have often tried to scandalize me. I want to love and be loved' and confounding religious logic she says, 'Krishna is with me ... I have just had to rename him Mohammed' (141).

Leela Menon wrote in the *New Indian Express*, 'Certainly her action has electrified Kerala's somewhat moribund social scene. The State, many feel, is evolving into a land of widows, with women outliving men and depression stalking the Land. In such a scenario, Kamala may even appear to provide an alternative.'

Kamala's life becomes more public than ever before with news paper reporters and the political involvement, she is torn hither and thither to address crowds in Cochin, Thrissur, Kunnamkulam, Edapalli, Kotakkal, Calicut, until she is almost dropping down with fatigue. She stands exposed in all her vulnerability.

The memoir goes on to explore the nuances of co-writing during which there are moments of despair and fear, the writing of the present events and the repeated movements into the past, the swing between the two locations, Cochin and Montreal with the two writers moving into each other's spaces and becoming a part of each other's society and families. Kamala visit's Montreal again in 2000, this time as Suraiya, free from the restrictions of Kerala society. The loss of her Hindu family with her conversion is substituted by the warmth of the Jewish family in Montreal. The two aunts revive her spirits once again and she puts herself totally at the hands of Merrily to write her story. Merrily sees through her ironic confession of celibacy reminding herself of the many times Kamala has talked of sex and rape. Merrily draws the conclusion that 'for fear of reprisals and to prove her 'purity', she has spent a life time, dissimulating and spreading misinformation about her sexual history. It is difficult to separate sexual fact from fiction in Kamala's life ... . She best describes herself in these words: 'I speak for the cause of female emancipation, attack the hypocrisy of conventional morality, but seek fulfillment within the nest of traditional values'(200) and 'I am my greatest creation.'

Seen through, Merrily's eyes, we witness a society that rips her apart, each sect claiming her to be theirs. The Hindus angered at her betrayal, the Muslims claiming her to be an icon and the Christian who looks on and would like a piece of her, as she says, 'After death you can have the deadly carcass ... If the Muslims want one bone, they can take it'. Hindus take another bone. Christians take the head. It doesn't make a difference to me'(256). Her death on 31 May 2009 is the final sacrifice she made in the cause of love, reaching across religions and cultures. She was buried in the mosque, and for the first time in India women stood near the graveside for the funeral rites. She died as she had lived freely giving herself through her writing to a society that found it difficult to place her within a conventional mode.

Kamala/Merrily's co-writing is as much a journey through the spirit of Kerala as Maria/Griffiths is through that of Metis community. Their acceptance and positioning in society is as much a concern as their attempt to make bridges across cultures. The texts under consideration exhibit the kind of transcultural positioning that is reflexive of both the subject and the object, the writer and the critic. The doubling of the self and the reaching out to translate the experience, reveals a frighteningly disturbed world in which one's own self becomes the smallest particle of social reality seeking to construct a coherent story out of a life. The social formations, the cultural taboos, the contextualization of a period in the history of a country, the gendering of experiences, the regional and local flavour exhibited in these works get reflected in different ways as women writers reach across physical, cultural and psychological boundaries in attempting to understand one another. Constructing a text of the self and reliving and distancing oneself from one's stories, creates a dialogic of life writing that explodes conventional narrative structures and translates traumatic experiences.

References

Campbell, Maria, *Halfbreed*, Toronto: McClelland and Stewart, 1973.

Das, Kamala, *My Story*, New Delhi: Sterling, 1988.

Grant, Agnes, 'Canadian Native Literature: The Drama of George Ryga and Tomson Highway', *Australian Canadian Studies* 10.2 (1992): 37–56.

Griffiths, Linda and Maria Campbell, *The Book of Jessica: A Theatrical Transformation*, Toronto: Coach House, 1989.

Weisbord, Merrily, *The Love Queen of Malabar: Memoir of a Friendship with Kamala Das*, Montreal: McGill-Queen's University Press, 2010.

13

Crossing the Boundaries

Feminist Archives and the Redemptive Power of Sisterhood

Sachidananda Mohanty

It must be an irony of postcolonialism that despite the rhetoric of anti-essentialism and emphasis on local histories and particularism, indigenous feminisms in India, are yet to find their foothold in the larger cultural history of the land. Such work must necessarily be negligible in the context of the globalization of knowledge when the Euro-American academy reigns supreme and Indian languages, the gateway to multiple histories, are in a state of retreat everywhere. Barring honourable exceptions, indigenous feminist research in India, is yet to come up in an effective and forceful manner to answer to challenges posed by South Asian feminists like Chandra Talpade Mohanty in her pivotal work 'Under Western Eyes: Feminist Scholarship and Colonial Discourse'. Admittedly, there are critics like Susie Tharu, K. Lalitha, Jasbir Jain, Madhu Kishwar and others who have done pioneering work in this regard. But clearly, much more needs to be done if we were to have a meaningful dialogue across cultural barriers. It is in this sense that I wish to thank the organizers of the conference: 'Gender, Diversity and Cultural Pluralism'. Canada and India for the invitation to share my research findings that would hopefully be useful to feminist scholars in India and Canada.

I

To begin with, the adage that 'difference is not division' is easier to accept as a notion than as part of our lived experience. Contemporary multiculturalism that pins its hope on the public acceptance of diversity and difference must descend from the realm of constitutional governance to democratic living: diverse and pluralistic. The debates about multiculturalism would be relevant here. The best way this can be done is by the internationalization of an alternative set of attributes through syllabus reforms. But can a new pedagogy in the academia come in the absence of original archival research?

Part of the reason for this sad state of affairs is because of the hierarchy of Indian languages and the particular trajectory that English education has taken in India. The centres of learning that sprang around the British settlements in India in Kolkata, Mumbai and Chennai, and missionary efforts in the Danish settlement of Serampore and elsewhere are two of the many significant factors that contributed to new thinking in domains pertaining to female citizenship. The Orientalist Anglicist debates went hand in hand with the discourse over the woman question. In many parts of India, the discourse over the new woman shared simultaneous space with what came to be known as the 'conduct book' tradition. No effective knowledge of Indian women is possible without adequate awareness of this body of archival knowledge. And yet, forget about western feminists, how many Indian scholars – men and women have bothered to delve into this neglected domain?

This fact became increasingly clear to me since 1994 when I began to do serious archival research in the context of Colonial Orissa. The findings in the form of research publications are in the public domain. I wish to share here my latest work, a literary monograph based on the life and work of one of the greatest literary women of India in the first half of the 20th century, namely Sarala Devi.

It is not my aim here to chronicle the fascinating life story and career of this outstanding but completely neglected literary feminist. What I propose to do instead is to offer a brief life sketch and then centre stage some of her notable critical feminist concerns. And finally, I shall suggest how these concerns are relevant to others elsewhere including Canadian scholars and feminists. For, like Sandra Gilbert who argued that feminism must go beyond the academia, Sarala Devi too spoke for the need for conscious raising involving both women and men in the larger society. She would have been in complete agreement with Audre Lorde who wrote insightfully:

> Survival is not an academic skill. It is learning how to take our differences and make them strengths. For the master's tools will never dismantle the master's house. They may allow us temporarily to beat them at their own game, but they will never enable us to bring about genuine change. (Lorde, 1983: 94–101)

Born on 9 August 1904, in a conservative aristocratic family, in the Narilo village of Balikua in the undivided Cuttack district of Orissa, Sarala Devi carved out a place for herself in modern India by the sheer dint of her own efforts. She studied up to class seven but was largely self-educated. A born rebel, she developed strong reservations against orthodox religion when she came across this scriptural indictment: 'Woman is the veritable gateway to hell'. In an autobiographical essay entitled, 'The Story of My Revolutionary Life', she wrote: 'The God who does not belong to woman and is only a property of man, the sin in whose committing only woman becomes fallen and a man remains untouched, that religion and that custom gradually became bereft of meaning for me.'

An active member of the Congress Party, Sarala and her idealistic minded spouse Bhagirathi Mohapatra, a lawyer by profession, plunged into the national freedom struggle. She was the first Oriya woman to take part in the Satyagraha movement, and first Oriya woman to court imprisonment. At the Vellore Jail for women in the Madras Presidency she was a prison mate of other distinguished women such as Durgabai Deshmukh and Kamala Devi Chattopadhyaya. She was the first elected woman member of the Orissa Legislative Assembly in 1936 and has to her credit numerous achievements of similar kind.

It is important to see Sarala's life and times against the backdrop of the national imaginary. What kind of imaginary did Sarala uphold? How did this imaginary feed into the complex set of priorities and objectives she upheld? How did these aims deal with the nation and its fragments that the historian Partha Chatterjee spoke about?

Like her mentor Gandhiji, Sarala Devi believed that a true emancipation of the nation is not possible without a corresponding liberation of women. We must therefore see the rationale of the two significant essays she wrote as two sides of the same coin: 'The Rights of Women' and 'How Gandhiji influenced My Life'. Unlike the traditionalists who saw women, necessarily confined to the domestic and spiritual sphere, Sarala advocated full and active participation of women in the public domain.

II

It is however in the realm of ideas that Sarala Devi distinguished herself the most. These straddle many genres and disciplines. She wrote poetry, prose, criticism, novels, plays, letters, biographies, and pamphlets. Above all, her writings on women, both conceptual and practical, are pioneering and noteworthy. Her literary output includes over 30 books and over 300 essays. Some of the prominent books are: *Rabindra Puja, Utkal Bharati, Kabi Pratibha, Maru Kahani, Pancha Pradipa, Sarala Mahabharater Nari Chitra* (The Portrayal of Women in *Sarala Mahabharata*), *Bharatiya Mahila Prasanga, Utkalara Nari Samasya, Nari Jagata, Beera Ramani, Biswa Biplabini, Raja Ramananda Katha Ramayana, Amulyanidhi, Narira Dabi,* and others.

It is the essays of Sarala that concern us here. These deal with issues of society, culture, philosophy, nationalism to the plight of peasantry and other socio-economic ills. Her essays on women were particularly trenchant and were based on a rare maturity of vision.

There are several aspects of Sarala's essays that will be of interest to contemporary Euro-American and Canadian feminists. One is the majestic range and sweep of her interests. The allusions were truly global and international: from ancient Greece to modern England and America, she brought in the position of women in Turkey, Egypt, Palestine, Spain, Russia, Persia, India, and Afghanistan, often with statistics. Secondly she disproved the notion of women as 'universal depends', a view that finds favour with contemporary feminists. Thirdly, she discarded the homogenous nature of women's experience across societies and culture. In the 1980s, Chandra Mohanty would speak of the notion of the third world woman as a 'singular monolithic subject' who lacked agency. Similarly, Sarala saw little merit in categories such as 'biological, sociological and anthropological universals and steadfastly argued that Indian women, with all their differences of caste, class and region are capable of shaping their destinies'.

Next, while many feminists, then and now, have spoken of the uniformly oppressive nature of religion, Sarala argued that our critique must be context specific and be informed by particular histories of women in given societies and ideologies. For instance, she refers to an essay, 'Does Islam favour seclusion?' by Khawaja Kamaluddin and answers by drawing a contrast between the original tents of Islam *vis a vis* the later dictates of the Mulla based orthodoxy. Providing a detailed knowledge of the place of women according to the Holy Koran (*Hindustan Granthamala*, 1936: 11–12), she concludes that indeed

Islam has an egalitarian attitude towards women. Under the heading 'Progress of Indian Women', she wrote 'Many wise men believe that national slavery is the root cause of the backwardness of women. However, it could very well be that the plight of women could also be a significant cause of the national crisis' (Raju, 1995: 53).

Elsewhere, she spoke of phantoms or make-believe images that men create women, a view point that significantly anticipate Naomi Woolf's *Beauty Myth*. As she observes pointedly:

> A great many of educated men in India marry an image (or phantom) of their making. Very few are successful in acquiring an embodiment of the image; the rest get disappointed and often their marriage suffers from mental unrest. They lost all interest and attachment for women; at the most, they have compassion for women. (Mohanty, 2011: 20)

And finally Sarala spoke of the marital rape and the right of women over her body and reproductive self much ahead of her times. Quoting Justice Mecard, she said:

> I maintain that the wife's body can never be owned by her husband. It's her own property and not her husband's. She can leave her husband at her will; she can select her business or join the political party of her choice. She has full right to decide whether or not she is going to have a child and at what point in time. No man can keep a woman under her control on the basis of the fact that she is married to him. The woman of this country has won independence; she is a citizen and not a slave. (Mohanty, 2005: 157–158)

It would be seen that many of the feminist insights of Sarala Devi have found echoes in later feminists among the African-American, South Asian, Chicano-American and Canadian traditions. Audre Lorde, Cherrie Moraga, Margaret Atwood and others have underlined, in varied manner, the concerns raised by Sarala Devi in non-Western societies.

Sarala Devi published the best of her writings in the thirties of the last century while Margaret Atwood was born in 1939. Unlike Sarala, Atwood was more privileged. She studied myth criticism and Jungian ideas at the University of Toronto, Victorian Literature at Harvard (1962–63, 1965–67). *The Edible Woman* (1969) and *The Handmaid's Tale* (1985), a dystopia, are works of science fiction, admittedly different from Sarala's thematic concerns, that deal with the subject of women through the prism of irony and keen observation. In *The Handmaid's Tale*, the first person narrator's perspective is limited: 'I try not to think too much. Like other things now, thought must be rationed. There's a lot that does not bear thinking about. Thinking can hurt your chance, and I intend to last.'

The Edible Woman deals with the story of a young woman who works for a consumer company. After getting engaged, Marian experiences a strange separation between her body and herself. She begins to invest food with human qualities. In the process, she is unable to eat affected by 'metaphorical cannibalism'. The shifting from the first to the third person in the narrative suggests Marian's gradual disassociation from the reality. At the end, the return of the first person narrator indicates the character's ability to take possession of her life again. In the foreword written in 1979 for the Virago Press edition, Atwood terms *The Edible Woman* as proto-feminist rather than feminist.

Similarly, Atwood's *The Handmaid's Tale* (1985), a dystopia, was influenced by George Orwell's *1984*. The troubling narrative is set in the imaginary Republic of *Gilaad* whose governing ideology is one of religious fundamentalism. It is a regressive State where women have lost their freedom; language is granted to only the dominant male elite. The narrator Offred's reproductive system has survived chemical pollution and radiation. Unlike Harold Pinter's 1990 screen play of the novel where the protagonist becomes an active revolutionary and metes out instant brutal justice, Atwood's principal character uses irony and detached observation. There are throwbacks in the narrative to Offred's earlier life with her husband Luke and her five-year-old daughter.

III

It would be interesting to stage conversations among feminist thinkers across space and time. Sarala Devi and Margaret Atwood belong to a different time span. And yet, they have much in common. The dialogues between them are best carried out in the archives. As Audre Lorde aptly wrote:

> For women, the need and desire to nurture each other is not pathological but redemptive, and it is within that knowledge that our real power is rediscovered. It is this real connection that is feared by the patriarchal world. For it is only under patriarchy that maternity is the only social power open to woman. (Lorde, 1983: 26)

Are science fiction narratives of the feminist kind the preserve of Western women alone? Not quite! For, we see the example of Rokaya Hussain as well in the Indian context.

Sarala Devi's early theorization of freedom for women in her essays and novels find interesting echoes in the works of Margaret Atwood. Archival research in India that retrieves the feminist texts of literary women like Sarala, could serve as a gateway to the contemporary fiction of Canadian writers like Margaret Atwood, despite the manifest differences. The sisterhood they embrace could indeed lead to the blossoming of new ideas.

References

Atwood, Margaret, *The Edible Woman*, Toronto: McClelland and Stewart, 1969.

——, *The Handmaid's Tale*, London: Jonathan Cape, 1986.

Hindustan Granthamala, Cuttack: Nari Jagata, 1936.

Lorde, Audre, 'The Master's Tools will Never Dismantle the Master's House', in Cherrie Moraga and Gloria Anzaldua (eds), *This Bridge Called My Back: Writings by Radical Women of Colour*, New York: Kitchen Table Book, 1983.

Mohanty, Sachidananda, *Early Women's Writing in Orissa 1898–1950: A Lost Tradition*, New Delhi: Sage, 2005.

——, *Sarala Devi: Makers of Indian Literature*, Kolkata: Central Sahitya Akademi, 2001.

Raju, Rajendra, *Sarala Devi*, Berhampur: Bijay Book Store, 1995.

14

Narrating History/Herstory

Memory Work in Anita Rau Badami's *Can You Hear the Nightbird Call (2006)?*

Smita Banerjee

If it is a given that Diaspora[1] is always about identity and homeland, then the pertinent question to ask is how History/history, memory and the Diaspora negotiate these questions of identity and the homeland? Who do the contemporary Indo-Canadian diasporic writers write to? Is it possible to read these narratives as finally moving away from the binary of the centre and the periphery which was the dominant critical trope for the earlier Indo-Canadian poco interventions?[2] If the contemporary Indo-Canadian diasporic literature is transnational, given the flows of both culture and capital, then what are the questions that we need to ask of these writings?[3] The contemporary writers such as, Rohintan Mistry, M.G. Vasanji, Anita Rau Badami seem to be writing not to India, but to Canada. These writers need to be differentiated from the earlier generation; these are educated professionals whose impetus to articulate their identitarian politics is of an entirely different nature. Conflicts of identities, issues of cultural belonging, and deep seated desire to be accepted as equals but with difference, these seem to be driving tropes for most of these writers. Critiqued as being overdone, dated or done to death themes with hardly any new concerns, they still are being given newer outings by the contemporary Indo-Canadian diasporic writers. Without getting into the critical quagmire of why 'older' themes are still being articulated it might be more engaging to foreground some conceptual and pragmatic problems that are being filtered through these issues. Within the conceptual grid, one could ask questions of the articulation of the authoritative voice and its point of location (not to be confused with the 'locale' of the novel). Pragmatically the deployment of the rhetoric of resistance and atonement can alert us to the larger politics of identity formation in the global paradigm. Lastly we need to ask if these articulations are promoting assimilation, integration, or are leading to further polarization for the diaspora. To my mind, it is pertinent to filter the criticisms against Indo-Canadian diasporic writers through this critical grid. Perhaps if we could see the location and articulation of the critic's voice it might alert us to the varied subject positions inhabited by the Indians in India, and the Indians in Canada. In this sense, not only the history, but geography too will become an entry point to ask questions, which might allow us to reflect and contemplate diasporic writings without getting into hierarchies of old and new, of the marginal and peripheral, or the centre; this is not to devalue critical insights but to think through rhetorical positions that are very often left unquestioned and unchallenged. Only then can we begin to see the relevance or lack thereof of the poco/pomo defining of both 'difference' and 'value', to cite Linda Hutcheon's position on the question of Canadian identity.[4]

Writing on the imaginary of new fictions of Canada, Pedro Rodriguez summarizes some of the key concerns of the contemporary poco theory.[5] Quoting Kanishka Chowdhury, he argues that the 'newness' of much contemporary poco arises from its engagement with three different concepts. First, by drawing from Appiah's ideas of liberal cosmopolitanism, second 'post nationalism' via Baliber and third by referring to disjuncture, via the premise of diasporas and the movements of people/s across borders in Appadurai or Bhabha's formulation.[6] This brand of engagement has actually meant a parting of ways from the Marxist analysis, since it makes no room for the relevance of capital, market consumption and its assumptions. While it has a lot to offer in terms of its demystification of colonial ideologies and structures of power, it has in its modern incarnation, especially in its allegiance to the 'new' disavowed the Marxist tradition for an interpretive model based on cultural ambiguity, hybridity and cosmopolitanisms. I think this is an extremely relevant intervention in this age of the transnational global flow of voices and their locations that I have already referred to earlier. While we might be celebrating the 'new' voices, we might pause and also see the 'masking' that underpins most of this writing.

Igor Maver suggests that this new writing emerging in Canada is different from the earlier literary negotiations that foregrounded the idea of the cultural mosaic.[7] The sheer diversity of the writer's geographical roots lends a peculiar charge to the expressions of the new self image as a multicultural country. 'It can range from Africa, Asia, Caribbean, South America or Eastern Europe and despite being liberated from a spatial concept of location can nevertheless be deeply embedded in terms of its cultural memory of its community or his/her personal biography. These writers are opening up increasingly pluralized and globalized spaces that transcend traditional categories of Canadian-ness especially with regards to locale and volatility of cultural memory'.[8] His position challenges Linda Hutcheon's argument cited above. This is not to suggest that the 'deep sense of marginality'[9] has disappeared for the Canadian writer, but that in the critical template of multicultural and Area Studies, we need different conceptual and theoretical paradigms. It is important to engage with it since it can enable us to ask different questions given the nature of transnational global flows of culture, capital and markets, questions that are generally not articulated in our literary engagements with Diasporic writers. There is a pronounced shift in recent writing in that there seems to be reversed migration back to a home place by a Canadian who does not want to return home, unlike the previous generation, but writes back home. I shall examine this issue a little later in my essay, when I discuss Makrand Paranjape's intervention. He too refers to this phenomenon, where these writers do not visit the 'home' through nostalgia but look at it dispassionately. India as 'home' emerges as a fertile ground which provides them with rich material that can be tapped. They want to dissect what is wrong with India through their writings. Maver feels that these writers are more interested in the idea of imagined community rather than the notion of imaginary homeland (though Paranjape counters this and works with Rushdie's idea of imaginary homeland). This notion of the global transnational culture imbues these new diasporic voices with more empowerment. They are able to negotiate their displacements, transplacements and their fluid identities and 'homes' in ways that are more dynamic and contemporary. 'This suggests that all the variegated pluralist diversity of Canada today and offers new conceptions of global(ized) identities *per se*. The spaces they have created in their diasporic writings thus fully open and invite constant constructions, deconstruction and reconstruction'.[10]

What of the Indian writers then? Makrand Paranjape[11] provides an answer. In a witty inversion of Badami's statement[12] he captures the peculiar position that both fires this new writing yet haunts its textures of experiences. They are different from the earlier category of writers, in their ability to inhabit the homeland without the debilitating trope of loss and longing, yet they manage to revisit their 'history' of their home in interesting and illuminating ways. His central thesis revolves around the following: 'dialectics of longing and belonging, about the ways in which diasporic fictions relate to the idea of homeland, their out of India experience and how this reciprocal relationship unfolds through their fictions. Quoting Victor Ramraj on diasporic writers, he argues that the 'attachment' to the homeland, makes these writings both transitional and liminal. While the writers can be grouped into two kinds of diasporas, the first group having a traditionalist engagement and retaining separate identity, the second gradually merging with the mainstream of the host country. Citing Uma Parameswaran he suggests that Badami is 'second generation Canadian of South Asian origin who realize that home is here not elsewhere, ... but 'here' is not exclusively English ... but a place where one can be oneself, assimilating if one is comfortable doing so, being different if one chooses to be so'.[13] Paranjape's essay provides an answer to Chowdhury bemoaning of the absence of the Marxist tradition referred to earlier. He unmasks the attitude of these writers to the homeland and how their writing is both a response to and a consequence of the market logic and the global terrain that they choose to inhabit. As he suggests, 'They do not celebrate the homeland, but mourn its relentless and innumerable atrocities and tragedies. They enact a farewell to India not a passage to India' (85). This transnational impulse according to him is a movement towards Canada, even when the narrative is located in India or the homeland. The absence of a nostalgic tone is a major departure from the earlier generation of diasporic writers. This new writing is imbued with an elegiac tone that foregrounds a self legitimating logic of leaving the homeland. The subtext of desiring cultural acceptance in the host country on a more equitable and less racist plane, of inhabiting a less alienated or strange Canada emerges as a defining trope. It is neither a simple rejection of the homeland or acceptance in the home-country, but rather a working out of Bhabha's idea of hybridization. Badami, Mistry, Vasanji et all are the new writers who in his words are in the 'privileged position of actually seeing the distinct strands of their lives merge to create a new type of culture ... that have access to the Indian and the Canadian, both separately and together' (79–80). And of course the citation is to Uma Parameswaran's formulation in *Ganga in the Assiniboine*.[14]

II

The idea of memory works in my title refers to the imaginary of a sociological intervention. This is largely related to identity work, often associated with displaced persons. These could be narratives of repressed, traumatic memories, events, or could be what Pierre Nora had termed as 'lieux de memoiré/sites of memory',[15] that revisit distorted history, or cultural memories that continue to haunt the present and need constant retelling to enable the community to exorcize the trauma.[16] The historical events that are imaginatively reconstructed and narrated could be ascribed the status of foundational events, acquiring mythic proportions in popular imaginary. These events form the corpus of collective or communitarian memories that the Diaspora[17] revisits with each articulation. The rewriting then operates to suture the fissures engendered by traumatic events in the popular imaginary. It is precisely this interpretive model that can provide us multiple grids to unpack the uses to which memory, History, identity is being put to in Badami's *Can You Hear the Nightbird call* (2006; hereafter *CYHNC)*. I would suggest that the intervention of Nora is central to formulating our discourse of cultural memory and its expression in the novel. The intermeshing of the private and the public, the fluid movement across time and space, and the storehouse of cultural memory enables Badami to open up spaces that can enable articulations of repressed memories. Following Nora we can suggest that Badami's enterprise is akin to creating an archive of the Sikh Diaspora through her imaginative reconstruction of its traumatic history. If the Diaspora is the tale of economic prosperity, it is equally culpable in its support of the communal and sectarian politics of the Khalistan movement. However as her retelling shows, this enterprise is a fraught one. Narrating tales of violence, terror and sectarian politics is not an easy enterprise, especially if it foregrounds the recent history. The section narrating Bibi ji's transformation and Jasbeer's embracing of the separatist cause brings to fore the terrifying consequences of having a warped sense of history. Both fall prey to acts of violence and become victims of the same violence they themselves helped engender. In the aftermath of the Kanishka bombing (1985), Bibi ji is left alone, 'an old woman living in a dead house, on the western edge of the world, only ghosts and guilt for company'(*CYHNC*: 395). Jasbeer's letter to Preethi makes us confront our own demons of fostering communal fanaticism. We realize how the 'other' who we consider an enemy is inside all of us, waiting to rear its self, straining to come out as the known faces of erstwhile friends and neighbours who in their moment of madness kill and maim. How the familiar and quotidian becomes the playground of terror, how attempts of rewriting 'other/separatist' histories can quickly turn into enterprises that can consume and suck people into endless spiral of more terror and violence.

From her first novel, *Tamarind Woman* (2002) Badami taps the reservoir of 'Memories(that) were like ghosts, shivery, uncertain, nothing guaranteed, totally not for sure',[18] in all their contradictions and selectiveness to spin tales that play on the fictions that we create to retell our stories. Like Saroja is that novel she hoards them, and through her writings leaves her readers with 'memories of an old story teller, a weaver of myths' (TW: 266). If *Tamarind Woman* deals with the intensely personal memories to narrate the search for self, Badami's *Can You Hear the Nightbird Call*, foregrounds the play of the personal and the public histories/History to 'write' the Diaspora. In this novel she taps the sad and the ugly, dusting off the cobwebs and revisits the dead and the living. Like Kamini in *Tamarind Women*, Badami too cannot let the memories be, she is driven by them.[19] It is with this novel that Badami tries to use the trope of collective memory, when she asks like Kamini of all of us to remember, remember unpleasant sad memories that we try desperately as people, as a community or nation to brush aside, cloak it with denial or silence or what Ashis Nandy has called the 'cultivated aphasia' in the context of Partition history and memory.[20]

Divided into five episodic parts, the novel charts the journey of its principle characters, inhabiting diverse geographical locations; these stories are interconnected not only through the trope of memory, but also intersecting pasts and presents. I use the novel to reflect on one of the core issues concerning Indo-Canadian diasporic writers, namely; literary retellings of histories and geographies of peoples and events. Badami's novel has an epic scale; moving from 1928 Punjab to Canada, ending finally in Delhi and Vancouver in 1986. The public events, the Komagata Maru (1914), the Partition riots (1947), Delhi riots (1984), and the Kanishka air crash (1985) collide with and impact the private stories of the three women, Bibi ji, Nimmo and Leela, in ways that are fascinating chronicles of the intermeshing of private and the public. These women find themselves caught in historical events, sometimes by choice, at others because they happened to be victims of those events. The first three sections are narrated in third person by the three women, Bibi ji, Leela, and Nimmo. In each, we are given glimpses into their childhood and growing up years, but the narration is framed by their attempts at reconstructing their memories of what they remember. The selectiveness, random and sometimes distorted nature of their memories gives a glimpse into the larger grid of remembrance and forgetting that Badami's novel signposts. The last two sections narrate the collisions that are engendered by these intersecting stories. All three women and their families become victims of events that are being played out in the larger public domain. It is as if Indra's net that fascinated Preethi as a child sets in motion events that 'caused a series of tremors'(*CYHNC*: 106). These tremors not only tear asunder the social, but have horrific repercussions on the individual and the personal. The other important trope is the relationship of history and memory. Recent scholarship has of course moved away from the earlier hierarchical position whereby the academic historical study of the past was considered superior to the popular engagements with the past via folklore or other expressive forms of memory, and the collective or the individual.[21] In her retelling, Badami uses both, History as well as 'histories/herstories', layering them with palimpsest of personal narratives.

The idiosyncrasies of memory are fore grounded early in the novel. It needs its place to grow, in the absence of its locale it seems to be selective, rudderless. In Sharan's remembering of her childhood, she only remembers some details. Immigration to Canada just before independence saves her from experiencing the trauma of Partition, but it makes her lose her moorings, her village 'And since after Partition, Panjaur itself disappeared into that grey zone ... she could not even return to the place of her origin, a necessary thing if memory has to kept fully alive. Yet some of those days remained in her mind, sharp and clear as shards of glass' (*CYHNC*: 4). She only remembers the day her father disappeared for good, the odour of cow dung, and her mother's anger overpowering everything else her memory of the smell of the scented soap, that Jeeti's father send from faraway Canada. Refusing to be cowed down by her mother's admonitions she dares to take her chances when she can. 'Beware of anything that begins with the troublesome question Why not,' Gurpreet would warn her younger daughter ... And although Gurpreet Kaur did not know it then, ten years later, sixteen year old Sharan would stick out her lower lip mutinously, murmur Why not question under her breath and change her sister's fortunes and her own a well' (*CYHNC:* 18). Unlike Harjot, who lets go of life after his failed voyage on the Komagata Maru, she is driven by the 'irresponsibility of dreams'(14) and 'when chance came galloping towards her she would leap on its back and ride like the wind'(18). Married to Pa ji, she does become the 'two edged sword' that he wants her to be and transforms herself into the successful immigrant, realizing her dreams of having the luxury of beautiful things. She surrounds herself with the smell of lavender, a luxury that she remembers envying her friend Jeeti for, something that she sent for her sister Kanwar, and the smell that Nimmo, her niece associates with her mother's dead body. Sharan herself refuses to use lavender soap after she loses contact with Kanwar, reclaiming her luxurious indulgence years after when she finds Nimmo and visits her.

Nimmo, Sharan's niece is a victim of partition, losing her family in the carnage. Her memory of her childhood is evoked in the association of fear and the smell of lavender that her mother washes herself with after she has been raped. Her memory plays tricks on her as she tries to remember what her parents looked like. The only object she has is a tattered post card addressed to Kanwar w/o Pradeep, with the name of her village. What she cannot forget is the fear and the shame of having peed in the grain bin that her mother made her hide as the Muslim men attacked their house. Years later she writes to Sharan about all that she remembers, 'She wrote every detail of that terrifying night in Dauri Kalan, except for her memory of a pair of lavender –fragrant feet suspended above the floor ... By the simple act of writing to her, Nimmo realized, she had gathered up those shards of memory and looked straight at them for the first time'(161). However this woman, who cannot shrug off her fear and is extremely conscious of being careful is finally torn asunder when she watches her daughter Kamal being burnt inside the steel almirah, victim of Delhi riots in 1984. Both her younger son, Pappu and her husband Satpal are burnt alive by the mob in the same riots. All through the narrative, we see Nimmo grappling with her fearful memories, never certain if they were true or figments of her imagination. It is people such as Satpal with little or no imagination who seem to be able to live their lives with certainties born of their sense of belonging, or Leela's father-in-law, who can die with the assurance of being in his own home and die in his own bed. She survives after the first loss, yet she cannot rewrite 'herstory' with a happy ending. Events beyond her control make her lose her entire family for the second time in her life. She thinks 'she is a careful woman, a fearful one, who is prepared for trouble. Not like her foolish mother, who left nothing behind except a small, frightened child and the smell of lavender soap' (*CYHNC*: 401). Try as she might, she is unable to exorcise the fear of the 'event' that forced her mother to kill herself. Years later, when her own daughter perishes in the carnage, she finally retires into the twilight of her memory of the time when they were alive. She withdraws into the mundaneness of her everyday chores of cleaning and cooking, doing it repeatedly and incessantly as she waits with feasts of food for her husband, son and daughter who she is sure would come back to her. She is unable to comprehend how one woman could lose her family twice over, so she lives on, clinging to her perception of her belief. If as Pierre Nora suggested, 'The quest for memory is the search for one's history',[22] Nimmo's history is wiped out twice, she becomes a piece of news briefly after the riots and her memories too seem to be stuck in a curious time wrap. Badami's narrative brings it to the fore, and the readers are left with a sense of disquiet to ponder on the vagaries of chance and fate. It is her writing of Nimmo that brings alive the sites of memories, created by a play of memory and history. It is her will to remember that makes this articulation possible.[23]

In this novel, two tropes, memory and maps are significant. In different ways all the characters try to redraw their personal maps in the manner that they choose to. If Pa ji, Bibi ji are the quintessential success story, Leela too manages to adapt to her in between state. Mukherjee and Balu reinvent their professional selves to fit into what is expected of them. As Bibi ji tells Leela, since they are all in the 'minority boat', they need to have 'bad memories' too, the ability to forget, it 'was necessary for a person wishing to settle in, to become one of the crowd, to become an invisible minority' (*CYHNC*: 137). Badami narrates the negotiations involved in this attempt of settling down, from the banal and funny to the serious. Lalloo learns to fit in by watching soaps, he makes all the new arrivals in Vancouver sprawl in front of the television and gives lessons in Canadian society. The novel also signposts the fictionality involved in this reinvention. Of reimagining histories to create selves that have no moorings. It is visible in Pa ji's attempt at creating a grand history of his father. Even if

Bibi ji cannot like Pa ji 'spin history using longing for yarn and imagination for a loom' (*CYHNC*: 203), she understands Pa ji's need to rewrite his familial history, 'she knew all about keeping dreams alive. What harm, she thought, could his small private fictions do in a world where larger truths were reshaped to suit those in power?' (204) Pa ji was able to 'scribble truth' the way he wanted. He built entire families out of thin air, 'use new relationships and stories to patch up the holes created by lost and left-behind ones' (203). Displaced from one's place of origin, without the certainties of belonging, these people acquire the ability of creating new maps or of learning to read maps. Both Bibi ji and Leela try to make use of their abilities to have their feet in two worlds, they learn the advantage of living 'neither here nor there'(84).

Yet maps become symbols of discontent and separation in Dr Randhawa's evocation. In his visits to Delhi Junction he displays maps of his imagined future state. Pa ji who ' loved maps: they were integral to the history of Sikhs. It was maps that caused countries to exist or expire; maps caused bitter wars, maps erased people and landscapes just as efficiently as they created them. Maps, Pa ji knew, were a bane and boon' (254). However in Dr Randhawa's reinvention, they become 'the imagined Independent Country superimposed on the map of India' (254). Pa ji realizes that it would mean another displacement and fragmentation while for Bibi ji these maps were like 'A series of tracings, a palimpsest of images, the product of so many histories, some true, some imaginary, all valid, but surely not all necessary' (255). However Pa ji is clear-sighted about his love for his Homeland and its fraught history, 'Pa ji wouldn't deny that he was fond of India that was part of his being and was where his memories often turned. But history was a picture hanging on a wall, something of the past to spur the imagination, to write books about. It wouldn't do to let swallow you whole' (166). But is precisely this need for history that forces Jasbeer to believe whole heartedly in the stories of his origins, his community's heroic valour. In trying to give shape to Jasbeer, to mould his sense of pride in his Sikh roots, Pa ji does not realize how it made Jasbeer's mind a fertile ground for Dr Randhawa's bitter communal schemes to take root in with disastrous consequences. Jasbeer allows his history to swallow him. His religious indoctrination propels him to choose a path that leads to death, incarceration and ultimately the destruction of his entire family. At the end, after he is released from jail he goes back to Nimmo, but she is a shadow, living in the curious grey zone of her memories of her dead family. He thinks he has come back home, but we the readers know how that space has turned into an empty shell, devoid of the living, only a storehouse of his mother's imaginary of her past.

However it is not only the personal mapping that is central to the negotiation of diasporic identity. If these reconstruct histories, then the social maps reconfigure the spatial relation of the personal and the social, the idea of 'location', of space is central to this imaginary. The multicultural or the Transnational does not seem to be completely devoid of the centrality of the ethnic ghettoization. The sense of comfort or the idea of 'desis' hanging out together still drives the narrative impetus. For the older generation, it is the coming together of other immigrants that fosters a sense of belonging and camaraderie. In typical Diaspora fashion, it is the smell, the rituals, the language, the spices, food etc. which Badami evokes to give a sense of the everyday lives of people uprooted from their villages. As a surprised Leela realizes, it is Punjab in the Taj Mahal. She herself wonders how long would it take her to belong in the new world, or would her move to Vancouver always be besieged by her earliest memory of being 'half and half' or her subsequent attempt at reinventing herself through marriage to Balu, at being the only daughter-in-law of the Kunjoor Bhatt's. In the novel, it is only with Leela's son Arjun and his white girl friend that we see the 'other' becoming a part of the family. And predictably, Leela does not know how to deal with the 'other' becoming a part of her 'self'. She would prefer the whites to remain outside, comfortable in her realization that, 'Abroad had turned into Home' and 'Nowadays, goras who came here wandered around with a dazed look in their eyes as if they were foreigners in their own country' (*CYHNC*: 308). Unlike them, she has managed to 'read' the city, 'She had taken the woman's map from her hands and without hesitating for even a moment had traced the route for her with her red pen ... a recognition of one who belonged, one who needed no maps to find her way' (307). Leela who had once grudged her move abroad now finds herself being astonished by how 'real India had overtaken her memories of it', how pictures of Indians back home look 'like her children-Indian, but with a subtle glossy western-ness coating their brown bodies' (308).This is precisely why we need to unmask the contemporary diasporic offering, because it manages to capture all the fissures and contradictions that immigrants need to negotiate and encounter in trying to create their histories. While the invocation of cultural and communitarian memories do help in solidifying their self imaginaries, the spatial interfaces remain exclusionary and hierarchical.

The 'hegemony of the historicism'[24] needs to be placed alongside, the geographical if we have to unmask the deployment of history, memory and identity. This hegemony has occluded a 'compatible critical sensibility to the spatiality of social life, a practical theoretical consciousness that sees the life world of being creatively located not only in the making of history but also in the construction of human geographies, the social production of space and the restless formation and reformation of geographical landscape: social being actively emplaced in space and time in an explicitly historical and geographical contextualization' (Soja 1999:136). It seems a kind of truism to evoke the home and host country as given categories that inflect the immigrant experience. It is not only the historical imaginary but the spatial as well that the immigrant identity has to contend with in its quest for belonging. In *Can You Hear the Night Bird Call* Badami's geographical imagination and the spatial life story of the characters is given what Soja calls 'a triple dialectic of space, time and social being; a transformative retheorization of the relations between history, geography, and modernity.'[25] Intertwined with the threads of memory and history, is a rich tapestry of space that the three women live in and weave their life stories. To my mind, Delhi Junction that Bibi ji and Pa ji establish in Vancouver is not merely symbolic of the immigrant success story in 1950s Canada. It is significantly that space where the Hindus and Sikhs come together over cups of chais to discuss the pink goras. It is the space where all fraught transactions of identity politics, ethnicity, faith and belief are played out. From its comforting avatar, where Sam Hunt comes for his fix of Mutton curry and prompts Bibi ji's condescending reflection on grouchy old man, 'the Englishman transplanted to Canada, was doing the splits between two cultures, just like the desis were' (*CYHNC*: 58), it soon turns into a battlefield. What we are left to wonder is how in the present, old rages and enmities get reconfigured and renewed. How questions of faith and beliefs continue to breed fanaticism and hatred. Bibi ji becomes an ardent supporter of the Khalistan movement, opening her home and restaurant to the Separatists meetings and going for demonstrations. In her grief at Pa ji's demise at the Golden Temple siege, she lets hatred and rage overcome all other emotions to take over her life. 'The Indians had humiliated the Sikhs and they had killed her Pa ji. Now it was a question of defending the faith, the thing that gave them, as a tribe, a face and a distinction'. (*CYHNC*: 343). And being away from the homeland is no safeguard against those differences, nor do they guarantee harmony and peaceful existence. 'The world had come apart since then and had fitted itself together with altered borders. Old countries had become two or three new ones, walls had gone up and had been torn down, ancient enmities had been buried and then renewed with greater rage'(307). The immigrants play out all the factionalism in the far away land with as much enmity as they are played out in India, making Balu wonder, 'us and them, Balu though uneasily. When did we split into these groups? The Singhs were family' (341). The immigrant dream of success and economic prosperity becomes redundant in the face of unfolding terror. As lives are torn apart, Leela dies suspended in the air, in between two continents. She dies as she had lived, 'half and half', leaving a grieving family. Bibi ji and Nimmo lose everything and become ghosts of their former selves. The shards of memory that both lived by, keep pricking their selves.

To conclude with Carlos Fuentes's words from a different context:

> 'Reality is not the product of an ideological phantasm. It is the result of history. And History is something we have created ourselves. We are thus responsible for our history. No one was present in the past. But there is no living present with a dead past. No one has been present in the future. But there is no living present without the imagination of a better world. We ... made the history of this hemisphere. We must remember it ... We must imagine it ...' times in which the present contains past and future, because the present is the place of both memory and desire'.[26]

Notes

1. Igor Maver, *New Diasporic Literature in a Post-Ethnic Transcultural Canada*, Slovenia: University of Ljubliana, 2011, p. 1. Maver's article provides a lucid summary of the concept of Diaspora, identity and homeland. He suggests that these writers translate their reality and personal experience in two or more different systems. Hence their work contributes to the enrichment of both cultures and is an important part of the emerging cosmopolitan culture *per se*. Diaspora, often caused by major historical and political changes, carries with it the collective cultural memory and capital of the past, overseas or across border.
2. See Stephen Slemon's argument that postcolonial writers are necessarily compelled to rewrite or reimagine history because of their colonial past. But Slemon's argument forces one to only think of this

interface in binaries of the 'centre' and 'periphery', in 'Post Colonial Allegory and the Transformation of History', *Journal of Commonwealth Literature* XXIII.1 (1988).

3. Maver says that Diasporic writing today connects the past and the present and forges new notions of fluid and transnational identities; it opens up spaces for new expressions of a transnational global culture. Thus, it also seriously challenges the centre-periphery positioning central to 'traditional' poco studies.
4. Linda Hutcheon suggests that the self imaginary of Canada is always that of the marginalized. Quoting Bharati Mukherjee, she suggests that this sense of 'ex-centricity' drives the Canadian writer to be obsessed with its dialogues with History. Her position, similar to that of Slemon is a 'traditionalist' poco position and is challenged by newer paradigms that deploy the 'transnational' critical grid. "Circling the Downspout of Empire': Post-Colonialism and Post-Modernism', https://tspace.library.utoronto.ca/bitstream/1807/10262/1/tspace0171.pdf. Accessed on 10.01.2012
5. Pedro M. Carmona Rodriguez, 'Beyond the Edge of the Century: The Post-Colonial Imagination in the 'New' Fictions of Canadas', *Miscelanea: A Journal of English and American Studies* 38 (2008): 29–45.
6. Ibid., p. 35.
7. Maver, 2011, op. cit.
8. Ibid., p. 10.
9. Bharti Mukherjee in Linda Hutcheon's essay.
10. Ibid., p. 10.
11. Makrand R. Paranjape, 'One Foot in Canada and a Couple of Toes in India: Diasporas and Homelands in South Asian Canadian Experience', in Paranjape (ed.), *Diaspora: Theories, Histories, Texts*, New Delhi: Indialog, 2001, pp. 161–170 (Makrand Paranjape official website: 10 January 2012).
12. Badami has referred to her situation as 'one foot in India and a couple of toes in Canada'. CNN Interview. (Available online)
13. Uma Parameswaran, 'Ganga in Assiniboine: Prospects for Indo-Canadian Literatures', in Makarand Paranjape (ed.), *Diaspora: Theories, Histories, Texts*, New Delhi: Indialog, 2001, p. 85.
14. Ibid.
15. Pierre Nora, 'Les Lieux de Memoire', *Representations* 26 (Spring 1989): 13.
16. I am indebted to the insights offered by Trauma theory. It has generally been associated with Holocaust studies, in the Indian context, Partition studies has drawn on this theoretical intervention.

17. Diaspora is the dispersal of various people around the world. In the classic sense it is associated with the Jewish experience of dislocation and displacement. However, it has since been used to productively engage with immigrant narratives.
18. Anita Rau Badami, *Tamarind Woman*, Chapel Hill: Algonquin Books, 2002, pp. 72–73.
19. In fact, Badami has referred to the actual incident that she had witnessed during her travel in north India during the 1984 riots. See her website for details of the burning of a Sikh man and the Kanishka bombing of Air India 182, that stayed in her memory and were retold in this novel. (CNN Interview with Badami. Available online)
20. Ashis Nandy refers to the complete cloak of denial surrounding Partition in our public and private discourse. According to him, it is deliberate as the victims and civil society prefers to brush the shame and trauma of their suffering aside and not to engage with it. See his Introduction in *Mapmaking*, Debjani Sengupta (ed.) New Delhi: Shristi, 2003.
21. The works of Memory theorists such as Maurice Halbwachs or Pierre Nora or Paul Ricouer despite differences in their theoretical positions, consider history and memory as different phenomena. The works of others such as Nerone, Burke, Samuel, etc. see the fluid transitions between both history and memory.
22. Nora, op. cit., p. 13.
23. Ibid., p. 22.
24. Edward Soja, 'History: Geography: Modernity', in Simon During (ed.), *Cultural Studies Reader*, London and New York: Routledge, reprint 1999, p. 136.
25. Ibid., p. 137.
26. Carlos Fuentes, *Myself with Others*, New York: Farrar, Straus and Giroux, 1988, pp. 75–76 and p. 214.

Reference

Badami, Anita Rau, *Can You Hear the Nightbird Call*, New Delhi: Penguin Viking, 2006.

15

Body as Text and Context in the Works of Atwood and Goswami

Shraddha A. Singh

Atwood asserts, 'As for Woman, capital W, we got stuck with that for centuries. Eternal woman. But really 'Woman' is the sum of women. It doesn't exist apart from that, except as an abstracted idea' (*Conversations* 201); and Cixous' 'The Laugh of the Medusa' (1976) is a tool that can be used to analyse women's textual self-representation and their strategy for challenging patriarchal discourses. It also offers a lens through which Atwood's and Goswami's writing of their female protagonists can be productively interpreted. This paper examines how Atwood and Goswami are alike in refusing to idealize totalities and insisting on writing the realities of women operating within a historically specific socio-culture, but the bodies they write are nevertheless subversive carriers of a female language and thus of coded meanings. They repeatedly write the female body in terms of the culture that determines it, simultaneously throwing light on that body and on that cultural process which is always and inescapably political.

Atwood's *The Blind Assassin* (2001) and *The Handmaid's Tale* (1998) and Goswami's *The Moth-Eaten Howdah of the Tusker* (2005) and *Shadow of the Dark God* (1987) are survival narratives in which the bodies of the protagonists provide coded versions of socio-political and interpersonal struggles. Both authors exploit the relationship of the body with clothes to create a frame to discuss the complex interrelationships among representation, voice, gender, and culture; into relationships which tie into the overarching project of survival.

In *The Blind Assassin*, Atwood's protagonist Iris, who is a writer, puts forth her story using her body as primary text and constantly refers to it. She faces domestic violence and writes about it in terms of 'a kind of code, which blossomed, then faded, like invisible ink held to a candle. But if they were a code, who held the key to it?' (371). Using the simile of 'invisible ink' to refer to her bruises she looks at her torment as a type of writing, where her body is the medium on which it is performed. At another point she says, 'I was sand, I was snow – written on, rewritten, smoothed over' (271). Therefore, her body becomes a blank page, a medium on which some code is structured by her abusive husband and she loses all autonomy over it. She does not possess the key to access this code and, thus feels effectively destroyed as an ındividual. This disempowerment of Iris makes her a victim of forces that are beyond her control and situates the body as a figurative text.

In Goswami's novel inspired by her experiences of the *sattra* at South Kamrup, Assam; *The Moth-Eaten Howdah of the Tusker*, she reflects upon the horrifying practice of marrying off young girls before they reach puberty in order to avoid the labelling of the family as outcasts. The social taboo emerges from superstitious beliefs which are centuries old and part of the local culture which label the female body as impure and unwanted once the rite of passage from childhood is crossed. The onus of morality and honour lies on the women. When Giribala, the young and recently widowed daughter of the Damodar Gossain, is brought back to her maternal home a crowd of local women of the *sattra* gathers in the courtyard making speculations about the ill-treatment of the girl by her wastrel husband to which she violently reacts asserting her active presence:

> With an explosive sound, the door of the sandal *puja* room burst open and Giribala rushed out like a tigress in rage. Her hair had come undone and flew wildly. Her *gatala* had come off and her clothes were in a disarray. Her eyes blazed at the group of women, she screamed 'You came here to see me, didn't you? You have seen me now. I am still alive! I will live on and have a better life than all of you .... (34)

The Gossainee, Giribala's mother, blames the women for prying on her young daughter's clothes for signs of menstruation which lead to her being married off to the first possible suitor. This alarming degree of surveillance to which women are subjected is a concern with Atwood and Goswami, as is reflected in their works and is manifested at both macro and micro levels in the novels of Atwood, especially when the state imprisonment of Offred is matched by the metaphorical imprisonment of Iris, and the inspection of Giribala.

Offred in *The Handmaid's Tale* and Eliman in *The Moth-Eaten Howdah of the Tusker*, are similar in the way their bodies are reinscribed by the biological discourse of the respective communities they belong to and their oppressive sexual practices. Ironically the only real hope for the women centres on the use of their bodies. Though Eliman does not have much of a choice, her only escape from her current situation is through marriage with the Gossain's son, Indranath. For him, it is the lure of her body ('He would remember this pair of legs the rest of his life .... Yes, what a pair of legs they were!') (20); but it is not powerful enough to make him rebel against the expected codes of conduct. For Eliman, any encounter with Indranath is dangerous and she suffers from an overpowering sense of guilt which stems from traditional morality which has seeped into her subconscious. A scandal of a woman is a scandal forever in the *sattra*, but even then she makes her bold attempt to meet him for the sake of survival.

In Offred's case, she has no choice and has to perform the duties of a Handmaid, but she does attempt defiance in the ownership of her body that she displays throughout the text. She takes pride in this and it reflects in her statement, 'I sink down into my body as into a swamp, fenland, where only I know the footing' (83). This goes well with Cixou's advice: 'Write yourself. Your body must be heard' (338).

Gayatri Spivak argues that 'there is no such thing as an uncoded body', drawing attention to ways in which the body is always marked by 'codes' that bear witness to wider cultural and political forces acting upon it.[1] As such, in the fiction of Atwood and Goswami the female bodies are bodies that are run on a system of codes written by patriarchs or women who act as agents of patriarchy where these bodies are constantly watched, examined, contained, and silenced according to the prevailing customs of the society in which these bodies are placed in the narrative. Thus, the ways in which a body image may be managed both by and for culture are significant.

The Handmaid's Tale, which may be classified as distopian literature, presents a horrifying account of reproductive rights. Atwood's corporeally oppressed protagonists often dissociate or physically remove themselves from their bodies. In Goswami's fiction as well there is no sentimentality about motherhood. In many of her stories we find women crudely inducing abortion, for example in 'The Offspring', the woman sells her body to a rich man who wants a child but aborts her pregnancy because she cannot bear the child of a man belonging to a lower caste. Sex for her protagonists must be both emotionally and socially acceptable. What occupies her most is the unfolding of desire in a protagonist and deals with the dangers of her existence. How can a woman achieve her self-fulfilment in a world where she is hemmed in by restrictions imposed by religion, social custom, and the fear of assault?

In *Shadow of Dark God*, Mrinalini, Sashiprabha and Saudamini live in the shadow of death; their guardians and protectors are either old or dying. Each one of them is haunted by the prospect of joining the *Radheshyamis*, the destitute widows of Vrindavan, who have been abandoned by their families in the name of religion and live on the edge of survival in foul-smelling, ramshackle hovels, begging near the temples or singing devotional songs at the *bhajanashrams* for a pittance. The money provided for their upkeep by the rich donors or temple trusts is pocketed by corrupt officials and the younger women are forced into prostitution or 'united in prayer' with priests and pandas. Some of them belong to educated and respectable families but have been degraded by extreme poverty, incurable diseases, sub-human living conditions and are subjected to every kind of physical indignity. Many of them just wait for death with their meagre savings tied in their waistbands, hoping to be given a decent funeral. Frequently their corpses are plundered by the pandas or even their own mates for any chance possessions, and then thrown unceremoniously into the Yamuna.

The *Radheshyamis* are portrayed with shaved heads, their foreheads covered with turmeric and sandalwood paste, their limbs crippled by leprosy and their starving bodies showing through their tattered saris. The dependence of and the threat from the agents of patriarchy is such that even in a group, these women who are widows, and therefore have no ties with any male; are perceived as a threat to society. They are assigned a space outside domesticity and it is considered to be an inauspicious omen if the shadow of a widow falls on a married woman. Thus, by their performative roles in the social arena, women are classified into groups that are worse or better off than the others.

When Saudamini approaches the *Radheshyamis* in a spirit of compassion and friendliness, they surround her and begin to molest her, pulling her cheeks and hair, and seem to be ready to tear her limbs apart till she is rescued by a Sadhu and warned to stay away from them. Such an act of a violent reproach by a peer group is also enacted in *The Handmaid's Tale* where accusations are levelled at one of the Handmaids for being responsible for the sexual violence that happens to her. The other Handmaids are made to point fingers at her under the supervision of the Aunts. The recurrent emphasis on erasure becomes conjoined with ideas relating to incarceration and surveillance in the writing of the female body by both authors. Ideas of nullity and absence often dominate symbolic activity in these stories as if these images and symbols alone attest to the storyteller's deletion from the body politic through such acts of violence and negation.

Thus, in the fictive worlds of Atwood and Goswami, identity is actively self-fashioned in response to context. Dress and adornment define identity as either identity that is expected or desired or identity that is reflected or assumed. For the female protagonists in the novels, codes of 'femininity' often determine their choice of clothing. Both authors suggest that feminist resistance to such structures can be figured in the body and its coverings, especially when we see Atwood's protagonists fashioning themselves; and Goswami's protagonists donning a certain garb due to the socio-cultural obligations.

As pointed earlier in this paper in the case of Iris, Atwood often describes storytelling in terms of designing or weaving, which aligns her with a particularly female tradition. Traditional English phrases, like 'spinning the yarn', are associated with storytelling and tailoring. Atwood's reflection on the stereotype of how she was expected to dress up, when in the literary circles, is quite revealing:

> I had no idea, for instance, that I was about to step into a whole set of preconceptions and social roles which had to do with what poets were like, how they should behave, and what they ought to wear, moreover, I did not know that the rules about these things were different if you were female .... I did not know that to be told I had transcended my gender would be considered as a compliment. I didn't know – yet – that black was compulsory (Waterstone's Poetry Lecture 2).

As Atwood realized that dressing in a certain way would bring into question traditional cultural binaries like masculine/feminine, self/other, individual/society, styling the self, or self-fashioning through dress, became an important method of survival. Clothes are a reflection of a culture that is laced with ideology and power. They work as codes that easily distinguish between the dominant and the marginal, the normative and the deviant. In Goswami's texts, dress is culturally prescriptive and part of the dominant patriarchal social order.

Individuals define their social positions through their clothes which can signal the possession or lack of power. In *The Moth-Eaten Howdah of the Tusker*, it is Eliman's blood stained *mekhala* that is of prime importance in her given social context. Her old maid's appeal to Indranath highlights the desperation of Eliman's situation. 'There are certain loathsome, malicious women who might visit the backyards secretly at night, just to find out whether the girl of the house has reached puberty ... those old Brahmins will declare her and her father social outcasts ... this girl is like a frail creeper! Who will protect her?' (50). It is the society which wants to control the natural cycles of a woman's body and she is dependent on a man for survival, as a victim of societal pressure.

Thus, Goswami's characters are always involved in negotiations of familial, rhetorical, political, and gendered networks and codes. When Saudamini's restlessness reaches its peak, one night her father helps her unite with her Christian lover on a boat on the river bank. As she moves towards the river bank she hears the sweet melody of the *shehnai* coming from the temple and her feet are caught in a red scarf of a married woman who was fortunate enough to die before her husband. Her lover, a shadowy figure, takes her into his boat and they make love while a storm rages outside. It is the presence of a red scarf that symbolizes her transition from the gory world of suffering, but Goswami ends the possible emancipation via Saudamini's death. Unlike Atwood, where characters tend to react strongly; Goswami's fiction hints at possibilities within confines. The radical steps are contained and often questioned or reprimanded.

In Atwood's *The Handmaid's Tale*, colour-coded uniforms are prescribed in order to define the roles of women in Gilead where women like Offred who can reproduce wear red, the wives of the men in power wear blue, domestic servants ('Marthas') wear gray, and prison guards/instructors ('Aunts') wear brown. When asked to dress up in provocative lingerie for her outing with her master/owner to the nightclub Jezebel she displays discomfort as she is accustomed to wearing her uniform, but is delighted when she sees a fashion magazine:

> Staring at the magazine, as he dangled it before me like fish bait, I wanted it. I wanted it with a force that made the ends of my fingers ache. At the same time I saw this longing of mine as trivial and absurd, because I'd taken such magazines lightly enough once .... I remembered now. What was in them was promise. They dealt in transformations; they suggested an endless series of possibilities, extending like the reflections in two mirrors set facing one another, stretching on, replica after replica, to the vanishing point. (*Handmaid's Tale* 200–201)

Examining the presence of uniforms in Atwood's fiction, Lorraine M. York (1990) suggests that 'to enter the world of uniforms is to enter a dark realm of experience and suffering' (8). Atwood's 'strategy', York argues, is 'to explode the myth of the uniform', which represents negative aspects of conformity (*Habits* 16).

The colour coded uniforms stand in sharp contrast to the whites worn by the widows in Goswami's fiction; yet it is the uniformity of representation that brings the widows together as an oppressed group. In *The Moth-Eaten Howdah of the Tusker*, poor women of the village are depicted by the drab clothes they wear, pertaining to poor health, or poverty as a result of being widowed. The central image of 'the moth-eaten howdah' is also of a drab colour, lying now in a corner of the house. It symbolizes the decline of a feudal order but does not hint towards hope or change. When women gather to witness the argument between Indranath's widowed aunt Durga and his mother, they notice that the clothes of these women, including Durga, 'had taken the colour of sheep's skin' (29).

Naomi Wolf in *the Beauty Myth* (1991) explores the phenomenon as a 'violent backlash against feminism that uses images of female beauty as a political weapon against women's advancement' (10). According to Wolf, 'the closer women come to power, the more physical self-consciousness and sacrifice are asked of them'; the 'central rule' is that '(f)or every feminist action there is an equal and opposite beauty myth reaction' (28). Whether Atwood's protagonists define their stories through their bodies or Goswami's protagonists are reprimanded for not adhering to the socio-cultural stereotypes; dress and clothing are an important indicator of oppression, struggle and independence.

In Atwood and Goswami's fiction, women who attempt to go beyond the female sphere reproduced in traditional literature must make difficult choices or face punishment. Both authors, in their writings, have been observed to constantly foreground ways in which notions of gender identity, and of cultural identity; have been shaped by media and other popular representations and their protagonists are seen struggling with the same. The body becomes the site of contest. Dress illuminates body and gender within a cultural context, and a focus on cultural representations of the female body is a significant aspect of Atwood's and Goswami's fiction. Their protagonists consistently style themselves or are forced to adhere to normative styles of presentation in response to divisive cultural codes. Thus, it is argued here that self-fashioning becomes a survivalist act.

In the writings of both the authors, issues of gender, interactions between the two sexes in a heteronormative patriarchal scheme of things, sexuality and the discourse on the nation collapse together. It is this which elevates their writing from being gendered/personal to being universal/global while being contextual at the same time.

Atwood unflinchingly examines culture in her writing. 'A writer's job', notes Atwood (1996) 'is to tell his society not how it ought to live, but how it does live' (*Survival* 42). Atwood and Goswami focus on systems of power and their effects on individuals, addressing everything from politics to consumerism to gender issues. Atwood's writing is regularly connected with terms like 'subversion' or 'transgression',[2] and dress contributes to the project of cultural critique by illuminating complex connections among dress, body, gender, art, and power in the works of both the writers.

Notes

1. Gayatri Spivak in Lukas Barr, 'An Interview with Gayatri Chakravorty Spivak', *BLAST unLtd* (Summer 1989), p. 12.
2. See Eleonora Rao's, *Strategies for Identity: The Fiction of Margaret Atwood, Vol. 9: Writing About Women: Feminist Literary Studies*, New York: Peter Lang Publishing, 1993.

References

Atwood, Margaret, *Survival: A Thematic Guide to Canadian Literature*, Toronto: McClelland and Stewart, 1996.

——, *The Blind Assassin*, New York: Anchor Books, 2001.

——, *The Handmaid's Tale*, New York: Seal Books, 1998.

——, 'Waterstone's Poetry Lecture', Delivered at Hay On Wye, Wales, June 1995, Margaret Atwood Information page, 27 paras, 13 July 2008, http://www.web.net/owtoad.html, para 12, p. 2.

Goswami, Indira. *Shadow of Dark God and the Sin*, New Delhi: Gaurav Publishing House, 1987.

——, *The Moth-Eaten Howdah of the Tusker*, New Delhi: Rupa and Company, 2005.

Barr, Lukas, 'An Interview with Gayatri Chakravorty Spivak', *BLAST unLtd* (Summer 1989): 12.

Cixous, Hélène, 'The Laugh of the Medusa', Translated by Keith Cohen and Paula Cohen, *Signs* 1.4 (1976): 873–893.

Ingersoll, Earl G., *Margaret Atwood: Conversations*, New Jersey: Ontario Review Press, 1990.

Rao, Eleonora, *Strategies for Identity: The Fiction of Margaret Atwood, Vol. 9: Writing About Women: Feminist LShariterary Studies*, New York: Peter Lang Publishing, 1993.

York, Lorraine M., *Literary Celebrity in Canada*, Toronto: University of Toronto Press, 2007.

——, 'The Habits of Language: Uniform(ity), Transgression and Margaret Atwood', *Canadian Literature* 126 (1990): 6–19.

Wolf, Naomi, *The Beauty Myth: How Images of Beauty are Used Against Women*, New York: Morrow, 1991.

16

Gender and Identity

Indigenous Women as Symbols of Power

Santosh Bharti

> In their words we saw their sadness, desperation, anger and pain, but we also saw their strength, courage, wisdom and hope. Throughout history, Aboriginal women have made many adjustments to cope with the circumstances facing them, and they continue to do so today.
>
> (RCAP, 1996E: 7)*

These lines are echoed by Royal Commission on Aboriginal Peoples (RCAP) reflecting the realities of indigenous women in Canada. Indigenous women across Canada, in spite of their subjugation, oppression, and discrimination, show a strong will and positive attitude to overcome their past injustices. The process of colonization had a drastic effect on indigenous peoples, but the greatest impact was on women. While racism was experienced by all indigenous peoples, indigenous women suffered a double curse. Racism and sexism had served to dramatically undermine the place and value of women in indigenous cultures, leaving them vulnerable both within and outside of their communities. Not only have women been subjected to violence in both white and indigenous societies, they have also been subjected to patriarchal policies that have dispossessed them of their inherited

---

* Royal Commission on Aboriginal Peoples (RCAP) (1996 E), Perspectives And Realities, Vol. 4, Minister of Supply and Services, Canada: Canada Communication Group Publishing.

rights, lands, identities, and families. Indigenous women continue to experience discrimination through the Indian Act, are inadequately represented in indigenous and mainstream organizations, lack official representation in discussions on self government, under- and/or unequal employment. The educated indigenous woman also suffers from ghettoization. Emma LaRocque highlighting this disadvantage states that, 'the tentacles of colonization are not only extant today, but may also be multiplying and encircling indigenous peoples in ever-tighter grips of landlessness and marginalization, hence, of anger, anomie, and violence, in which women are the more obvious victims' (LaRocque, 1996: 11–12).

Acknowledging this, Royal Commission on Aboriginal Peoples states that, 'with the onset of colonization, the position and role of Aboriginal women were undermined by imported ideas and values that displaced and devalued them' compared to pre-contact period when, 'women were highly respected' and 'their thoughts and views were sought before decisions affecting the community'. Joyce Courchene an indigenous woman affirms:

> Before colonization, Aboriginal peoples had social and political organizations with distinct social classes, which ranged from simpler structures to highly complex systems of social order, social control in governments. Every individual filled a particular role and had a specific purpose within the community life unfolded with much harmony. Since European contact, or tradition, dignity and self-respect have been systematically taken away from us. (RCAP, 1996E: 7–8)

Indigenous women in Canada, who once, in their traditional gender role behaviour, were considered 'to serve as the chief providers for – and sustainers of – their families over time', had certain rights and duties. As mothers and grandmothers, they were able to 'direct the affairs of their communities', towards legal, economic and political equality. In other words, gender relation within indigenous was based on egalitarian principles and women who played a very special role as 'nurturers of families' and 'keepers of cultures', were considered an important part of an indigenous communities (Valaskakis, 2009: 8).

> First Nations believe the eagle flies with a female wing and a male wing, showing the importance of balance between the feminine and masculine contributors to a more complete understanding of gender relations and reinforces relationships. (ibid.: 9)

Karen L. Anderson further, points out that, prior to the arrival of the Jesuits, 'men and women, for the most part occupied different roles, but retained equal capacity to exercise power' so power, in words of Anderson ' should not be seen as something that women and men had or possessed. Power, can be usefully be conceptualized in terms of the working out of social forces, through specific social institutions' (Anderson, 1991: 7). Since gender balance was woven in all aspects of indigenous life, 'sexual division that permeated all aspects of the native people's world-in rituals, the exercise of authority, productive and reproductive activities, spatial arrangements, and food distribution – profoundly influenced how women and men faced the vicissitudes of daily living' (Devens, 1992:10). In other words, different roles were expected of both genders but neither was considered above the other. They were equals and efforts of neither men nor women were superior as both were essential for functioning of society. It was believed that the balance between the two, creates harmony. So much so, 'the existence of distinct men's and women's roles, then, does not indicate in itself either an equality of genders or a superiority of one gender over the other' (Klein and Ackerman, 1995: 14).

However, this gender equality and balance was disrupted with the arrival of Jesuits to North America, affecting women most. Their 'idea of womanhood' revolved around women domesticity and confinement to the household, subordinating their wills to their fathers, husbands or to any other male relative. She was defined as a nurturer directing her energies towards selfless support to the family. Further, she was burdened with the responsibility of her children. This 'ideal' women emerged as the prime symbol of civility, represented female emancipation (Stevenson, W., 2011: 46). Soon, this image of European ideal women began to be projected on indigenous societies, where indigenous women 'appeared antithetical to the presumed natural condition of women'. This led to two types of colonial images of indigenous women: one of pure and innocent 'Pocahontas' who was the saviour of the righteous white man; other is sexually oriented 'Squaw' who sold herself for economic benefits or pleasure (Weist, 1983: 38–39). The first image represented the romantic image of an 'Indian princess', who is presented in European terms as 'royalty', 'rejecting the standards and traditions of her people for European views of morality and romantic love' while image of a squaw indigenous woman appears to have no social input, no choice in spouses, and no respect. She is inferior to her husband and necessary only for her labour and for her sexual and reproductive duties. Her sexual favours can be sold by her husband while she meekly acquiesces. Canadian indigenous women, then, were 'viewed as demeaned drudges who followed, or were mired in, the backward traditions of their cultures or as picturesque ladies who took on the virtues of upper class European society and left Native American traditions behind them' (Klein and Ackerman 1995: 5–6).

Whether glorified in the figure of the 'princess' or denigrated in the image of the 'squaw', indigenous women have existed in European myths since classical times (Albers, 1983: 3) and 'in the real world, Native American women still find themselves type cast, burdened by white people's unrealistic images' (Katz, 1995: 7). As Gretchen M. Bataille states:

> The histories of Native women from the past such as Pocahontas, Sacagawea, Lozen, or Dahteste resonate with fabulous tales of sacrifice or exploits, achieving for Native women explorer or warrior status, but much of what has been published perpetuates myths which have been repeated by scholars for so long that the complete truth will probably always remain hidden. (Bataille, 1993: xi)

Such images of indigenous women especially dehumanizing portrayal of 'squaws', over the years, have made them suffer from low self-esteem and self-worth and undermined their status/social position in their own communities which even encouraged indigenous men to look down upon their own indigenous women and made 'all aboriginal female persons vulnerable to physical, verbal and sexual violence' (LaRocque, 1994: 74).

Though little domestic violence against indigenous women existed in indigenous societies prior to European contact however introduction of western patriarchy system in indigenous communities became one form of oppression and subjugation of indigenous women, due to the fact that colonization deprived indigenous men of their traditional and ancestral roles 'which led them to move away from their gender relations based on shared power to a stance of domination' treating indigenous women as inferiors (Weaver, 2009: 1554). Further, Neelima Kanwar posits that, 'the native men would give, in a common meeting place, the white women respect but would treat their own women with contempt'. In this sense, indigenous women, suffer double marginalization – first for being indigenous and second for being women (Kanwar, 2008: 24). This is also noted by

Native Women's Association of Canada: 'Many indigenous men have learned Eurocentric patriarchal values and have treated Indigenous women with disrespect by abusing or violating them in one way or another' (NWAC, 2003: 9). Further, indigenous men considered indigenous women as 'burden of beast', who could be bought and sold by her husband, father, brother or any other male. This way, indigenous women were considered as 'the greatest wealth an Indian possesses next to his horse' (Cited in Weist, 1983: 33).

Since coming of White-Europeans altered indigenous affairs and redefined male/female gender roles in indigenous societies leading to gender inequality. Such gender imbalance still exists in Canada. According to a recent study by Shannon Brennan for *Statistics Canada*, most victimization of indigenous women is committed by males. 'Over half (52%) of Aboriginal women who were victimized by a current or former partner stated that they feared for their lives, compared to 31 per cent of non-Aboriginal women' (Brennan, 2011). These all indicate that, the traditional base of women's power in various indigenous groups such as the Iroquois and Cherokee have eroded. Further, with the imposition of Judeo-Christian values, efforts to assimilate indigenous women into Euro-American society through education changed the status of women (Bataille, 1993: xiii). Therefore, indigenous women recognition as equal persons and member of their communities has been denied which still continues till date.

Emphasizing on inequality and marginalization experienced by Canadian indigenous women Amnestry International research titled *Stolen Sisters: Stop Violence Against Women*, revealed that 'indigenous women between the ages of 25 and 44 with status under the federal Indian Act are five times more likely than other women of the same age to die as the result of violence' (Amnesty International Report, 2004: 14). Subsequently, in 2005, Native Women Association of Canada launched an initiative titled 'Sisters in Spirit' in 2005, to address violence against First Nations, Inuit and Metis women and reported that 580 indigenous women and girls across Canada have either gone missing or murdered (NWAC, 2010: i). Calling it as 'national tragedy', Vancouver Police Department position paper reports that ' despite making up only four per cent of the Canadian female population, women of Aboriginal descent make up the majority of women who are missing and murdered' and that 'the issue of violence against Aboriginal women is a complex one involving social, economic and cultural factors'(VPD, 2011: 7). Therefore, today, the issue of missing and murdered indigenous women has become serious, disturbing and unacceptable level of violence against indigenous women in Canada, and through grassroots research like 'Sisters in Spirit', Native Women Association of Canada has 'developed education and awareness kits to improve safety and foster a preventive response' at all levels (SWCC, 2011: 56).

No doubt violence against indigenous women stems from colonization in Canada, their identity has always been administrated through Indian Act 1876. For years, this piece of legislation denied indigenous women legal access to their communities and identities. Provision in the Act stated that any indigenous women who married any non-indigenous men lost both their 'Indian' status as well as membership to the local band whereas indigenous men, on the other hand, were permitted to marry non-indigenous women without losing either 'Indian' status or band membership and their wives too acquired both status and membership (Russell, 2000: 91). A report on indigenous women conducted by Canadian Council on Social Development and Native Women's Association of Canada in 1991 states that, 'it was aboriginal women, in particular, who felt their role and status corrupted. Once an influential member of her society, participating in the governing process and commanding the highest respect as the life-giver of her people, the aboriginal woman was reduced to a subservient role by the Indian Act of a foreign and patriarchal system' (Canadian Council on Social Development and NWAC, 1991: 3).

Hence, through various colonial and post-Confederation legislations, indigenous women have been increasingly marginalized. After the 1876 Indian Act, 'Indian women were denied the right to vote in band elections or to participate in reserve land-surrender decisions' and if their husbands passed away without a will, 'they were required to be 'of good moral character' in order to receive any of their husband's property'. The cultural identity was shaped by that of the husband. 'A woman who married a man without Indian status lost her own status .... The children of such a marriage would not be recognized as Indian either' (RCAP, 1996E: 23).

Amanda Pezzutto says, 'though the Indian Act had many severe provisions that applied to men, without a doubt, Indian legislation was harsher for women' (2004: 14). Taiaiake Alfred called it, 'internal racism' or 'internalized oppression'. According to him, 'to say that an Indian woman who marries a white man does not have any rights – that's not based on tradition, yet it's so ingrained' in colonization (Alfred, 2009: 126). Moreover, 'once a woman left the reserve to marry, she could not return to her reserve, so she lost all property rights'. In contrast, an indigenous man who married a non-indigenous woman retained his Indian status and his wife gained Indian status under the Act. Such imposition of Eurocentric views directly disrupted traditional indigenous communities (Bourassa, 2010: 78).

Apart from this, indigenous women suffer from social and economic marginalization. According to a recent study, they are 'afflicted by higher levels of poverty, lower educational attainment, higher unemployment, family violence, poorer physical and mental health and lack of housing (CCPA, 2010: 37). In the words of Sharon Donna McIvor, 'today, aboriginal women are among the poorest of the poor in Canada' and their legal and political inequality further deprive them of social and economic benefits, even their right to basic adequate standard of living. Scholar further states that indigenous women are also 'denied opportunities to leadership positions within their communities and organizations and have been excluded from high-level negotiation among Aboriginal and Canadian political leaders. Male Aboriginal leaders and male Canadian politicians have colluded in excluding Aboriginal women from participation in governance' (McIvor, 2007: 96–97).

No doubt, indigenous women have suffered and are still suffering marginalization and oppression inside and outside their communities but now indigenous women in Canada have started to struggle for their recognition and assertion of their indigenous rights:

> In these struggles, Aboriginal women are seeking recognition from the Canadian government and from men in their own communities of their rights as equal persons to be Indians, to pass on their Indian status to their children and grandchildren, to hold property on an equal footing with men, and to participate fully as Aboriginal women where decisions are being made about the rules for their communities and the distribution of resources and opportunities. (ibid.: 98)

To address issue of violence against indigenous women, first ever National Aboriginal Women's summit was held in 2007 in Corner Brook, Newfoundland and Labrador, led by Native Women Association of Canada, and the province of Newfoundland and Labrador involving many national and sub-national indigenous groups as well as many national representatives of indigenous organizations. Under the theme of 'Strong Women, Strong Communities', indigenous women discussed many issues such as violence against indigenous women, poverty, child welfare, health as well as equality and empowerment of indigenous women with the premiers of Canada's provinces and territories and federal level ministers (Wessendorf, 2008: 60). In the following year, in 2008, in the name of 'Walk for Justice', a group of people from British Columbia walked across Canada to Ottawa to demand justice for the missing or murdered indigenous women. To address the severity and critical situation of indigenous women, in 2009, two members of parliament named Anita Nevill of Winnipeg and Todd Russell of Labrador, demanded investigation into thc rcasons of high rate of such crime and violence against indigenous women (Anderson, 2010: 1).

Such steps illustrate the growing public efforts both at national and international level, to create awareness of the violence against indigenous women in Canada and given such concrete expression in a wide range of social, demographic and economic indicators, this marginalization has in the last 10 to 15 years gained increasing attention within the country's policy and research communities. A growing literature focused on the exploitation of Aboriginal women's lives and cultural contexts has provided a means of addressing the myriad challenges which they face during the course of their day to day lives' (Stout and Kipling, 1998: iii).

In this context, it can be stated that colonization is considered as a gendered process which undermined the status of women in indigenous societies. But now, indigenous women in Canada have begun 'decolonizing themselves' which means reverting to revitalization and reaffirmation of ways of governing indigenous communities and trying to heal, unite, and re-establish 'good relations' among various indigenous peoples. This, revitalization would lead to 'acknowledgement of the role of women in protecting Mother Earth'. An attempt to restore clan system was considered as a good way of moving forward because 'clan system provided the Haudenosaunee League with a mechanism for bonding all members of each nation and all nations of the broader league while also establishing a way to balance responsibilities' between genders which forms a core component in establishing system of governance (Sunseri, 2011: 156–157).

Since, Indian Act forcibly displaced indigenous women and their descendents upon marrying non-status or non-indigenous men. Children of these women, formerly known as Metis, are now struggling to locate their identity with respect to their mothers and grandmothers. Struggling for their social and cultural rights, indigenous women have become politically active in mainstream Canadian society.

This resulted in an amendment to Indian Act in 1985 and passage of Bill C-31 which restored their 'lost' indigenous identity and band membership. Many indigenous women organizations were formed such as the Native Women's Association of Canada, Women of the Metis Nations (Alberta province), Saskatchewan First Nations Women's Council, Ontario Native Women Association, Inuit Women's Association of Canada and so on, who have attempted to defend and improve indigenous women's rights in Canada and restore their multiplicity of identities as mothers, as head of household, as grandmother and so on.

However, women lack the support from within their communities but this has only strengthened the will of indigenous women to fight for self-government rights. Shelley Thomas et al. writes, 'Despite the tremendous challenges, Aboriginal women today are claiming their voices and positions as leaders and healers within their communities. They are becoming increasingly politically active. Particularly within their own government structures, and are pushing for social and gender issues that are often marginalized by male-dominated leadership' (Thomas, 2004: 155).

Indigenous women hold various posts and offices leading their communities as band chiefs and educators. There are politicians like Nellie Cournoyea, (who was the first indigenous woman premier when she was elected premier of the Northwest Territories in 1991), actresses like Tantoo Vardinal, singers like Susan Aglukark and Butfy Sainte-Marie, are well known throughout Canada. In 2006, the federal government dedicated Women's History Month to indigenous women (Kacll, 2011: 216). During Oka crisis in 1990, indigenous women were visible as protestors and community leaders. Similarly, in 1992, to have equal participation in discussion of Charlottetown Accord, indigenous women through their indigenous women organization like Native Women's Association of Canada (NWAC) lobbied federal government to take part in drafting of the Charlottetown Accord because NWAC participation would have ensured a share in the amount indigenous men organization received for their active participation in drafting the Charlottetown Accord. Sharon McIvor, states: 'The Canadian government has a habit of financially supporting organized Aboriginal men's groups to suppress the Aboriginal women of Canada in Court, in public forums, and even on the streets' (McIvor, 2006: 256). However such exclusion of indigenous women from high level negotiations among indigenous and Canadian political leaders never deterred or stopped them from raising their voices against biased male society.

Parallel to such protest movement, is the indigenous women literary movement started in late 19th and early 20th century when an indigenous writer (Mohawk) and performer Pauline Johnson begin to write. Through her various characters presented in her writings as well as through her stage performances 'she portrayed Native women as not only the equals of white women, but at times their superiors'. She further considered indigenous women to be 'virtuous, hardworking and dignified, they were never 'squaws', a derogatory but commonplace term that signaled sexual licence, indolence, and disrespect'. Such Johnson's reclamation of the social value and moral character of indigenous women has been considered as courageous and praiseworthy for example indigenous women (Iroquois) writers like Patricia Monture-Angus and Beth Brant recognized Johnson's unusual portrayal and in current times indigenous women writers (First Nations) like Lee Maracle, Jeannette Armstrong and others consider Johnson as their enabling foremother (Gerson and Strong-Boag, 2005: 47–48). So it can be said that there has been a rise in indigenous women writers like Maria Campbell, Lee Maracle, Beatrice Culleton and Jeannette Armstrong. These indigenous women writers are 'involved in a host of socio-economic issues, including legislated and social discrimination, poverty, violence, health, (in)justice, education, identity and cultural renewal' (LaRocque, 2009: 157).

In an attempt to assert themselves and desired to be heard, indigenous women have also started to tell their stories, their history from indigenous point of view. This urge of writing back and telling the story from indigenous point of view has its origin in the oral tradition in the form of storytelling which includes myths, legends, folklore, traditional stories, etc. transmitted from generation to generation verbally. These oral traditions which are didactic in nature, helped to communicate indigenous histories, beliefs, religious and cultural practices (Petrone, 1990: 3). Canadian indigenous woman activist and scholar Bonita Lawrence states that for indigenous peoples writing back means telling their histories which involves recovering their own stories of the past and asserting their epistemological foundations. 'It also involves documenting processes of colonization from the perspectives of those who experienced it' (Lawrence, 2010: 39).

Though indigenous women writings have been considered as insignificant but it outrightly critiques dominant mainstream white narratives as Julia V. Emberly elaborates:

> The use of the label 'Native Women' or 'Indian Women' writers contains, on the one hand, a political and historical inscription of subjectivity that delimits 'authenticity' and, on the other hand, delimits a cultural politics of autonomy in which Native women writers engage in a critique of dominant ideological representations of 'the' Native women, remaking subjectivity through the very act of writing. Native women's literature can be read, then, for a critique of sexism, racism, colonialism, and economic exploitation as well as for its mark of cultural, and not essential, differences. (Cited in Kanwar, 2008: 14)

Before 1960s indigenous literary writings were sparse. The politics of 1960s and 1970s, leading to the publication of *White Paper* in 1969 by the Trudeau government, led to the growth of indigenous literature in Canada. Known as 'postcolonial protest writing', this literature emerged out of experience of colonization and have emphasized their differences from their nation-states. These indigenous writers/authors both male and female narrate the stories of dispossession, loss of land, language, marginalization, disruption, displacement, and identity. Expressing their anguish and dissent, indigenous writers emerged to counter the colonial subversive interpretation of indigenous peoples and their cultures and attempt to reconstruct indigenous history for their survival and development. Since indigenous women writers form a separate small canon of indigenous writings, they are gradually gaining prominence at national and international level expressing their marginalization and victimization and through their personal experiences in the form of autobiographies, short stories, fiction, prose work so on narrate the realities of indigenous women in Canada.

However, there is no denying the fact that today indigenous women continue to experience violence of all forms – racism, sexism, discrimination, social and economic marginalization, lack of education, so on but through their continuous struggle, these indigenous women have led efforts at healing and rebuilding their communities, even when male-dominated governments sidelined them. Their struggle for recognition of their rights represent their efforts to shed the shackles of their oppression, domination and colonialism and attempts to restore their sacred position as mothers, grandmothers, teachers, and healers of life.

References

Alfred, Taiaiake, *Peace, Power, Righteousness: An Indigenous Manifesto*, Don Mills: Oxford University Press. 2009.

Albers, Patricia C., 'Introduction: New Perspectives on Plains Indian Women', in Patricia Albers and Beatrice Medicine (eds), *The Hidden Half: Studies of Plains Indian Women*, New York: University Press of America, 1983, pp. 1–28.

Amnestry International Report, 'Stolen Sisters: A Human Rights Response to Discrimination and Violence against Indigenous Women in Canada', 2004.

Anderson, Karen L., *Chain Her by One Foot: The Subjugation of Women in Seventeenth-Century*, New York: Routledge, 1991.

Anderson, A. Brenda, 'The Journey from Awareness to a Conference to a Book...and Beyond', in Anderson et al. (eds), *Torn from Our Midst: Voices of Grief, Healing and Action from the Missing Indigenous Women Conference, 2008*, Saskatchewan: Canadian Plains Research Centre, 2010, pp. 1–17.

Bataille, Gretchen M. (ed.), *Native American Women: A Biographical Dictionary*, New York: Garland Publishing, 1993.

Bourassa, Carrie, 'The Constitution of Aboriginal Identity: A Healing Journey', in Brenda Anderson et al. (eds), *Torn from Our Midst: Voices of Grief, Healing and Action from the Missing Indigenous Women Conference, 2008*, Saskatchewan: Canadian Plains Research Centre, 2010, pp. 75–85.

Brennan, Shannon, 'Violent Victimization of Aboriginal Women in the Canadian Provinces, 2009', *Juristat Article* (85-002-x), Ottawa: Statistics Canada, Minister of Supply, 2011.

Canadian Centre for Policy Alternatives (CCPA), *Getting the Job Done Right: Alternative Federal Budget 2010*, Ottawa, 2010.

Canadian Council on Social Development and Native Women's Association of Canada, *Voices of Aboriginal Women: Aboriginal Women Speak Out About Violence*, Ottawa, Canada: Canadian Council on Social Development, 1991.

Devens, Carol, *Countering Colonization: Native American Women and Great Lakes Missions, 1630–1900*, California: University of California Press, 1992.

Gerson, Carole and Veronica Strong-Boag, 'Championing the Native: E. Pauline Johnson Rejects the Squaw', in Katie Pickles and Myra Rutherdale (eds), *Contact Zones: Aboriginal and Settler Women in Canada's Colonial Past*, Vancouver: University of British Columbia Press, 2005, pp. 47–66.

Kacll, Hillary, 'Canada', in Mary Zeiss Stange et al. (eds), *Encyclopedia of Women in Today's World*, California: Sage, 2011, pp. 215–217.

Kanwar, Neelima, *Resistant Voices*, New Delhi: Anamika Publishers, 2008.

Katz, Jane, 'Introduction', in Jane Katz (ed.), *Messenger of the Wind: Native American Women Tell Their Life Stories*, New York: One World Ballantine Books, 1995, pp. 1–20.

Klein, Laura F. and Lillian A. Ackerman, 'Introduction', in Laura F. Klein and Lillian A. Ackerman (eds), *Women and Power in Native North America*, Norman: University of Oklahoma Press, 1995, pp. 3–16.

LaRocque, Emma, 'The Colonization of a Native Woman Scholar', in Christine Miller and Patricia Chuchryk (eds), *Women of the First Nations: Power, Wisdom, and Strength*, Manitoba: University of Manitoba Press, 1996, pp. 11–18.

——, 'Reflections on Cultural Continuity Through Aboriginal Women's Writings', in Gail Guthrie Valaskalis et al. (eds), *Restoring the Balance: First Nations Women, Community, and Culture*, Manitoba: University of Manitoba Press, 2009, pp. 149–174.

——, *When the Other is Me: Native Resistance Discourse, 1850–1990*, Winnipeg: University of Manitoba Press, 2010.

——, *Violence in Aboriginal Communities*, Ottawa, Canada: Health Programs and Services, March 1994.

McIvor, Sharon Donna, 'Aboriginal Women: Working in Coalition to Advance Sex Equality', in Elizabeth Sheely and Sheila McIntyre (eds), *Calling for Change: Women, Law, and the Legal Profession*, Ottawa: University of Ottawa Press, 2006, pp. 253–262.

——, 'Aboriginal Women Unmasked: Using Equality Litigation to Advance Women's Rights', in Margot Young et al. (eds), *Poverty: Rights, Social Citizenship, and Legal Activism*, Vancouver: University of British Columbia Press, 2007, pp. 96–118.

Native Women's Association of Canada (NWAC), 'Our Way of Being: Gathering of Indigenous Women on Self-Government', *A NWAC Position Paper*, 2003.

——, 'What Their Stories Tell Us: Research Finding from the Sisters in Spirit Initiative', 2010.

Petrone, Penny, *Native Literature in Canada: From the Oral Tradition to the Present*, Toronto: Oxford University Press, 1990.

Pezzutto, Amanda, *An Indian Through and Through: First Nations Women, Activism, and the Indian Act*, Vancouver: University of British Columbia Press, 2004.

Royal Commission on Aboriginal Peoples (RCAP), *Perspectives and Realities*, Vol. 4, Minister of Supply and Services, Canada: Canada Communication Group Publishing, 1996 E.

Russell, Dan, *A People's Dream: Aboriginal Self-government in Canada*, Vancouver: University of British Columbia Press, 2000.

Saskatoon Women's Calender Collective, *Herstory 2012*, Canadian Women's Calender, Saskatchewn: Coteaubooks, 2011.

Stevenson, Winona, 'Colonialism and First Nations Women in Canada', in Martin J. Cannon and Lina Sunser (eds), *Racism, Colonialism, and Indigeneity in Canada: A Reader*, Don Mills: Oxford University Press, 2011, pp. 44–56.

Stevenson, S. Ronald, 'Toward a Shared Narrative of Reconciliation: Developments in Canadian Aboriginal Rights Law', in Hester Lessard et al. (eds), *Storied Communities: Narratives of Contact and Arrival in Constituting Political Community*, Vancouver: University of British Columbia Press, 2011, pp. 271–286.

Stout, Madeleine Dion and Gregory D. Kipling, *Aboriginal Women in Canada: Strategic Research Directions for Policy Development*, Ottawa: Status of Women Canada, 1998.

Sunseri, Lina, *Being Again of One Mind: Onida Women and the Struggle for Decolonization*, Vancouver: University of British Columbia Press, 2011.

Thomas, Shelley et al., 'Aboriginal Women and Home Care', in Karen R. Grant et al. (eds), *Caring For/Caring About: Women, Home Care, and Unpaid Caregiving*, Aurora: Garamond Press, 2004, pp. 147–166.

Valaskakis, Gail Guthrie et al., 'Introduction', in Valaskakis et al. (eds), *Restoring the Balance: First Nations Women, Community, and Culture*, Manitoba: University of Manitoba Press, 2009, pp. 1–10.

Vancouver Police Department (VPD), 'The Tragedy of Missing and Murdered Aboriginal Women in Canada', *A Position Paper*, 2011.

Weaver, Hilary N., 'The Colonial Context of Violence: Reflections on Violence in the Lives of Native American Women', *Journal of Interpersonal Violence* 24.9 (2009): 1552–1563.

Weist, Katherine M., 'Beasts of Burden and Menial Slaves: Nineteenth Century Observation of Northern Plains Indian Women', in Patricia Albers and Beatrice Medicine (eds), *The Hidden Half: Studies of Plains Indian Women*, New York: University Press of America, 1983, pp. 29–52.

Wessendorf, Katherine (ed.), *The Indigenous World 2008*, Denmark: International Work Group for Indigenous Affairs, 2008.

IV

Practical Applications

17

Knowledge Keepers – Canadian Cinema About the Indigenous

Special Focus on *Atanarjuat* and *Unnatural and Accidental*

Prem Kumari Srivastava

> *The role I have in my family is as an archivist, recorder of history and knowledge-keeper.*

Using this statement by Jeannette Armstrong as a starting point, the present paper is a spreadsheet of diverse Canadian indigenous concerns alongside discussions with Jeannette Armstrong, the renowned indigenous novelist of Canada. The interview, conducted in Vancouver in November 2010 lasted some hours and was aimed at getting her responses on Native Canadian Literature and its adaptations in cinema. It yielded, in turn, rich material on a range of global literary issues, native stereotypes, her authorial intentions to write an oral narrative with the typical elements of orality such as non-linearity, use of first person voice in her first novel *Slash* (1985); her response to 'indigenous cinema in Canada'; the APTN (Aboriginal Peoples Television Network); setting up of the En'owkin Center[1] and her role as a knowledge keeper for her Okanagan community in Pentictin, Kelowna. The paper uses this frame to weave into this discussion two examples of Canadian Cinema about the indigenous: *Atanarjuat: The Fast Runner* (2002) based on an Inuit oral legend by Zacharias Kunuk, and Carl Bessai's film adaptation of the Métis playwright, actor, and artistic director, Marie Clements' play The *Unnatural and Accidental Women* (1997). The paper's sole aim through a thin lens of gender, is to establish how both the texts masterfully archive and capture the 'history' and 'knowledge' of Canada's native community and in this process, become 'keepers' of their people. Thus, broadly, this paper is structured in three parts. Part one looks at the concept of Knowledge Keepers by using Jeannette's interview (2010) as a frame. The second part discusses *Atanarjuat: The Fast Runner* (2002) and the third part focuses its gaze on Carl Bessai's adaptation *Unnatural and Accidental* (2007) of Marie Clements' play, *The Unnatural and Accidental Women* (1997).

I

Stepping back from the above for just a while, what is also useful for the dynamics of this paper are some of the anxieties that often grip researchers researching about the indigenous. Julie Cruikshank, the renowned anthropologist at University of British Columbia, Vancouver, Canada, in her famous studies' *Life Lived Like a Story* (1992) and *The Social Life of Stories: Narrative and Knowledge in the Yukon Territory (2000)* cautions researchers about, 'how meanings of the original stories shift, as tellers (researchers: Julie explained this in a personal discussion with me on 31 October 2010 at UBC, Vancouver) address different audiences, situations and historical contexts' (2000: xi). How do scholars see beyond the norms they use to frame the experiences of others unless those norms are interrupted and exposed so that scholars are vulnerable, seeing what they believe as possibly wrong or at least limited?' (Greg Sarris in Cruikshank, 2000: xi).[2] Similarly, Margery Fee (2010)[3] from UBC, an expert on Canadian and aboriginal literatures raises foundational queries about the objectives and methodology of research in oral and indigenous cultures, and stresses on the 'act of collaboration' between researchers and the indigenous communities in material collection. Researchers point out that when white anthropologists who are genuinely sympathetic with the cause of indigenous peoples become interested in their stories, they are interested in them for anthropological reasons and thus marginalize their literary qualities, hence exhibiting what could be called a very subtle racism. Jay Miller says that the first Native American indigenous novelist, Mourning Dove or Christine

Quintasket's letters show that while she was working on the Coyote stories, 'McWhorter was concerned that *Indian* themes and concerns be highlighted, whereas Mourning Dove wanted to express her knowledge and literary talents' (Bowering, 33).[4] Almost contrapuntally, Linda Tuhiwai Smith, the famed Maori indigenous scholar and the Vice Chancellor of Maori University, New Zealand, (in her keynote address to Chotro III in Delhi 2010) positively states that 'the dialogue between the indigenous and non-indigenous can be constructive and non-exploitative'.[5]

On the same register, the paper draws your attention to the key concept of 'knowledge keepers'. In the specific context of the indigenous, knowledge keepers/keeping can be sharing, preserving, passing of culture with the wider community, as explained in the following examples:

1. In May 2011, the head of the Aboriginal Initiatives for the University of Alberta (Edmonton) hosted an event that drew together First Nations, Inuit and Métis knowledge keepers. They shared their stories and helped in the building of a sense of reflection and understanding for Aboriginal ways of being.
2. In February 2009, 'The National Centre of First Nations Governance' gathered in Winnipeg, Manitoba along with the University of Winnipeg's Aboriginal Governance Program and hosted a 'Sacred Sharing Circle' in which 50 elders and knowledge keepers shared their thoughts on the meaning of traditional governance and its role in First Nations today.[6]
3. Recently, a project called 'Knowledge Keepers' is running at Mildura Primary School, Swan-Hill, Victoria, in which preservation is done in various forms such as art and book exhibitions. 'The actual aim of the project was to teach the children about culture, what is important about culture, our connection to culture ...' says the coordinator, Charlie Davis.[7]
4. Setting up of Friendship centres all across Canada also preserves specific cultural knowledge: Sun dancing or the concept of pipe carriers amongst many others is preserved as part of Okanagan Culture at Pentictin, Kelowna.
5. Closer home, the Adivasi Academy at Tejgarh, Gujarat, a one-off of its kind in India, is primarily about knowledge keeping of endangered and dying adivasi languages.

Why Knowledge Keepers/Keeping?

Recent scholarship and contemporary theoretical formulations suggest an interesting turn as the need for Knowledge Keepers and keeping is examined closely. According to Sherene Razack of the University of Toronto, and Penny Petrone, author of *Native Literature in Canada, First People, First Voices* (1984) and *Native Literature in Canada: From the Oral Tradition to the Present* (1990), pedagogically and institutionally, the need to be Knowledge Keepers arose because of an ongoing 'callous disregard' of the indigenous body and indigenous histories in the (postcolonial?) academy and in dominant culture at large.[8] Both stress on European Cultural imperialism and its purist attitude towards native literature as another important reason.

Jeannette's role as a Knowledge Keeper is very well-known. Her desire to preserve the knowledge of the Okanagan Culture can be summarized through innumerable examples and her initiatives: the setting up of the En'owkin School of International Writing as the first credit-giving creative writing school in Canada operated entirely by and for Aboriginal people (Petrone 140 and *Voices*), setting up of the first printing press, Theytus Books at Kelowna, her creative oeuvre: novels and poems in which she preserves the oral tradition of story-telling. It is her role as a knowledge keeper and the novel *Slash*[9] that has earned Jeannette critical catchet. In the interview she says:

> One of the things that I have always been very much aware of is that I come from a family of knowledge keepers and that informed me at a very early age, as soon as I entered my teens that, that was an academic responsibility. In our tradition we are trained in certain ways to be able to not only retain and pass on the knowledge but the various areas of knowledge that are required for us to be able to say we are knowledgeable. So many people in our communities are knowledgeable in one area or two or three areas and so part of our tradition is that people who are recognized and knowledgeable in certain areas, all have responsibility and stature in the community as teachers and later on as elders.
>
> (Interview of Jeannette Armstrong with the author on 3 November 2011, Vancouver)

II

Though Alanis Obomsawin is the subject of the first-ever book on Native filmmakers,[10] the two films under discussion in this paper also lend a set of unique voices to the role of knowledge keepers in the context of indigenous cultures. They are firsts in their own right in the recording of history and use of native language. With the sole aim of unpacking 'Four thousand years of oral history silenced by fifty years of priests, schools, and cable TV' director Zacharias Kunuk's film *Atanarjuat*: *The Fast Runner* (2002) is the first feature-length film in Inuktitut language (Canadian Eskimo). Having won several awards for best direction, camera, screenplay, etc. at several renowned film festivals,[11] this epic tale recounts the ancient Inuit legend of *Atanarjuat,* the Fast Runner. Set some thousand years ago in the settlement of Igloolik,[12] North of the Northwest Territories, beyond Hudson Bay, in the eastern Arctic wilderness of Nunavut, with a population of 1,200,[13] 'Atanarjuat' relates how shamanic forces 'the major frame of reference for Inuit life' (Angilirq, Cohn and d' Anglure, 2002: 113–115)[14] lead to deep divisions within a community of nomadic Inuits. It also shows us, without sentimentality or political correctness, what life must have been like in Igloolik before the arrival of Europeans. The film espouses something profound about the sources of an ethnic group's well being and its destruction.

Evil in the form of a mysterious, unknown shaman enters this small community and upsets their balance and spirit of cooperation. The stranger leaves behind a lingering curse of bitterness and discord: after the camp leader Kumaglak is murdered, the new leader, his son Sauri drives his old rival Tulimaq down through mistreatment and ridicule. Power begins to change when Tulimaq's two sons – Amaqjuaq, the Strong One, and Atanarjuat, the Fast Runner, the camp's best hunters repeatedly clash with the loutish son of Sauri, Oki (Arnatsiaq). The latter is incensed by the fact that Atanarjuat has won the heart of the beautiful and flirtatious Atuat (Sylvia Ivalu), to whom he has been betrothed since childhood. Shot in the serene landscape of the remarkable Arctic region, it almost seems that social tensions have been airbrushed out of existence. But this is not the case at all. Supported by his henchmen, Oki plans an ambush that will eliminate his rivals that eventually result in the murder of Amaqjuaq.

Far from being just simple objects of ethnographic curiosity, the robust Inuit cast, succeeds in bringing alive this mythic drama of good versus evil. *Atanarjuat* 'is an important step for an indigenous people who have, until recently, seen their culture recorded by outsiders' alone, wrote Doug Alexander in the Canadian historical magazine 'The Beaver'[15] (2002: 48). The film is also an impressively vivid and detailed depiction of a 'particular way of life': shelter is provided by carefully-constructed igloos, clothes are fashioned from animal skins, transport consists of husky-drawn sleds, whilst the staple food is walrus or seal meat. Ritualistic events, such as a grieving ceremony and a head-thumping contest between the two adversaries, immerse us yet further into Inuit culture.

Aided by the remarkable Arctic light, the camera captures the forbidding expansiveness of the tundra landscapes, which sometimes dwarf the protagonists. Yet the 20-minute chase sequence involving a naked Atanarjuat being pursued on foot across the ice floes is genuinely extraordinary. Towards the end, Atanarjuat regains his spiritual strength, avenges his brother's death and brings harmony back to the tribe (Wyndham Wise, The Canadian Encyclopedia).

The Inuits believe the story of Atanarjuat to be more than five centuries old. The takeaways from the legend are that evil can occur when personal ambition (Sauri's and Oki's, in the film) is put before the needs of the community; secondly, if one (Atanarjuat) defies the camp leader, he may end up fleeing alone across the ice.

Over the course of five years, writer Paul Angilirq consulted the sketches from the journal of Admiral William Parry's 1922 expedition and interviewed eight elders/knowledge keepers for their versions of the story to form one story.[16] Despite the emphasis on accuracy, the film takes liberties with the original Inuit myth: Just like the legend, 'At the film's core is a crucial lie', which is that the original legend ended in a revenge killing, whereas in the film, Atanarjuat stops short of doing that Zacharias found this 'message more fitting for our times' (Shubow, 2003).[17] The Fast Runner is '... not some aboriginal folk-art curio but an enthralling and sophisticated work that fully exploits cinema's potential as a visual medium' (Anderson).[18] Hailed as a 'masterpiece' and an instant 'classic' by *The New York Times*, an 'astonishing epic' by Roger Ebert in the *Chicago Sun-Times*, the goal of the film, amongst many, was to introduce the new storytelling medium of film to help Inuit communities survive long into the future. In all, it is the allegiance to knowledge keeping of their community that is the core ethical force behind the film, echoed well by Cohn:

> We're Inuit storytellers in a history of 4,000 years of Storytelling. And if we are successful, this story and storytelling will last for another 4,000 years. It just so happened that in our moment, to do our job, film and television exists on earth. We see ourselves in this Inuit

storytelling history, not in the Hollywood history of storytelling by the likes of DW Griffith or Steven Spielberg. (Alioff, 2005: 19)

Sophie McCall does raise the question of complicated and multiple authorship in oral narratives and she cites the example of *The Fast Runner.*[18] But, struggling past indifference, condescension, funding catastrophes, tough shooting conditions, untimely deaths of Paul Apak at 44 years only and a year later of his wife Amelia, the Zacharias team succeeded in bringing ... an ambitious epic story involving dramatic, comedic and romantic notes strung neatly and strummed melodiously.

At one level, *Atanarjuat* can be appreciated as a faithful reproduction of a lost way of life and a beautiful rendering of ancient folklore. On the other, '*Atarnajuat* is bold and emotionally generous' (ibid.: 13). This led to an interrogation that not many scholars and reviewers of *Atanarjuat* have done or written about: the gender perspective. In many ways *Atarnajuat* is a voyeuristic peep into the everyday world of women who inhabit the serene blue landscape of the Arctic region. In its portrayal of women characters, it does both, setting in motion along with dispelling, a host of clichés regarding stereotyping of women. In this slow paced scenic extravaganza and wanting in spoken words or voiced statements once a while, the film does guide us through the complexities of women's layered social structures. Director Zacharias Kunuk, faithfully recreates a world composed of women cleaning animal skins, children chasing each other across the drifts, men racing dogsleds across the barrens, couples making love, families feasting on raw walrus meat, throat singing, rituals, startling Arctic light, and endless snow. But Puja's insistent blossoming youth and sexual exhortations; Atuat's evolutionary tragedy of sorts: from flirtatious pursued Belle to motherhood, secondary positioning and victim of revenge rape; Amaqjuaq's wife, Uluriaq's frustrated anger, compliance and widowhood; and grandmother Panikpak's coming of age, from protecting Atanarjuat with a prayer to her dead husband quite early on during the head butting contest and tolerance (she puts up with her own grandson Oki's horrendous act of revenge rape of Atuat) to ridding the community of evil and teaching lessons in forgiveness, thereby becoming a surrogate camp leader towards the end-uncover that there is no fixed recipe for a real understanding of female desire and acceptance.

The film uses the domestic space creatively to comment on the multi layered subtle power-mongering. For example, Ataut complains to Atarnajuat that Puja does not help the women with household chores. Atarnajuat in turn cuffs Puja on the head, whereby, she goes like a cry baby back to her father's camp. Here in the guise of domestic control, Atuat exercises her power as a first wife (*Patrani* in the Indian context),[20] over Atarnajuat too.

Adultery is an ugly word. But it has been stripped off, of its ugliness by masterpieces such as *Anna Karenina* and *Madame Bovary* (Lal, 2003)[21] *Atanarjuat* joins this league but with a difference. Here, it is the male protagonist who commits the adultery and there are no overt moral judgements. Not just in examples like this one and the following where a man pursues a woman betrothed to another man, and later wins and marries her after a head butting contest, *Atarnajuat* is bold in several other interpretations. Not fearful of hankering feminists, polygamy seemingly is an acceptable norm; Atuat is quite flirtatiously open in her liking for Atarnajuat; the amoral sexy (Alioff, 2005: 13). Puja, hellbent on getting Atarnajuat tricks him into taking her with him on a caribou hunting expedition, sings songs with him in the night, teases him with sexual innuendoes and wins him over. The question of the man abandoning a woman after having sex with her is not a part of Inuit psychology. She automatically becomes his wife. The silent acceptance by Atuat of the horrendous revenge rape with a quietude and tolerance can bypass a multitude of social meanings about the condition of women among the Inuits. In the film's mythic, intimate plot, involving a rivalry for a beautiful woman and a very human susceptibility to evil, ribald humour feeds into like a down-to-earth feel, particularly when a strong elder brother tells the younger brother who is learning to grow strong, to think of a boulder he is trying to lift, as a woman's butt! As an aside, when Alioff asked Zacharias kunuk whether the film's uninhibited sensuality disclosed a particular Inuit attitude toward sex, Zacharias found the question incomprehensible and hilarious, but tried to answer, 'Sex. You can't top it. That's why there's so many of you. Every time I go South, I wonder where all these people came from' (ibid.: 15).

With two desirable women at the centre, their faces traced with delicate, felite tattoos – the beautiful but flirtatious Atuat and the teasingly demanding sister of Oki, Puja (Lucy Tulugarjuk), women are only seemingly at the receiving end. Atuat has to contend with long absences of her husband and later on share him with another woman, Puja, the amoral sexy (ibid.: 13) second wife of Atarnajuat, is only one example. But like Atanarjuat and the Inuit community in general, these women are also seeking ways of re-establishing that lost harmony under new social conditions and relations. Whether they can run fast enough is an open question.

The characterization in general never limits itself by locking up the characters into one mode and *Atanarjuat* is not like one of those films about aboriginal peoples that stereotypes most of the characters, men and women as nature gurus, martyrs, booze-addled, gas-sniffing losers (ibid.: 13), prostitutes or alcoholics.

The legend and film *Atanarjuat* depicts a duel between the forces of continuity and those of destruction. Eventually, betrayal linked to love is forgiven because that's human weakness (it is here that women once again show the way). However, betrayal with its roots in evil will not be pardoned. You have to love to survive, but when evil gets into love, it has to be exorcized lest it destroys the community. It is a story about communal exorcism in ancient times.[22]

III

This part of the paper discusses the film *Unnatural and Accidental* (2007). Based on an acclaimed stage play by the Métis[23] playwright, actor, and artistic director, Marie Clements, filmmaker Carl Bessai's *Unnatural and Accidental* adaptation received its world premier at the 2006 Toronto Film Festival. The play, *The Unnatural and Accidental Women* (1997) focuses on serial killings of Native women in Vancouver's downtown eastside between 1965 and 1987. The women were killed by alcohol poisoning; but all reported in the press to be 'unnatural and accidental'. The play as a 'site for struggle' (Schryer, 108 quoted in Ried, 2003: 126)[24] critiques state apathy to racial and gendered violence, and celebrates the women as life affirming and interconnected, even after death. The despair of Canada's native community in the 21st century dovetails easily in this moody and haunting drama of mystery and murder.

Rebecca (Carmen Moore) is a woman in her early thirties of aboriginal heritage living in the rough East Side of Vancouver. Here crime, drugs, and prostitution are common and many native Canadians have been caught in a downward spiral of self-destruction. Rebecca also looks after her ailing father, and shortly before he dies, he shares some startling news with her – Rebecca's mother Rita (Tantoo Cardinal), who she has long thought to be dead, is actually still alive and living in downtown Vancouver. Shattered by this disclosure, Rebecca desperately wants to reconnect with Rita, but she begins to scour the East Side in search of her mother at a very dangerous time. Norman (Callum Keith Rennie) a motor garage owner is a psychotic killer obsessed with aboriginal women. As Rebecca looks for Rita she unwittingly puts herself in Norman's path. Towards the end, egged on by the chantings and early native wisdom imparted to her by her mother, Rebecca gains strength to avenge her mother and sisters. *Unnatural and Accidental* powerfully revisits the theme of survival in a brutal environment and the power of sisterhood.

The contemptuous treatment of these women: prostitutes and alcoholic and poor and indigenous, is the central political comment of the play. Woven into this comment are larger questions of the need for love and family, and to find a space (both physical and psychological) for native values in the violent city. Told in the present, this story connects the individual stories of the women. On the way, the protagonist develops relationships with the dead women, who appear as embodied memories or spirits. These women lead the protagonist forward in her quest while living out their own sad lives in this memory narrative. The true resolution at the end occurs peacefully as Rebecca forgives her mother for leaving her as a child. As Rebecca and her mother, a former murder victim turned trapper, reunite in mythic time, the narrative ends in a spiritual/cultural space where freedom, pride, and the collectivity of women triumph.

Conclusion

Thus far, in the conclusion, the paper makes the following observations that reach out of the confines of particularities to larger debates about the cinema about the indigenous:

Firstly, there is no denying the fact that the space of global politics is not neutral but underpinned by a powerful hegemonic normative framework that circumscribe *who* and *what* we can hear and see. The exclusion is the result of what Judith Butler says 'a normative violence' that denies the excluded, the possibility of a culturally intelligible and politically qualified subject position. The narratives under discussion perform the role of knowledge keeping of cultural history and accord them an intelligible subject position in that history.

Secondly, often in our rush to make sense of confusion we look for simple explanations. Many point out that the media serves a useful purpose: they help us understand the surface reality of a complex world (Warry 2009: 69). They have also raised apprehensions of this kind too. It is naïve to assume that the purpose of the media is to educate the public about complex social issues of a culture! But what if cinema, as one of the dominant technologically progressive modes of cultural transmission, which has positioned itself as integral to the development of the culture of 'sense' and 'meaning' in modern societies (Srivastava, 2010:192)[25] chooses to promulgate truths about distorted history and visibilize oral legends through its adaptations? Further, isn't this true that '... in order to account for doubly marginalized cinema cultures operating in the space of a 'fourth' or 'indigenous' cinema, received theories of audience, genre and form need to transcend the fixity imposed by the 'national' framework and engage with the inherent openness and fluidity of film as text and practice' (Sawhney in Devy et al., 2009).[26]

Thematically, demands on the audience for such kind of cinema about the indigenous, is a certain locus of believability, distinct from that of melodrama/fiction. Often, these films are made from an advocacy point of view, with the objective to generate an awareness of their history and to preserve their cultures. Often, such cinema attempts to undo history by re-writing it. What is crucial about this cinema is much more than an artistic expression: it is a 'fight for survival'.[27] Closer home, as the first and probably only indigenous documentary filmmaker Dakxin writes, 'My sole intention in making films is to effect *change*. Where I or my theatre cannot reach, there my films should be able to reach. They should be able to sensitise the audience to the voices and issues of the most marginalized communities' (Dakxin Bajrange, Chhara theatre producer and filmmaker of Gujarat, India, quoted in Sawhney in Devy et al., 2009).

This sensitizing about their communities (Dakxin), preservation of the Inuit culture showcased in the Inuktitut language (*The Fast Runner*) or uncovering truth and facts about the traumatic history of the disappearance of aboriginal women in downtown Vancouver between 1965 and 1987, to set right a distorted unnatural history which was not accidental, with truth (Unnatural and Accidental), and setting up of academies for preservation of dying languages and cultures (En'owkin Center, Pentictin, Kelowna and Adivasi Academy at Tejgarh, Gujarat, India) are examples of unique knowledge keeping in an ingenuous way.

Last Words

Sometimes, there are surrogate knowledge keepers: researchers, academicians, cultural anthropologists: the so-called outsiders. They contribute towards community development by helping to preserve dying or soon-to-disappear cultures and narratives. A good example is a completed and documented project on gender that recovers the older women's narratives of the Gaddi tribe of Chamba and Bharmour in Himachal Pradesh.[28] To quote Linda Tuhiwai Smith once again, 'development is recovering of knowledge and preserving it ... it is a huge community project'.[29]

In short, the discussion on the two films has been book-ended by two projects in which I have been intrinsically involved, the aforementioned Chamba project and the Canada Project with my interview with Jeannette Armstrong as its centrepiece! Twinnily, both remain the fulcrum on which I rested my entire story!

Notes

1. The objectives of the society, which governs En'owkin, as Armstrong describes, are 'to record and perpetuate and promote 'Native' in the cultural sense, in education, and in our lives and our communities' (quoted in Lutz, 1991: 27). To support these objectives, the En'owkin Centre created the Okanagan Curriculum Project as a component of its institution ... that presents Okanagan history in an accurate and dignified way (ibid.: 27). Armstrong and her fellow members on the Okanagan Tribal Education Committee believe that Okanagan people must tell their own stories; therefore, the curriculum project created the Learning Institute, which provides adult native people with skills in research and writing so that First nations' individuals can develop quality, correct, and appropriate information for the project (ibid.: 28).
2. Greg Sarris, *Keeping Slug Woman Alive: A Holistic Approach to Native American Texts*, Berkeley: University of California Press, 1993 and Julie Cruikshank, *The Social Life of Stories: Narrative and Knowledge in the Yukon Territory*, London: University of Nebraska Press, 2000.
3. Professor Margery Fee of Department of English at the University of British Columbia, Vancouver, and an expert in Canadian and Aboriginal literatures – in her inaugural lecture: 'What does Oral Culture Mean?: Aboriginal Language Loss and Revitalization in Canada' in the Seminar titled 'Managing Diversity: Oral Cultures as Resource in Indigenous Communities in Canada and India' conducted on 3 March 2010 at the University of Delhi, South Campus in New Delhi, India.
4. George Bowering, 'The Autobiographings of Mourning Dove', *Canadian Literature* 144 (1995): 29–38, http://cinema2.arts.ubc.ca/units/canlit/pdfs/articles/canlit144-Autobiographings(Bowering).pdf, accessed on 27 December 2010.
5. Keynote address Chotro III Convention Hall, University of Delhi, North Campus, Delhi, India, 11 September 2010.

6. http://fngovernance.org/news/news_article/elders_and_knowledge_keepers_gather_in_winnipeg, accessed on 12 January 2012.
7. http://www.abc.net.au/local/videos/2011/07/08/3264606.htm, accessed on 27 December 2011.
8. Sherene Razack in her work on aboriginal deaths in custody in Aruna Srivastava's, 'Reconciling Pedagogy: Ethics and Dilemmas in 'Teaching' and 'Learning' Reconciliation', University of Calgary.
9. *Slash* relates a history of the North American Indian protest movement through the critical perspective of central character Tommy Kelasket, who is eventually renamed Slash. Despite the intolerance that Tommy encounters in an assimilationist school system and racist North American society, his family encourages him to be proud of his Okanagan heritage and he eventually becomes an activist for Aboriginal rights. Armstrong clearly states that *Slash* is not a chronicle of AIM (American Indian Movement) rather, the text provides a personalized account of the origins and growth of Native activism since the 1960s (Lutz, 1991: 22). The scholarship on *Slash*, however, is more abundant and varied. In a 1989 interview with Hartmut Lutz, Armstrong relates that some feminist scholars question her decision to select a male central character for her novel; however, Armstrong compellingly contends that female strength and male development are portrayed effectively through the perspective of Slash (18). In the same interview, Armstrong notes, 'I've been criticized by non-Native critics in terms of character development' (quoted in Lutz, 1991: 15–16). She explains that she could not isolate the character of Slash from his community in order to depict his individual nature and still compose the story for her people (ibid.: 16). Significantly, and consistent with the view she expresses in 'Land Speaking', Armstrong argues that Slash's personal growth can be perceived through his relationships with his family and community (ibid.).
10. Randolph Lewis, *Alanis Obomsawin: The Vision of a Native Filmmaker*, Lincoln: University of Nebraska Press, 2006.
11. When the film was premiered at the 2001 Cannes Film Festival, Kunuk won the Caméra D'Or, an award given to first-time directors. It also won the Best Canadian Feature Film Award at the 2001 Toronto International Film Festival and later five Genie Awards, including best picture, director and screenplay.
12. 'For Torontonians or Montrealers, Igloolik is so distant, it might as well be on the moon', says Maurie Alioff (2005).
13. Archaeological evidence suggests that people have been living continuously in Igloolik for 4,000 years. *Atanarjuat, the Fast Runner* (2002), http://projects.chass.utoronto.ca/soc101y/brym/SocAtMovies.html, accessed on 26 January 2012.

14. Bernard Saladin d'Anglure, 'An Ethnographic Commentary: The Legend of Atanarjuat, Inuit and Shamanism', in Paul Apak Angilirq, Norman Cohn and Bernard Saladin d'Anglure (eds), *Atanarjuat, the Fast Runner*, Toronto: Coach House Books and Isuma Publishing, 2002.
15. Doug Alexander, 'An Arctic Allegory', *The Beaver* 82.2 (April–May 2002): 48.
16. As told to Nancy Wachowich (2002: 17).
17. Jason Shubow, 'Cold Comfort: The Misrepresentation at the Center of *The Fast Runner*', *The American Prospect Online*, retrieved 2 March 2007.
18. *Atanarjuat, the Fast Runner* (2002), Reviewed by Jason Anderson, *Eye Weekly*, accessed on 7 December 2006.
19. Sophie McCall, 'I Can Only Sing This Song to Someone Who Understands It: Community Filmmaking and the Politics of Partial Translation in *Atanarjuat, the Fast Runner*', *Essays on Canadian Writing*, 83 (2004): 18–46.
20. The first wife amongst many wives of the erstwhile Rajas of India, were called *Patrani*. Though, having failed in their attempts to disallow their husband (Rajas) to get more wives, they exercised some control over the domestic sphere and once a while over the Raja.
21. Malashri Lal, 'After Emma', Book Review of *In the Country of Deceit* by Shashi Deshpande, 3 November 2008, http://www.outlookindia.com/article.aspx, accessed on 27 January 2012.
22. Alioff (2005: 19).
23. In Canada, the term 'Métis' usually designates a constitutionally recognized individual born of an Aboriginal group, descended primarily from the marriages of Scottish and French men to Cree Saulteaux and Ojibwa women in Southern Ruperts land.
24. Here, Schryer is employing Bakhtin's notion of the centripetal and centrifugal within utterance; see Bakhtin, 60–102 in Ried (2003).
25. Raymond Williams, Tony Bennett and Francis Mulhern refer to culture as 'sense' and 'meaning' in their discourses on culture in Prem K. Srivastava's 'Cultural Diversity: A Pedagogical Negotiation', *Indian Literature* 256 (2010): 192.
26. R. Sawhney, 'Through the Lens of a 'Branded Criminal': The Politics of Marginal Cinema in India', in K.K. Chakravarty, G.N. Devy and G.V. Davis (eds), *Indigeneity*, New Delhi: Orient Blackswan, 2009.
27. Rashmi, writes about Dakxin Bajrange (Chhara theatre producer and filmmaker) and Chara documentaries.
28. Malashri Lal and Sukrita Paul Kumar (eds), *Chamba-Achamba: Women's Oral Narratives*, New Delhi: Sahitya Akademi, 2012.
29. Refer to the Keynote address of Chotro III, 11 September 2010.

References

Acoose, S. et al., 'Beginning with Our Voices: How the Experiential Stories of First Nations Women Contribute to a National Research Project', *Journal of Aboriginal Health* (December 2009): 35–43, http://www.naho.ca/jah/english/jah04_02/04_V4_I2_Beginning.pdf.

Alioff, Maurie, 'From the Edge of the Earth: Zacharias Kunuk's *Atanarjuat, the Fast Runner*', *Take 1* 14.50 (June–September 2005): 13–19.

Atanarjuat, the Fast Runner, 2002, http://projects.chass.utoronto.ca/soc101y/brym/SocAtMovies.html, accessed on 26 January 2012.

Bowering, George, 'The Autobiographings of Mourning Dove', *Canadian Literature* 144 (1995): 29–38.

'Bringing Ancient Knowledges Home', *Art Direction*, 2002, http://www.atanarjuat.coni/art_direction/index.html.

Cruikshank, Julie, *The Social Life of Stories: Narrative and Knowledge in the Yukon Territory*, London: University of Nebraska Press, 2000.

——, *Life Lived Like a Story*, Lincoln: University of Nebraska Press, 1992.

d'Anglure, Bernard Saladin, 'An Ethnographic Commentary: The Legend of Atanarjuat, Inuit and Shamanism', in Paul Apak Angilirq, Norman Cohn and Bernard Saladin d'Anglure (eds), *Atanarjuat, the Fast Runner*, Toronto: Coach House Books and Isuma Publishing, 2002, pp. 197–227.

Devy, G.N., *Painted Words: An Anthology of Tribal Literature*, Delhi: Penguin Books, 2002.

Dickinson, Peter, *Screening Gender, Framing Genre: Canadian Literature into Film*, Toronto: University of Toronto Press, 2007.

Fee, Margery, 'Upsetting Fake Ideas: Jeannette Armstrong's Slash and Beatrice Culleton's April Raintree', *Canadian Literature* 124.5 (1990): 168–180.

——, 'Writing Orality: Interpreting Literature in English by Aboriginal Writers in North America, Australia, and New Zealand', *Journal of Intercultural Studies* 18.1 (1997): 23–39.

Igloolik Isuma Productions, 1994–95, 'Our Company', *About Us*, 2003, http://www.isuma.ca/about_us/index.html.

Kunuk, Zacharias, 'I First Heard the Story of Atanarjuat from My Mother', in Paul Apak Angilirq, Norman Cohn and Bernard Saladin d'Anglure (eds), *Atanarjuat, the Fast Runner*, Toronto: Coach House Books and Isuma Publishing, 2002, pp. 13–15.

——, 'The Public Art of Inuit Storytelling', Spry Memorial Lecture, Burnaby: Simon Fraser University, 25 November 2002, http://www.isuma.ca/news/zach_spry.html.

Lal, Malashri and Sukrita Paul Kumar (eds), *Chamba-Achamba: Women's Oral Narratives*, New Delhi: Sahitya Akademi, 2012.

Lutz, Hartmut, *Interview, Contemporary Challenges: Conversations with Canadian Native Authors*, Saskatoon: Fifth House, 1991, pp. 13–32.

McCall, Sophie, 'I Can Only Sing This Song to Someone Who Understands It: Community Filmmaking and the Politics of Partial Translation in *Atanarjuat, the Fast Runner*', *Essays on Canadian Writing* 83 (2004): 18–46.

Petrone, Penny (ed.), *Northern Voices: Inuit Writing in English*, Toronto: University of Toronto Press, 1988.

Petrone, Penny, *Native Literature in Canada: From the Oral Tradition to the Present*, Toronto: Oxford University Press, 1990.

Raheja, M., 'Reading Nanook's Smile: Visual Sovereignty, Indigenous Revisions of Ethnography, and *Atanarjuat, the Fast Runner*', *American Quarterly* 59.4 (2007): 1159–1185.

Ried, Gilbert, 'Marie Clements's *The Unnatural and Accidental Women:* 'Denaturalizing' Genre', *TRiC/RTaC* 24.1–2 (2003): 125–146.

Sawhney, R., 'Cinema and the Adivasis of India', *Moving Worlds: A Journal of Transcultural Writing* 9.1 (2009): 102–115.

——, 'Through the Lens of a 'Branded Criminal': The Politics of Marginal Cinema in India', in K.K. Chakravarty, G.N. Devy and G.V. Davis (eds), *Indigeneity*, New Delhi: Orient Blackswan, 2009.

Scott, A.O., Rev. of *Atanarjuat, the Fast Runner*, Dir. Zacharias Kunuk, *New York Times Online* 30 March 2002, http://www.nytimes.com.

Smith, Andrea, 'Native American Feminism, Sovereignty, and Social Change', *Feminist Studies* 31.1 (Spring 2005): 116–132.

Smith, Linda Tuhiwai, Keynote address, Chotro III Convention Hall, University of Delhi, North Campus, Delhi, India, 11 September 2010.

Srivastava, Prem K., 'Interview with Jeannette Armstrong' (unpublished), Vancouver, Canada, 3 November 2010.

——, 'Cultural Diversity: A Pedagogical Negotiation', *Indian Literature* 256 (2010): 189–198.

Warry, Wayne, *Ending Denial: Understanding Aboriginal Issues*, Toronto: University of Toronto Press, 2009, pp. 69–83.

Wachowich, Nancy, 'Interview with Paul Apak Angilirk', in Paul Apak Angilirq, Norman Cohn and Bernard Saladin d'Anglure (eds), *Atanarjuat, the Fast Runner*, Toronto: Coach House Books and Isuma Publishing, 2002, pp. 16–23.

18

Diversity and Questions of Alliance

A Case Study of the Assam Mahila Samiti, India and the Mahila Shanti Sena, Canada

Hemjyoti Medhi

This paper explores why and when questions of diversity/pluralism/intersectionality gain currency or emerge as crucial academic and policy engagements. What does it tell us about the nature of coalition and alliance that we seek across borders – national, geographical, communal, linguistic. I shall try and explicate these questions by turning to specific moments in the history of the *mahila samitis* in Assam and compare with the Mahila Shanti Sena. While we already have a macro picture of India and Canadian multicultural and diverse plural society, I would like to site a micro scenario. I use macro/micro not as oppositional terminology, but as a part trying to inflect the way the whole is understood. By raising issue of diversity in a women's association, I would like to problematize both identity politics and the politics and polemics of diversity.

In Assam, *mahila samitis* or women's associations were formed in urban centres in the first two decades of the 20th century – Dibrugarh (1907), Sibsagar (1916), Nagaon(1917), Tezpur (1919). The Assam Mahila Samiti (hence AMS) was established in 1926 at the provincial level with Chandraprabha Saikiani (1901–72) as its founding Secretary. It was reorganized as the Assam Pradeshik Mahila Samiti (hence APMS) in 1945. In early 2012, there are more than 25 district samitis and nearly a thousand primary mahila samitis in Assam.

Though the APMS was formed as the apex body, in practice most district samitis function independently of the APMS. In principle, the mahila samiti began as an apolitical institution. But key members were active in anti-colonial Gandhian mobilization and courted arrest and were imprisoned during the Indian nationalist movement in the 1930s and 1940s. The AMS aimed for 'the improvement of education, health and other aspects of Asamiya women' (Assam Mahila Samitir Uddeshya, 1928: 3). The Samiti demanded girls' schools, better facility for female travelers in railways and steamer networks, and separate seats for women in the Council, Municipalities and Local Boards during the late 1920s. The provincial Samiti started with a few hundred members in late 1920s and evolved and grew to become an organization of nearly 32,000 members by 1949 (Pradeshik, 1948: 173). Sucheta Kripalani (1908–74), who addressed the APMS 22nd Annual Conference in Dibrugarh in 1949, called it the largest democratic organization of women in India (Saikiani, 1961 15).

Mahila Shanti Sena, (Women's Peace Brigade International, hence MSS) was founded in 2002 in Bihar and is registered in Canada. It was the brainchild of Gandhian mobilizer Acharya Ramamurti who said, 'Give women a chance ... Make them agents of change' (MMS Newsletter, May 2013). Noted intellectuals from India and Canada and nearly 10,000 men and women participated in the Vaishali Sabha (2002) where a programme was charted. The ideal of the Gandhian Village Community with sustainable livelihood is central to its vision. The MSS movement has nearly 75,000 women involved in different parts of northern and eastern India – Bihar, Uttar Pradesh, Odisha, West Bengal, Assam, Tripura, Manipur, and Arunachal Pradesh. The MSS's slogan is Meet –Talk – Consensus. The movement has helped women tackle issues of petty conflict resolution, economic self-reliance, cooperation in *panchayati raj* and empowerment as agents of change. The MSS also engages in international collaboration especially with friends of the MSS in Canada.[1]

I

I shall try and enter the question of diversity in a women's association through membership. The initial members of the AMS belonged largely to the middle class. The lists of members published serially as Appendices of the women's journal *Ghar-Jeuti* through 1927–28 are testimony to this. These lists include women across castes and communities, both Hindus and Muslims.[2] Most of the listed members belonged to the urban middle class – wives of lawyers, doctors and bureaucrats. Only a handful of women were listed as professionals, mostly as teachers in girls' schools. Muslim women were actively involved in most early mahila samitis in the 1920s and 1930s. Majida Tayyebulla (d. 1935) in the Kamrup Mahila Samiti as Joint Secretary and later as Secretary, Chashme Nurjahan Begum in the Tinsukia Mahila Samiti, Z. Haque in the Uttar Lakhimpur Mahila Samiti and others in Tezpur are a few examples.[3] Theoretically, the mahila samitis were always open to all religions, communities and castes. Some samitis, like the Tezpur Mahila Samiti, made a strong point of their secular ethics stating in their first meeting itself that 'one may read essays in praise of one's own religion but may not demean another's' (TDMS Proceedings 1928–39 scan 0007).

However, the praxis of samiti meetings, conferences and other everyday activities regularly invoked rituals like starting meetings with the Vaishnava bargita, lighting lamps, performing an *uruli* (ululation) and so on. In an undated anecdote published in 2001, Usha Das, an active member of the APMS in the 1950s and 60s, relates how Gulanara Begum, an office assistant of the APMS, transformed herself into a Hindu woman. Gulnara wore vermilion during a field trip so that the Brahmin family providing shelter to the samiti workers would accept her. Das reads this act of Begum transforming herself into 'Renu Devi' as an 'example of sacrifice in a woman's organization' (32). But, this anecdote is representative of personal accommodation and sacrifice as well as a context where such 'sacrifices' were legitimized. Were such 'accommodations' expected? Muslim women were being mobilized separately in Assam by 1945 as the overall communal politics in the state had made such mobilization on communal ground possible ('Muslim Mahilar', 1945: 2). The old rivalry between the Congress and the Muslim League was temporarily buried for a few months in 1945 under a new agreement only to fall apart by October the same year (Guha 2006: 232–236).

Similarly, the tribal woman too largely remained outside the mahila samitis' constituency till the late 1940s. In March 1936, the AMS protested the denial of a seat in Guwahati for 'Assamese women' and sent a telegraph to the Congress Party Secretary Mr Satyamurti:

> Hammond Committee's recommendations permanently locate only available women's seat for Assam at Shillong, quite unjust and unthinkable. [The] Seat must move by rotation. If cannot be located

> in Gauhati, central and biggest town in Assam. Pray try redress injustice to Assamese women.' ('Assam Mahila Samitir Pratibad', 1936: 9 [quoted in English in the original newspaper report])

The AMS's demand for political representation had been a constant since 1929, after Prafullabala Chaudhurani's call for women's seats in the Local Boards, the Municipalities and the Council. The AMS Seventh Annual Conference in 1933 took a resolution stating that the Samiti did 'not support the current regulation on women's franchise' and demanded one woman's nomination from the entire province in the Central Legislative Council, three women from the Assam Valley, and two from the Surma Valley in the Provincial Council. The AMS strategically claimed that the two reserved seats for Hindus in the Surma Valley, which were being transferred to Assam Valley, must be reserved for women ('Assam Mahila Sanmilanir Prastabsamuh', 1993: 2). Amalendu Guha has discussed in detail how the colonial government strategized electoral politics through the dichotomy of Asamiya/Bengali, Hindu/Muslim as predominant modes of exercising political representation in a complex province like Assam with its multi ethnic, multi linguistic context. It seems, at least from the incident cited above, that the mahila samitis had accepted such divisions in principle. Thus, women's mobilization could be well entrenched in a particular regional or communal conceptualization of the world.

I do remain alert to the fact that a popular weekly may have had its own politics in highlighting claims by the AMS about Brahmaputra/Surma valley divisions. However, my conclusion about the mahila samitis' limited theoretical conceptualization of their constituency is borne out in their own documents. For instance, the Tezpur Mahila Samiti supported Chandraprabha Saikiani's candidature in the 1936 elections as the members felt that the nominated Khasi woman would not represent the concerns of 'the Assamese woman' (TDMS Proceedings, 1928–39 scan 0099). The separation of the tribal from the Asamiya was well entrenched in the APMS even as late as 1948. In the APMS 21st Annual Conference held in Nagaon in January 1948, the Samiti overwhelmingly supported the decision of the Assam State Government to declare Asamiya as the language of the state. Bonnily Khongmen, who was a female member in the Legislative Assembly then, and was present at the APMS Nagaon conference, opposed the move. She gently suggested that it might be better to gradually work towards the spread of the Asamiya language among the hill communities (who have their respective mother tongues). Khongmen added, 'It is futile to try and impose a language on anyone.' Khongmen was completely isolated and a host of representatives from Tezpur, Lakhimpur and Guwahati such as Swarna Mahanta, Lilabati Bardoloi and Induprabha Barua protested Khongmen's position. Most members present strongly supported the motion for declaration of Asamiya as the state language and the APMS carried it forward (Assam Pradeshik Mahila Sanmilanir Ekoish, 1948: 177).

It has been a sustained criticism of Asamiya regional nationalism/sub-nationalism that the language policy was one of the major setbacks and a key reason for alienation of the tribal population, both in the valley and the hills. The APMS's support to the Asamiya language imposition policy of the government does not indicate that the mahila samitis had developed as a significant force to *determine* policies at this stage. Nonetheless, it definitely implicates the mahila samitis in a limited conceptualization of identity at this juncture.

Despite a wide-scale network of mahila samitis from Goalpara in Western Assam to Tinsukia in Upper Assam and Tarapur (Silchar) in the Surma Valley, the female tea garden labourer remained outside of the mahila samitis' pale till the late 1940s. Hemprobha Das, one of the founding members of the Dibrugarh Mahila Samiti and active in the AMS, in her reply to Shanta Bhalerao of AIWC wrote in a letter in English, dated 3 April 1939, 'I am indeed very sorry that I could not show you the gardens as you desired after [sic]. You see, I have no idea about the tea garden labourers and I know very few tea planters and specially I have no interest in them' (Letter, 1939: 13). While Hemprobha Das may have made a candid admission, it is clear that the AMS in its category of the 'Asamiya woman' neither recognized the tribal woman nor the coolioni (the female tea garden labourer).

The greater inclusiveness at the policy level in the late 1940s followed Congress's attempt to mobilize tea garden labourers, only after the Communist Party of India had already made inroads and forced a rethinking of representational politics in general.[4] Thus, the mahila samiti movement reinforced some of the institutional divisions such as Assam valley/Surma valley in questions of political representation, and derived these ideas from mainstream politics.[5] But, there were moments in independent India when the samitis did assert an independent analysis of state policies in the context of the weaving co-operative movement – a site where the mahila samitis had much at stake.

By the early 1930s, the AMS had successfully networked with select areas in South Asia. The outpouring of funds for Amrit Kaur and the Ceylon Malaria Relief Fund in 1935 was a reciprocal gesture for Kaur's fast to support fund-raising during floods in Assam (TDMS Proceedings, 1928 –39 scan 0088). It was a confident AMS that invited Muthulakshmi Reddy to be the President of the AMS Seventh Conference in Guwahati in 1933. However, Reddy declined as she was busy with the Women's Franchise Committee (Assam Mahila Sanmilanir Saptam, 1933: 7). Amrit Kaur came as President of the AMS 11th Annual Conference held in Guwahati in December 1937 (Assam Mahila Samitir Ekadosh, 1938: 3). In her presidential address Amrit Kaur praised the women of Assam for their expertise in spinning and weaving and urged them to fully participate in national and social work (3). Hemaprabha Mazumdar came from Comilla and graced the President's chair in one of the Goalpara Mahila Samiti meetings in 1931. Comilla, in East Bengal (now in eastern Bangladesh) near Tripura was connected to Goalpara through the railway network of Eastern Bengal Railways. This partly explains the ease with which women leaders from Comilla came and attended conferences in Goalpara. Secondly, Comilla was very vibrant during 1920s and 1930s with an active *Abhay Ashram* (1910). Similarly, Shanta Bhalerao toured parts of Assam as an AIWC representative in March–April 1939 to seek potential partnership with the AMS ('Correspondence', 1938–39: pp. 1–65). Bhalerao felt that the AMS was already a strong presence and 'in aim and objective [it was] much the same' as AIWC (Suggestions, 1939: 72). However, the AMS's opposition to joining the AIWC was not lost on Bhalerao. A handwritten letter accompanying the Bhalerao papers in the AIWC files explained that the AMS decision not to join the AIWC citing differences in rules was led by 'wrong impressions' (Correspondence, 1938–39: 26). The letter was not signed. As the letter writer identified herself as the secretary of the AMS in 1933, it was possibly Rajabala Das. The AMS's strategic dissociation from the AIWC highlighted the fissures within diverse constituencies of the women's movement, and the shifting paradigms of local, regional, national.

The affiliation with the AIWC was a contentious issue. It was agreed in a Working Committee meeting of the AMS that the secretary would correspond with the AIWC to discuss possible affiliation ('Correspondence', 1938–39: 26). But, in 1934, during the AMS 8th Annual Conference, Saikiani opposed this affiliation and asserted that the rules of AIWC 'seem to be a little strange' ('asahua') and the AMS rules would have to be changed substantially if it were to join the AIWC (Assam Mahila Sanmilanir Ashtam, 3). Rajabala Das, the then secretary protested at such a turnaround and formed a separate association, the Assam Pradeshik Mahila Sabha as a branch of the AIWC in Assam shortly afterwards (Assam Pradeshik Mahila Sabha, 7). This branch remained marginally active in the 1930s and 1940s in Assam. Rajabala Das led Mahila Sabha merged with the APMS in 1950 (Duyuo Khon, 8). The reasons for Saikiani's opposition and the overwhelming support she received from other members are difficult to determine as papers from this period are not available at the current APMS office. This might have been a reflection of the general disconnect from the Indian mainstream.

A certain level of disconnect with border provinces like Assam was apparent in the AIWC's own resolutions. In 1935, Omeo Kumar Das quotes the 9th Annual Report of the AIWC and its unilateral decision about women representatives from Assam: 'This being a backward province, most of its first representatives would be Bengali or of the domiciled community' (page 187 of the Report). Das adds, 'We know that women in Assam had organized themselves (AMS 1926) even before the AIWC was established (1927). How could the Conference [AIWC] write such a statement about women representatives from Assam in such a situation?' (Mahila Jagat, 1935: 623). Das supports the AMS against what he sees as marginalization by the AIWC in 1935. Yet, it may be recalled, that he was among the prominent Congress leaders who had persuaded the AMS to withdraw the legal notice against the groom during the Sarda Act controversy, only a year ago, in 1934!

The AMS worked successfully with various parallel organizations such as the Assam Sahitya Sabha, regional branches of the Indian National Congress, representatives of the AIWC, Local Boards, as well as individuals in colonial bureaucracy, local members of legislative assemblies, and ministers, eminent Congress leaders *and* a large section of women spread across villages and towns.

The mahila samitis were undoubtedly influenced by the nationalist frame, but they did achieve considerable success in inflecting the tenor of the local public sphere, sometimes by openly challenging patriarchal authority and power, and on other occasions by simply engaging with new modes of participation in the public (Medhi, 2012: 50). Yet, I remain alert that while the AMS could connect across distances, it remained alienated from specific groups and communities within the province.

A proper comparative study of AMS and MSS is awaited as the latter organization is new and both have had different trajectories. Women-based/focused social organizations come largely in four forms: government-initiated/funded, community-based but partially funded by government, non-governmental organizations (NGOs), and social movements which are unstructured and are not owned and operated by one group or an elected body. The AMS began in pre-independent India as a community based voluntary organization which started receiving government grants after India attained independence in 1947, so it overlaps category two and three. The MSS however is seen more as a movement towards empowerment of women within a larger Gandhian view of life. Compared to the AMS (1926), the MSS is a new organization started in 2002 in Bihar. However, despite the recent origin of the MSS organization, a few comparisons with AMS would be instructive.

Both organizations have privileged the constituency of women as their focus. The AMS was founded for the welfare of women and consisted in their promotion in education and employment, and participation in social and political organizations. The MSS seeks to raise women's self-awareness, to empower with women's collective strength. Both have evolved as social movements led by women but supported by both women and men. Unlike the AMS which formulated written Rules and Regulation (1927) and reformulated later in 1945, the MSS has no constitution, no elected body and no central office. MSS members, workers, leaders are distributed and are made up of people associated with various organizations, NGOs and educational institutions following or supporting the philosophy of MSS.

The initial and pre-independence membership of AMS cut across caste, class and religion as the nationalist movement perhaps subdued if not overpowered the communal and religious forces that generally divide the society. However the fragile nature of social harmony in contemporary India seems to be a hindrance for similar mobilization. The question of membership in the MSS is an indicator of this. In the MSS membership follows the line of the NGO with which the MSS is associated in a given area. During the initial years in Bihar the majority of the MSS members was primarily from the lower castes/classes (Dalit and OBC) with relatively few women coming from the upper classes. There were almost no women from the Muslim community.

MSS works with existing NGOs and creates new MSS chapters only if a local NGO cannot be found. This has the advantage of sharing resources and making use of social connections and know-hows that these NGOs have already worked out. The disadvantage is that some of these NGOs are dependent on government grants or on assistance received from funding agencies whose mandate is of a charitable nature rather than creating self-awareness and self-empowerment. If not careful, this conflict can hinder work and progress.

A final point of comparative interest is the financial base of the AMS and the MSS. The AMS could function with income generated from membership fees, voluntary work and hours put in by members, government grants and the proceeds from handloom and handicrafts managed by the organization and its local chapters. The MSS, on the contrary, has no such income generating mechanism and this seems to have been a major problem. The organization received some help in its initial phase from UNICEF (Bihar) and from its friends in Canada but it has not developed any local sustainable resources. As Rama S. Singh puts it 'MSS women, the majority coming from the poor classes, are always asking for jobs, even part-time jobs, some source of income, for a few penny in their pockets. A collaboration between MSS and SHGs (Self Help Groups) is a possibility, where the two organizations can complement each other'.[6]

The MSS has theoretically steered clear of identity markers. At an immediate level this facilitates transcending of borders, geographical, communal, and linguistic. Gandhian Village Development model through KVK at Khadigram, animal husbandry, issues of caste divide, village roads acquire centrality. This is significant because it indicates how conscious raising sessions transcend set objectives beyond political and economic rights. As Chandra Mohan writes about his experience of the MSS convention in Bhubaneswar in 2012, 'One MSS worker shouted and asked 'Why Mahila, why not 'Male' also?'' (12). However one of the challenges of the MSS is gender stereotyping. The naming of the women's school 'Grihini Vidyalaya' with its emphasis on 'kitchen gardening, sewing, cooking' may be read as sustainable livelihood training but has the potential to perpetuate traditional gender roles.

II

Judith Butler in *Gender Trouble* (1990) offers a critique of identity politics in general, and of a women's identity-based feminism in particular where she reads identity as performative rather than of representation. If all identities are performative, is my search for the Muslim woman, or tribal, coolie woman in the AMS misplaced? I try to conceptualize this as the recognition/segregation dilemma. What does recognition of difference signify? Does registering difference segregate rather than unify? Is recognition of difference really necessary for a sustained democratic engagement? There are examples in both AMS and MSS about how difference is constituted. In MSS Odisha network, women trained in 2005–06 are increasingly asking questions about caste divisions and similar exploitative structures.

In AMS, the *sipini bhoral* or the weavers' cooperative was an attempt that transcended caste and community markers. One of the key figures who headed this cooperative was Majida Tayabullah. She and her joint Secretary Sashiprabha Hazarika published reports of income and expenses of the bhoral regularly in the press. The sipini bhoral was an extension of the intense labour that people like Majida Tayabullah was accustomed to. In her daughter Jahanara Begum Hussain's words: Mrs Tayabullah was an 'expert weaver', she took good care of poultry at home and was very hard working. I had the good fortune of meeting Jahanara Begum in June 2010 to try and see if I could probe further this whole issue of Muslim women within the mahila samitis in Assam, and to know how she reads the question of diversity. I met her as part of a project to create a digital archive of the mahila samitis in Assam concentrating on three mahila samitis, the APMS and the Tezpur District Mahila Samiti and the Dibrugarh District Mahila Samiti.[7] Jahanara Begum seemed to have had a cosmopolitan upbringing who participated in festivals, acted in mahila samiti staged plays as a child with mostly Hindu friends. She sang marriage songs during the interview which are usually sung in Assamese Hindu marriages. In a situation where all three mahila samitis I worked with did not have a single active Muslim Executive Body member and I had not been able to get in touch with most descendents of Muslim mahila samiti members, meeting Jahanara Begum was extremely rewarding. There are Muslim general members in the mahila samitis as well as local Muslim women who are in leadership positions in primary samitis, but not in the district level of the samitis with whom I worked.

I encountered more questions after this meeting in my search to locate diversity and pluralism in the mahila samitis – 1. Was Jahanara Begum performing the allegedly expected role of a 'good Muslim' to a researcher who carried a Hindu name? Why did her narrative not invoke any sense of discomfort about the contemporary polarized society? 2. *Am I* constituting Majida Tayabullah in the category of a 'Muslim woman'? Did she function with that category? As one of the elites families in Assam, did the Tayabullahs function with a class index rather than a communal marker? Or is it my academic pretence towards secular pluralism? Similarly when Rama S. Singh notes that the MSS women are 'always asking for jobs', a source of livelihood, do we hear a different voice? Finally, is diversity an identity prism that could potentially blur the larger picture? Am I missing the whole while I see the parts? Is diversity ideological and political both in India and Canada where tropes such as reservation, immigration, citizenship, rights of groups x, y, z gain currency? I would like to posit if policy driven diversity privileges identity politics and has the potential to jeopardize the entire project of alliance formation across borders.

Epilogue

This paper was written over two phases. In the first phase I largely concentrated on the AMS, which is part of my doctoral study. In the second phase I received extensive help from Dr Chandra Mohan and Prof. Rama S. Singh who are both associated with the MSS. My understanding of AMS has evolved from a study of textual sources such as reports, minutes of samiti meetings, etc. as well as oral history, mostly interviews and conversations with past and present members. But I have not had the opportunity to interact with MSS members closely. Therefore this 'study' is more an attempt to enter the question of diversity through these two women's associations rather than a coherent explication of both organizations and their philosophy. I have also come to recognize that while academic studies like mine may be critical of some of the policies of these associations, I remain humbled by their achievements, the result of painstaking efforts of hundreds of women and men, hours of voluntary work and labour of love and passion.

Notes

1. I am grateful to Professor Rama S. Singh for forwarding me copies of the MSS Newsletters. The information here is compiled from my interaction with him and the Newsletters.
2. See 'Oporonchi' ['Appendices'] of the women's journal *Ghar-Jeuti* through 1927–28. 'Oporonchi' in *Ghar-Jeuti* 1.9 lists a number of Muslim women from Dhubri.

3. See Kamrup Mahila Samiti 5; Kamrup Mahila Samiti 3; Assam Mahila Samiti: Tinsukiat 4; and Uttar Lakhimpur Mahila Samiti: Purushar 9.
4. For a comprehensive study of tea, labour and trade union activities in Assam, see Rana Behal (2007).
5. For the political implications of the divisions of the valleys, see Guha (2006).
6. The last five paragraphs are written in collaboration with Prof. Rama S. Singh and inputs from Dr Chandra Mohan.
7. The project was funded by the Sephis Programme, International Institute of Social History, Amsterdam, and supported by Tezpur University, Assam (2009–2011).

References

Assam Mahila Samitir Ekadosh Adhibeshan: Srimoti Amrit Kauror Sabhanetritwat Guwahatit Sukalame Sampanna (Assam Mahila Samiti's Eleventh Conference: Mrs Amrit Kaur Presides in Guwahati), *Assamiya* (weekly) 8 January 1938: 3.

Assam Mahila Samitir Pratibad: Mr Satyamurtiloi Telegraph (Assam Mahila Samiti Protests: Telegraph to Mr Satyamurti), *Assamiya* (weekly) 21 March 1936: 9.

Assam Mahila Samitir Uddeshya (Aims and Objectives of the Assam Mahila Samiti), *Assamiya* (weekly) 11 March 1928: 3.

Assam Mahila Sanmilanir Saptam Barshik Adhibeshan: Abhyarthana Samitir Gohari (Assam Mahila Sanmilani's Seventh Annual Conference: Appeal of the Reception Committee), *Assamiya* (weekly) 7 April 1933: 7.

Assam Mahila Sanmilanir Prastabsamuh (Proposals of the Assam Mahila Sanmilani), *Assamiya* (weekly) 5 May 1933: 2.

Assam Pradeshik Mahila Sanmilanir Ekoish Barshik Adhibeshanor Karjya Bibarani (Assam Pradeshik Mahila Sanmilani 21st Annual Conference Proceedings), *Abhijatri* 1.4 (1948): 176–186.

Behal, Rana P., 'Power Structure, Discipline, and Labour in Assam Tea Plantations under Colonial Rule' in Rana P. Behal and Marcel van der Linden, eds., *India's Labouring Poor: Historical Studies,* c. 1600–c.2000, Delhi: Foundation Books, 2007.

Bhalerao, Shanta, 'Correspondence with Miss Bhalerao Concerning A.I.W.C. Conference in Assam and Miss Bhalerao's Visit to Assam', File No. 197, A.I.W.C. Papers, Microfilm Roll No. 12, New Delhi: Nehru Memorial Museum and Library, 1938–39, pp. 1–65.

——, 'Some Suggestions for the Extension of A.I.W.C. Organisation in Assam, Report on the Work Done in Assam, Delhi and Bihar by Shanta Bhalerao', File No. 198, A.I.W.C. Papers, Microfilm Roll No. 12, New Delhi: Nehru Memorial Museum and Library, 1939, pp. 71–76.

Butler, Judith, *Gender Trouble*, New York: Routledge, 1990.

Das, Hemaprabha, 'Letter of Hemprobha Das to Miss Bhalerao', File No. 197, A.I.W.C. Papers, Microfilm Roll No. 12, New Delhi: Nehru Memorial Museum and Library, 3 April 1939, pp. 12–13.

Das, Omeo Kumar, 'Mahila Jagat: Nikhil Bharat Mahila Sanmilan' ['Women's World: All India Women's Conference'], *Banhi* 23.10 (1935): 622–624.

Das, Usha, 'Padmashri Shradheya Chandraprabha Baideor Soaranat' ['In Memory of Padmashri Chandraprabha Baideo'], Barua and Bora 32–33.

Guha, Amlendu, *Planter-Raj to Swaraj: Freedom Struggle and Electoral Politics in Assam*, 1977, 3rd revised edition, New Delhi: Tulika, 2006.

Medhi, Hemjyoti, 'The Making of an Archive: 'Memory, Movement and the Mahila Samiti in Assam, India', *Global South: Special Issue Gender and Development* 8.1 (2012): 49–57.

Mohan, Chandra, 'Marathon MSS Convention in Bhubaneswar, Odisa (India), 4–5 February 2012', *MSS Newsletter* (March 2012): 10–13.

'Muslim Mahilar Anusthan' ['Muslim Women's Organization'], *Assamiya* (weekly) 19 May 1945: 2.

'Pradeshik Mahila Samitir 1946–47 Sonor Pradhan Jutia Sampadikar Bacherekia Karjya Bibarani' ['Chief Joint Secretary's Report on the Proceedings of the Pradeshik Mahila Samiti for the Year 1946–47'], *Abhijatri* 1.4 (1948): 169–175.

Saikiani, Chandraprabha, *Assam Pradeshik Mahila Samitir Itibritta* [*A History of the Assam Pradeshik Mahila Samiti*], Guwahati: APMS Office, 1961.

TDMS Proceedings 1928–39, scan 0007, 'TDMS Proceedings 1928–1939', Documents Archive, TDMS, DVD 1, SEPHIS, IISH, The Netherlands and Tezpur University Project, Co-ordinator Hemjyoti Medhi, 'Memory, Movement and the *Mahila Samiti* in Assam, India' (2009–2011), Project Advisor: Rimli Bhattacharya, Team members: P. Anbarasan and Reetamoni Narazary, Technical Asst. Mridusmita Baruah, A Digital Archive of the Mahila Samiti housed at Tezpur University.

TDMS Proceedings 1928–39, scan 0088, ibid.

TDMS Proceedings 1928–39, scan 0099, ibid.

19

Women and Work in India and Canada

A Kaleidoscopic View

Nilima Srivastava

Background of Women and Work

There is a new drive on, to change mindset about employing women. U.N., World Bank and Corporate Sectors all are paying more attention to women as employees. Some European Companies have already introduced quotas to get more women on Company Boards. It has become a capitalist compulsion to make the most of women professionals' potential.

In the rich world, most of the battles about legal and political rights have been won and on the economic front too women have come a long way. Even in the developing countries, women work force has become significant both in number and in work profile. Employers have a reason to be grateful for the boost to their labour pool, because talented and skilled work force is in short supply world over. A number of studies have shown that the presence of a critical mass of women in senior positions is positively co-related with company's performance and possibility of higher profits as companies benefit from a more diverse work force with broader set of ideas (*The Economist*, 26 November 2011: 5).

For women themselves, it has been unshackling, to be able to choose almost any kind of career for reasons ranging from economic independence to the desire for self-fulfillment. They have made great strides in all kinds of careers, but they still find it much harder than men to bag the coveted leadership jobs. On the face of it women have done all they possibly could do to prepare themselves by getting into all kinds of businesses and profoundly varied professions too. A lot of them make it to middle ranking jobs. But, a vast majority of them get struck at this level, because of decades old organizational structures that favour men more than women. The scene is pretty much the same everywhere that men and women graduating out of colleges or universities get recruited together, half way up the ladder a lot of women have already dropped out and at the top, there are hardly any left. Most organizations tend to be gender blind or profess to be gender neutral by treating women equal to men, but women's circumstances are often quite different.

It is mostly assumed that women are the secondary earners as in a patriarchal society, men are the bread winners and the primary wage earners in a family. Women usually earn a lower income and their decision to enter the labour force depends on the complementary economic need of the family and when the cost associated with household labour, such as child care, care of elderly, sick, disabled family members, etc. is lower than the income generated out of their paid work. This is to say that economic factors together with institutional structures shape women's work participation rate in most of the developed countries. In developing countries, women tend to get into gainful employment to meet the high cost of living, to save for old age and to meet any medical or economic emergency in the family (in absence of effective state instituted welfare measures). But, when job prospects are poor in the labour market and economy is sluggish, women are seen to be withdrawn from the job market first, irrespective of which part of the world they belong to.

Korabik and McEwain (2006) in their research found that when men and women have the same family responsibilities, pursue identical careers and work same number of hours, family demands tend to interfere more with women's careers than with men's. Another, interesting finding of the study is that career minded women do not ask for fewer hours of work but they would like to have more flexibility in choosing their hours and ability to work from different locations at times.

Women in modern times have more options but face a lot more pressure because of multiple roles they have to perform. Moreover, women are often more closely scrutinized. Shirley Addison, a psychotherapist avers that women tend to face troubled times even if they are blameless as they internalize problems and take the blame and responsibility of the things.

This paper looks at the status of women in two countries, one from the developed world, viz. Canada and another from the developing world, India. In the beginning, development indicators affecting women and the situation of working women in the two countries is discussed. Next, we will analyse the situation with regards to the similarities and differences in the Female Labour Force Participation Rates of Canada and India and also State mechanisms to support working of women in paid labour.

Status of Women in Canada

In Canada, women (50.4%) comprise just over half of the population. and in India, women (48.1%) are less than half of the population (http://www.statcon.gc.ca).

In Canada's immigration female population, Asian and Middle Eastern Countries (41%) have the highest representation followed by women immigration from Europe (36.0%) and Central and South America (12.0%). Majority of women are Catholic (40%) and 24 per cent as one of the other Christian sect and about 5 per cent women in Canada are Muslims, Jews, Buddhists, Hindu, or Sikhs.

Educational and Literary Levels

In Canada, according to an estimate in 2004, 37 per cent women had attended but not completed high school and just 16 per cent women couldn't go beyond Grade 8 (http://www.statcan.gc.ca).

Aged between 25–34 years, more women (33.0%) had a university degree, compared to men (25.0%). Proportion of men (24.0%) and women (25.0%) having a university degree is almost same (http://www.12.statcan.ca/census-recenscment/2006). Education indicators show that women generally do better than men and on an average have higher literacy skills than the male population (http://www.statcan.gc.ca/pub/89-503-x/2010001/article).

Labour Force Participation Rate (LFPR)

LFPR has received considerable attention in recent years in Canada. This is especially on account of problems of population ageing. This implies shortfall in labour supply, resulting in lowering of standard of living, weakening of welfare system and crumbling of health status of general population.

Canada, since mid 1990s has experienced an impressive increase in LFPR following reforms in the tax and benefit system especially for secondary earners. The aggregate LFPR (73.0%) has surpassed that in the United States (69.02%) and it is now only just short of the rate in Nordic Countries (75.1%) (Tsounta, 2006: 4).

The increased participation of women in paid work force has been the most significant social trends in Canada in the past quarter century and constitute 47 per cent of the employed workforce. In 2004, women aged 15 yrs and above, 58 per cent of them were part of paid work force. On the contrary, percentage of men in the same age group who were employed fell from 73 per cent to 68 per cent (Women in Canada Report, 2006: 103).

Policy initiatives at both the federal and provincial levels have been responsible for these changes in LFPR with benefits in tax wedges. Let us have a quick look at these policy initiatives:

- Government (at both levels – federal and provincial) floated National Children's Agenda in 1997 to support and enhance the health safety and development of all young children. Federal Government has particularly increased incentives for single mothers to enter labour market.
- In 2000, the Early Childhood Development Agreement was signed to provide federal funds to provinces and territories to improve and expand childcare and other services to children less than six years of age.
- Maternity and parental leave benefits, initiated in 2002, administrated under Employment Insurance System, were expanded. An eligible parent, enjoying a partial salary payment by federal government, can take up to 50 weeks off work, an increase from 35 weeks previously. Another improved provision is reduced hours of works from 700 to 600 hrs per week to avail this benefit.
- Multilateral framework on Early Learning and Childcare (2003) requires federal funds given to the provinces to be used to improve access to affordable, quality and locally regulated early learning and childcare programmes, thus supporting their parents' participation in employment or training.

There are other provincial support policies that include low cost full day universal childcare (in Quebec) and universal expansion of childcare to all children above two and a half years old.

In 2009, 58.3 per cent of women were employed, which has doubled since 1976, showing an upward trend over the past three decades (but declined during economic downturn in early 1990's). It is interesting to note that downturn's effect on employment of women were less severe than for men.

But there is another side to this story also. Even when the women are employed on full time basis the average earning of the employed women are still substantially lower than that of men, accounting for only 71 per cent of what their male counterparts make. Also, the gap between the earnings of women and men has not changed substantially in past decades. In Canada, women make a disproportionate share of the population with low income as measured by Low Income Cut-Off. (LICO). Unattached women are more likely to have low incomes. Families headed by female lone parents also have relatively high rates of low income. Women in Canada Report (2010) documents, 38 per cent of all female lone parent families had incomes which fell below the after tax LICO as compared to 13 per cent of male lone parent families.

Another fact that needs attention is that, even though the female visible minority women (Chinese, South Asian and Black, etc.) are better educated on an average than Canadian women but they are less likely to be employed. When these minority women get into paid labour they earn less at their jobs than do other women.

Child Care and Working Mothers

There has been particularly sharp growth in the employment rate of women with children in the past two decades. In 2004, 73 per cent of all women with children under 16 years of age living at home, were in employment, up from 36 per cent in 1976. Employment levels of women with very small children have sharply increased in last 10 years because of the proactive measures taken by federal and provincial governments to provide state sponsored child care provisions. Vast majority of employed women with children hold full time jobs. It is interesting to see that the age of children appears to have little impact on the likelihood of workers being employed full time. But, there is some hitch amongst women with pre-school children who are still less likely to be employed than those with school-aged children (ibid.: 104).

In the past one decade, there has been substantial increase in number of child care facility available to families. Majority (82%) of day care spaces in Canada are regular day care centres while a small percentage (18%) are licensed spots in a family home. Cleveland Gunderson and Hyati (1996) and Powell (1997) using Canadian data, found a substantial negative effect of childcare practices on labour supply. Lefebure and Mergain's (2005) study of Quebec shows that low-fee day care policy has substantial positive labour supply effects on the mothers of pre-school children (c.f. Tsounta, 2006.: 8).

Absence from Work

Employed women are far more likely than the males to absent themselves from work because of personal or family responsibilities. Women, on an average of 10 days in a year were found to be absent from work whereas employed men missed only about a day and a half of work for reasons of personal or family responsibilities (ibid.: 109).

Part-time Employment

Another phenomenon which is more commonly found with employed women is to work part-time (that is less than 30 hours per week). Women in all age groups are far more likely to work part-time than their male counterparts.

More percentage of women (26.9%) than men (11.9%) work part-time for the reason as childcare and other responsibilities (one in five women part-time workers), family or personal responsibilities (3.8%). Only 2.3 per cent of male part-time workers cited these reason for their not taking up full time work. Work part-time practice has a bearing on the age of the women workers, women aged 15–24 years were found to be studying while working, women between 25–44 years of age caring for their children and women above 45 years were most likely to not want full time employment (Women in Canada Report, 2010: 15). A substantial number of women couldn't get a full time job and therefore working part-time, a reason with 26 per cent of all female part-time employees (ibid.: 109). To conclude, the Report on Women in Canada says that 7 out of 10 part-time workers are women and this proportion has not changed in past three decades (ibid.: 13).

Self Employment and Temporary Work

At present, more than one out of ten employed women in Canada is self-employed and most likely to run self-businesses. Women are also more likely to be engaged in temporary employment with predetermined end date (14%), than the male employees (12%) (ibid.: 111). A small but growing share of employed women is in the multiple employment segments (6%). It is the women who are more likely to be seen as multiple job holders than their male counterparts.

Distribution Across Occupations

As a result of these policy measures, in recent years, Canadian women have increased their representation in several professional fields. In 2009, women constituted 51.2 per cent of business and financial professionals, more than one half (55.2%) of doctors, dentists and other health professionals and 72.5 per cent of professionals employed in social sciences or religion. Their visibility in managerial positions has also become better (37%) but their representation remains clustered at lower level managers than amongst those at higher level. Women professionals are still in minority (30.1%) in the natural sciences, engineering and mathematics (Women in Canada Report, 2010: 23).

Despite change in work scenario of women in Canada, women are still concentrated in traditional occupations. When we see it in comparison to men, we find 67 per cent of employment in teaching, nursing, administrative or sales and services occupations detained by women and only 31 per cent of employment in these sectors rest with men (ibid.: 21).

According to the Report, in comparison to 30 per cent employed men, 67 per cent of all employed women were working in traditional women occupations like teaching, nursing and other health related occupation, clerical or other administrative jobs, sales and service sector (ibid.: 113). Women have increased their representation in several professional fields in recent years. In Canada, women are increasingly making up majority of professionals in education related profession. However, women engaged in traditionally female dominated occupations have declined from 71.8 per cent in 1987 to 67.0 per cent in 2009. In contrast, percentage of women in teaching professions rose marginally from 3.8 per cent to 5.8 per cent over the same time period. For the same time span, women in nursing profession show an increase from 8.3 per cent to 9.1 per cent but there is decline in sales and service jobs held by women from 30.0 per cent to 28.9 per cent (ibid.: 22).

Women currently take up one in four farm operators in Canada. A large majority of female farm operators share the responsibilities of management with at least one partner while majority of male farm operators managed alone (ibid.: 144).

Unpaid Work by Working Women in Canada

Canadian women spend more hours working at home than women in other prosperous countries. Women in Canada spend 248 minutes in a day in unpaid work while others spend only 146 minutes, a difference of almost 100 minutes more (http://www.thestar.com/living/healthy-canadian).

Mental Health and Working Women in Canada

According to a study conducted by Leger Marketing for Wyeth Canada, 71 per cent respondents said that mental health problems, (viz., depression, anxiety) are more of a barrier to successful career and only 23 per cent respondents held pregnancy as an impediment in their career growth. The same study also projects that one in every five working women in Canada experience work related depression/ anxiety that make some women avoid or even quit work. Profile of the respondents show that these problems are more visible in women aged between 35 to 55 years, live in a city or sub-urban areas and have children to look after. But, types of occupation, their educational status or income level have no relationship with the issues of mental health. The findings also project the emergent need to address this issue at the place of work to increase productivity, improve morale and create amiable work environment (http://www.ctv.ca/CTVNews/Women_depression_041115).

Women in India

As per the census in 2011, India has 58,64,69,174 women in its population of 1,21,01,93,422. Sex ratio is 933 women per 1,000 men, signifying not a healthy demographic picture. Although, the Constitution of India not only grants equality to women but also empowers the State to adopt measures of positive discrimination in favour of women for removing the historic cumulative socio-economic, educational and political disadvantages faced by them

There has been a progressive increase in the five year plan outlays for women and children over the last six decades. There has been policy shift from 'welfare' oriented approach in the decades of fifties and sixties to 'development' and 'empowerment' in later five year plans. Let's take a look at development indicators with respect to women in India.

Education of Girls and Women

More men (82.14%) are literate than women (65.46) in India. The trend starts from the educational avenues provided to boys and girls in their early childhood.

Girls are lagging behind in enrollment-rates of all educational types. (69.5% for girls and 77.4% for boys) and the dropout rates for girls are also high (NPCCD Report, 2010).

Health and Nutrition

Although the life expectancy at birth has increased from 36.1 years in 1951 to 66.91 years in 2001–06, the health and nutrition status of women and girls remains a matter of concern. Maternal mortality in India is estimated at 301 per 1,00,000 live births. While, National Family Health Survey-3 (NFHS-3) shows reassuring decline in fertility ratio, birth and infant mortality ratio but anemia and malnutrition continue to be on rise among both children and adult women.

Labour Force Participation

Every media platform projects a very progressive and modern face of India's women workers. But when we sift the data, the reality, unfortunately, hasn't changed much.

As per the Census, in the adult working age group (18–59 years) barely 13 per cent of the Indian women are categorized as workers. Within this small section nine out of 10 women work in unorganized (informal) sector in difficult job environment. If we take a look at distinctive features of women workers in India, it comes to fore that it is the rural, poorer and less developed regions of the country where more women work against the urban India, implying that job is a necessity not a choice for most women in economically difficult circumstances.

India has 397 million workers out which 123.9 million are women. 106 million of these women workers are in rural areas and the remaining 18 million women work in urban areas. Almost 96 per cent of the women workers are in unorganized sector. The female work participation rates has increased from 19.7 per cent in 1981 to 25.68 per cent in 2001 (ibid.: 209), but it is still low when compared to men work participation which was 52.6 per cent and 51.9 per cent for the respective years. Although there has been an increase in women work participation rates but has been distress induced, compelling women to take up jobs which offer very poor wages and no social security. In the last decades, for the need of augmenting income in urban households, there has been a significant increase in women employed in petty retail trade, hotels and restaurants. But these are typically low paid jobs where women work for long hours without any benefits and face sexual harassment (http://www.cpiml.org/liberation/year_2004/women and workers.htm).

The women (81–87%) are most likely to be paid below the standard minimum wages against 40–50 per cent men workers; reports National Commission for Enterprises in the Unorganized Sector (http://www.economictimes.Indiatimes.com).

Subsidiary employment is much more prevalent among women workers because economically gainful activities have to be combined with their socio-culturally determined non-market household activities (Mukhopadhyay and Tendulkar, 2006: 8).

Occupation and Segregation of Women Workers

Being slightly below 36 per cent, women's Labour Participation Rate (LPR) in 2008 was extremely low in comparison to men (85%). Thus, the induction of female labour force into paid workforce has lagged considerably behind the males as a result of socio-cultural determinants that affect division of labour within household, compounded by low literacy rates of girls and women, their marital status, age, household size, number of dependent family members are other demographic features. Even if the women are required to be inducted into labour market because of pressing family need to augment income, average women would already have been at a disadvantage of being older than her male counterpart as marriage in Indian society is more important than a girl becoming economically independent. Even in educated, middle class families, girls are provided with unequal opportunities for acquiring educational and technical skills to compete on equal terms with men in labour market.

There remains employers' bias also. Given the cultural notion of bearing full burden of household responsibilities and the reproductive roles of women, employers in disguised manner prefer to hire a male worker over a female worker with equivalent qualifications as that of the hired man or pay a lower wage because in the perception of the employer, a woman employee may not be able to give her best to the paid labour. Also, in addition there are other gender based factors such as fear of harassment of women at the place of work, restriction on mobility of girls and women and lack of infrastructural support for women staff, all making labour market scenario less women friendly thus pushing down women's LFPRs. The female membership in Trade Unions remains low but strongholds of females organizing themselves as cooperatives/federations have emerged as a response to problems faced by women workers in informal labour.

Another interesting phenomenon that has been observed is the 'currently married' status of women that has a negative impact on their participation in labour force. For men it ('currently married' status) ensures probability of paying more attention to the paid job. In Indian society, men are still considered as bread winners while the women with their reproductive and care work can take up gainfully economic engagement after ensuring their household responsibilities are well taken care of.

There is another important feature that of biased measurement and faulty perceptions of capturing economic activities that woman perform in Indian economy. A range of expenditure requiring activities like fetching firewood and drinking water in rural areas; home based piece rate work in urban areas and other activities clubbed under 'care economy', all of which goes unaccounted.

Thus, it can be said that for women workforce in India, cultural and demographic factors turn out to be better predictors of women's work participation than they are for men.

Mukhopadhyay and Tendulkar (2006) have pointed to yet another significant pattern of women's participation in paid labour. Labour status of husband and wife remains fairly congruent. For the 'self-employed' and 'casual labour' categories, a large percentage of wives who are self employed or casual labours, have their husbands sharing the same status. However, the situation when studied for 'regular wage and salaried men workers', in urban areas, in 84.5 per cent cases their wives were found to be 'out of the labour force'. For rural areas, the percentage is 63.4 per cent for the same category. The chapter suggests that over and above the socio-cultural, demographic constraints faced by women in Indian labour market, the insecurity of income associated with self employed and casual work status of men has also a bearing on women's decision to participate in paid work (30).

The creation of flexible labour market and the myth of 'feminization of work' in reality have led to unemployment and under-employment in India.

Sectorial Employment of Women (1999–2000)

S. No.	Sector	Per cent
1.	Agriculture	64.3
2.	Live Stock	9.00
3.	Textiles and textile products	3.0
4.	Beverages and Tobacco	3.0
5.	Food products	1.1
6.	Construction	1.7
7.	Petty retail trade	3.4
8.	Education and Research	2.7
9.	Domestic servants	3.2

Source: Sundaram (2001).

According to an estimate in 2005, 50.16 lakh women employees were engaged in organized sector, out of which 58.0 per cent in public sector and 42 per cent in private sector (industrial relations, naukrihub.com/women-employment.html). In spite of a recent decline in public sector employment, the share of female workers are gradually increasing in central, state governments. Relatively high wages, maternity and sickness benefits and other social security benefits make public service attractive for young women.

Growth in employment in services is highest in IT/BPO industry (Business Process Outsourcing) with one third workforce comprising of women. The trend shows increasing share of women in this sector.

In case of women, though seen both in rural and urban India but particularly high incidences in rural women, Work Participation Rates in poor households are higher than those in the households above poverty line as a measure of what may be called compelling need based participation of women in work (Sundaram and Tendulkar, 2004: 3). It is estimated that about 60 per cent of all agricultural operations are handled exclusively by women, with appalling working conditions. Hourly female wages varying from 50–75 per cent of the rates given to men and women workers in agriculture remain perpetually entrapped in poverty (http://www.wageindicator.org/countryreport-india). Initiated in the last decade, Mahatma Gandhi National Rural Employment Act (MGNREGA), a public employment programme ensures the constitutional provision of minimum wage.

Legislative Measures and Public Policy

Since independence, several legislative measures have been instituted for the welfare of workers including women workers. These are:

1. The Minimum Wages Act, 1948
2. The Employees State Insurance Act, 1948
3. The Mines Act, 1952
4. The Factories Act, 1948 (amended in 1949, 1950 and 1954)
5. The *Bidi* and Cigar Workers (Condition of Employment) Act, 1966
6. The Contract Labour Act 1976 (Regulation and Abolition) Act, 1970
7. The Maternity Benefit Act, 1961 (Amended in 1995)
8. The Equal Remuneration Act, 1976
9. The Employment Guarantee Act, 2004
10. The Domestic Workers (Registration, Social Security and Welfare) Act, 2008
11. Sexual Harassment of Women at Work Place (Prevention, Prohibition and Redressal) Act, 2013
12. The Unorganized Sector Workers' Social Security Bill, 2007

The Government of India has undertaken several initiatives to provide support to women workers. Some of the important programmes are:

- Rajiv Gandhi National Creche Scheme for Children of Working Mothers
- Working Women Hostels with Day Care Centres
- Mahatma Gandhi National Rural Employment Guarantee Act
- Diversification and Extension of Vocational Training Programme for Women
- Funds to establish Women Industrial Training Institutes
- Schemes for leadership development of minority women
- *Swawlamban* programme for women provides skill training to women to facilitate their employment or self-employment on a sustained basis in traditional and non-traditional trades.

Several policy measures have been initiated by the central government in India for women's empowerment. A milestone enterprise undertaken by Committee on Status of Women in India was

'Towards Equality Report' of 1975 that brought to forefront how women's work is under valued and not accounted in national income. In 2001 another comprehensive national policy (National Policy for Empowerment of Women, 2001) was formulated for holistic development of women in the country. The objectives of this policy ensure (1) creating a positive environment through development of economic and social policies for full development and realization of women's full potential, (2) equal access to participation and decision making by women in social, political and economic life of the nation, (3)equal access to women to health care, quality education at all levels, career and vocational guidance, employment, equal remuneration, occupational health and safety, social security and holding public office, etc.

But, India does not have a publicly funded social security scheme. A small segment of the organized sector workers is covered by the Payment of Gratuity Act (1972).

India has ratified only four out of eight core ILO labour conventions but has a wide array of labour protection laws in its Constitution. By 2007–08, there were 43 labour laws enacted, albeit, no assurance of their compliance. The report on National Commission for Enterprises in Unorganised Sector (2009: 170) states that if we take the effectiveness of coverage of different labour regulations into consideration, the actual coverage of India is very small. The laws themselves apply to a small proportion of workforce and they are actually implemented in the case of even smaller segment. In the whole scenario percentage of women who are covered under these legislations is only dismal.

Conclusion

Human society has historically overlooked the value of wo performed by women.

According to Economic Survey 2010–11 (293), India ranks 122 out of 158 ranked for Gender Inequality Index (GIE) in 2008, whereas Canada ranks 16 on GEI (GEI captures the loss of achievements in the areas of reproductive health, empowerment and LFPR due to gender disparities). But, still Canada is plagued by gender disparity in the sphere of paid labour where women are provided work in stereotyped occupations, their wages less than those for men for the same work, do more of unpaid work at home and remain the primary care givers to children. As a consequence suffer more from health related problems.

Whereas, in India, in spite of democratic system of government, a progressive constitution and many laws to protect women's rights, implementation in true spirits and political remains lacking. Women are still expected to be the lead caregivers at home, thus limiting choices a woman has when she needs to work. The deck is stacked against women largely because our workplaces and our social and labour policies have failed to reflect the realities of women's life.

But, women continue to move into the workforce in even increasing numbers. More opportunities have opened up for them and the pay gap with men is getting smaller. It is taking a long time, but things are getting better.

Tsounta's study (2006: 1) states that policy initiatives to family-friendly policies introduced in Canada could boost female participation in paid labour in other countries and help policy makers meet the challenges especially that of population aging.

To sum up one can say that women are joining labour force in record numbers, raise families and participate in community work, but barriers remain in realizing their full potential. Women are still not equal to men, not even close, both in developed and developing world.

References

http://www.census2011.co.in/.

http://indiabudget.nic.in/es2011-12/estat1.pdf.

http://www.statcon.gc.ca.

http://www.12.statcan.ca/census-recenscment/2006.

http://www.statcan.gc.ca/pub/89-503-x/2010001/article.

http://www.thestar.com/living/healthy-canadian. Last accessed on 11 April 2012.

http://www.cpiml.org/liberation/year_2004/women and workers.htm. Last accessed on 11 April 2012.

http://www.ctv.ca/CTVNews/Women_depression_041115. Last accessed on 11 April 2012.

http://www.economictimes.Indiatimes.com.

http://www.wageindicator.org/countryreport-india.

Human Development Report 2010, New York: UNDP Publications.

Korabik and McElwain, 2006, 'Working Women More Influenced by Family' http://www.uoguelph.ca/news/2006/05/ working_women_m.html, last accessed on 11 April 2012.

Mukhopadhyay, Swapna and Suresh D. Tendulkar, *Gender Differences in Labour Force Participation in India: An Analysis of NSS Data*, New Delhi: ISST, 2006.

Special Report on Women and Work, *The Economist,* 26 November 2011.

Sundaram, K., 'Employment and Poverty in 1990s: Results from NSS 55th Round Employment-Unemployment Survey, 1999–2000', *Economic and Political Weekly* 36.32 (11 August 2001): 3039–3049.

Sundaram, K. and Suresh D. Tendulkar, 'The Poor in the Indian Labour in the 1990s', Working Paper No. 128, Centre for Development Economics, Department of Economics, 2004.

Tsounta, Evridiki, 2006, 'Why Are Working Women More in Canada', IMF Working Paper, www.imf.org/external/pubs/ft/wp/2006.

Women in Canada: A Gender-based Statistical Report 2010.

20

School Education and the Challenge of Diversity

India and Canada

Meenu Anand

International efforts over the last two decades in education have focused largely on gender equality in education. As agents of primary socialization, schools play a critical role in imparting and reinforcing gendered identities to girls and boys thereby contributing towards polarized conceptions of femininity and masculinity. The current paper attempts to build upon exploring the role of schools in reinforcing notions of gender identity through various classroom processes across India and Canada. The paper begins with an introduction to various national and international level commitments towards gender equality in education. It further cites evidence of research carried out in Canada and India on gender and education. The paper specifically focuses on findings of author's research conducted in 16 government and private schools of Delhi, India. It unveils quantitative as well as qualitative data gathered from over 339 respondents (teachers and students) covering issues such as gender specific behaviour in various classroom processes like sitting arrangement, allocation of roles and responsibilities and expectations of teachers/students from a gender lens. Based on these, the paper seeks to dwell upon building Indo-Canadian linkages.

India and Canada are two great democracies sharing a strong commitment towards education. The Indo-Canadian academic relations have been flourishing in recent years at both institutional as well as government levels. Significant among these include the Shastri Indo-Canadian Institute, the Department of Foreign Affairs and International Trade (DFAIT) Canadian Studies Program, The Commonwealth Scholarship and Fellowship Plan and Canadian International Development Agency (CIDA). Both countries have taken various steps to advance equality for women and remove the barriers to women's participation in society, putting emphasis on increasing women's economic security and eliminating violence against women. Both nations greatly highlight on the importance of education of women for nation's development and recognize the importance of schools as progressive institutions to nurture latent talents among children and grooming their personalities, enabling them to move beyond the traditional gender biases and stereotypes and sexist notions.

Indo Canadian National and International Commitments Towards Gender Equality in Education

Both India and Canada have demonstrated commitments towards gender equality in education and are a signatory to international conventions and taken steps towards the same in their respective countries. Let us trace some of the significant measures adopted by these nations that reflect dedication towards developing a gender perspective in education.

India

India is a signatory to the Convention on the Elimination of All Forms of Discrimination Against Women (CEDAW 1981), Convention on the Rights of the Child (CRC 1990). The CRC draws attention to the right to development as a basic set of rights which includes the right to education and non-discrimination among children. The Beijing Platform for Action (1995) was reviewed in 2000 (Beijing +5) with further commitments calling for the elimination of discrimination in education at all levels, the creation of gender-sensitive education systems with a particular focus on quality and gender-sensitive curricula, as well as emphasizing the critical impact of girl's education. Education for All Goals reaffirmed in Dakar in 2000, emphasized a focus on gender equality in education within two of its six goals where all children, especially girls, would have access to and complete free, compulsory primary education by 2005. It also aimed to eliminate gender disparities in primary and secondary education by 2005, and; achieve gender equality in education by 2015. India has committed to meeting the UN

Millennium Development Goals (MDG) (2001) where the MDGs two and three aim to achieve universal primary education and to promote gender equality and the empowerment of women. It is currently at the 132nd position of the Gender Inequality Index (HDR, 2013).

At the national level, the Indian constitution gives considerable emphasis to education. Article 45 of the constitution enjoins the states to provide for free and compulsory education for all children until they complete the age of 14 years irrespective of their sex. The Government of India in its 86th constitutional amendment of 2002 created Article 21-A, that seeks to provide free and compulsory education to all children aged 6 to 14 years 'in such manner as the State may, by law, determine'. Moreover, the National Policy on Education (NPE) and its Programme of Action (revised in 1992) is a landmark document in the Indian context that focused heavily on gender issues in education. Thus, a lot of programmes were initiated and were given a further impetus by a range of special projects initiated by Government of India like the *Shiksha Karmi Project* and *Lok Jumbish Project* in Rajasthan, Bihar Education Project, Andhra Pradesh Primary Education Project and *Mahila Samakhya*, Education Guarantee Scheme (EGS) of the Madhya Pradesh government, the bridge programmes of Andhra Pradesh and Karnataka, the District Primary Education Project (DPEP) and *Sarva Shiksha Abhiyan* (Ramachandran, 2003). The 12th Five Year Plan, Government of India builds on the view that development is a process of expanding freedoms equally for all individuals, and considers gender equality as a core development goal in itself (Ministry of Women and Child Development, 2011).

Canada

Canada is a world leader in the promotion and protection of women's rights and gender equality. Securing the 18th rank in the Gender Inequality Index (HDR, 2013), the country is committed to the view that gender equality is not only a human rights issue, but is also an essential component of sustainable development, social justice, peace and security. One of the first countries to sign and ratify the Convention on the Elimination of All Forms of Discrimination Against Women (CEDAW), Canada also ratified the Optional Protocol to the CEDAW in 2002. It participated in the development of the Vienna Declaration and Programme of Action in 1993, which affirmed that *women's rights are human rights* and called for action to integrate the equal status and human rights of women in the mainstream of UN system-wide activity.

Canada also played a key role at the 1995 Fourth World Conference on Women in Beijing, which identified 12 critical areas of concern and set out a course of action to ensure comprehensive protection and advancement of women's rights around the world. Committed strongly towards the MDGs, Canada has also set an example by being the first country to celebrate the first International Day of the Girl on 11 October 2012 (http://www.swc-cfc.gc.ca).

At the national level, the Government of Canada adopted the Federal Plan for Gender Equality in 1995 as a response to the Beijing Platform for Action created at the 4th World Conference on Women (1995). The key commitment of the Federal Plan was to 'implement gender-based analysis throughout federal departments and agencies'. The Canadian Charter of Rights and Freedoms (1982) and the Canadian Human Rights Act (1977) outline legal obligations to ensure gender equality in Canada. The principles of gender equality are also reflected in 1998 Multiculturalism Act, which introduced measures to protect and promote the rights of aboriginal women and foreigners. Moreover, the Canadian International Development Agency (CIDA) has identified its own Gender Equality *Action Plan 2010–2013* that aims to explicitly integrate gender equality in all policies, programmes and projects.

Evidence of Research Carried Out in India and Canada on Gender and Education

A lot of research has taken place in India as well as Canada that establishes the strong linkages between education and gender. A careful analysis of the research studies across India unveils that during the 1980s and early 1990s, the focus of research rested primarily on the issues related to primary education such as enrolment of girls in schools, their retention, factors associated with their dropout rate. During the 1990s a paradigm shift took place from primary education towards to elementary education. A lot of stress in the education sector was laid on the qualitative aspects such as importance of teacher's attitudes, their expectations, teacher's behaviour towards boys and girls, parental motivations, aspirations, etc. With the emphasis on Universalization of Elementary Education by 2010, the main focus of action currently has been on improving the functioning of schools and enhancing the quality of their outcomes. It has been realized that quantitative progress without attending to processes and outcomes would in the long run only lead to unviable and unproductive structures.

Thus schools in India are currently being looked upon as progressive institutions that enable the children learn values and ethics considered important for their overall personality development. With schooling being recognized as one key indicator of human development index, they are also viewed as 'corrective institutions' that play a major role in re-socialization of the child who has already acquired some understanding of gender based roles, behaviours, expectations from his/her family (Gandhi, 1995). According to the NUEPA (2014), percentage of girl's enrolment across all the states in India in 2012–13, was 48.66 per cent for grade VI–VII.

In Canada too, significant observations are being noted with respect to gender and schooling. According to 'Women in Canada: A Gender-based Statistical Report 2010–2011' (2012), young girls in Canada are doing better than boys. In 2006, Statistics Canada presented the results of an extensive study that found that 5-year-old girls exceeded boys of the same age in terms of readiness to learn. Girls scored higher than boys in communication skills, attention, self-control of behaviour and independence in dressing. However, boys ranked higher than girls with respect to curiosity.

According to Human Resources Skill Development Canada, school drop-out rate has declined steadily since the academic year 1990–91, reaching a low of 8.5 per cent in 2009–10. Drop-out rates for women were consistently lower than for men between 1990–91 and 2007–10, with an average disparity of 4.3 percentage points. Drop-out rates have decreased for both men and women, from 19.2 per cent for men and 14.0 per cent for women in 1990–91, to 10.3 per cent for men and 6.6 per cent for women in 2009–10. Drop-out rates have also been consistently lower for women than for men. Between 1990–91 and 2009–10, the average disparity was 4.3 percentage points.

The upcoming trend in Canada focuses on single sex education. David Holthouse (2010) in his paper *Gender Segregation: Separate But Effective* talks about the recent movement in Ontario based on the hypothesis that hard-wired differences in the ways that male and female brains develop and function in childhood through adolescence, require classrooms in which boys and girls are not only separated by gender, but also taught according to radically different methods.

Demers and Bennett (2007) in a collaborative study by The Ontario Association of Deans of Education and The Literacy and Numeracy Secretariaton *Single Sex Classrooms*, debate on increasing number of single sex schools in Canada. Their research suggested focusing on increasing student's intrinsic motivation, diversify teaching practices and ensuring attention in initial teacher education. Although recommended by some, single-sex classrooms were not the new paradigm for scholastic success.

We can assume from the evidence of recent research on gender and education in both countries that there is a definite focus on recognizing the gender perspective at the school level. Both countries recognize the importance of the school system in gendered socialization and the highly influential role of teachers in transmitting societal norms and values. Both however, seem to have taken a diverse stand with respect to segregated/mixed sex school education system.

Findings of Research on Gender and Elementary Schooling in Delhi, India

A comparative research was conducted in 16 schools of Delhi (eight government and eight private) to explore the classroom practices in schools of Delhi, India from a gender lens. The schools were selected from four different zones of Delhi with equal representation of both categories of schools. The study was designed with the following objectives:

- To analyse the classroom practices in elementary schools of Delhi from a gender perspective.
- To examine the beliefs and stereotypes of school teachers regarding gender biases in school practices.

School Category wise Disaggregated Data on Sitting Arrangement in Classroom

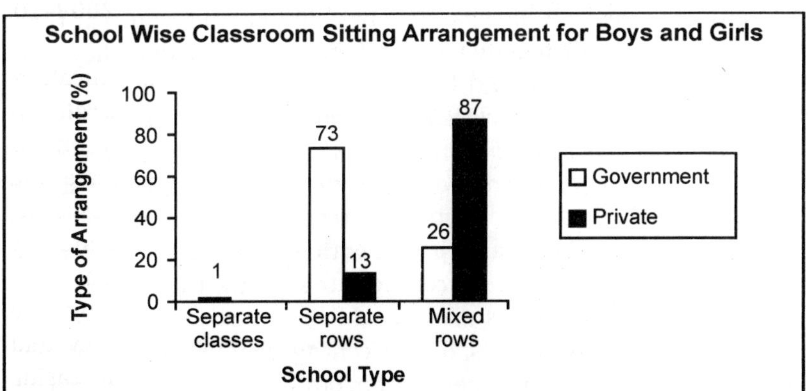

- To study the understanding of gendered roles and identity as imbibed by upper primary school children.
- To draw a comparative analysis between government and private schools with respect to gender and education.

Research Methodology

To meet the above objectives, quantitative as well as qualitative information was gathered from school teachers and children. A structured interview schedule was administered among 160 school teachers (80 males and 80 females) from the upper primary classes (classes VI–VIII). Analysis was done on the basis of findings of teachers' interviews, group discussions with students and observations made by the author. Major findings of the research may be discussed under the following broad heads:

Classroom Activities

Classroom processes are seen to have an impact on transmission of expected behaviours and traits from boys and girls. Being a little society in itself, it exerts a powerful socializing influence on the children affecting their personal characteristics, attitudes and behaviours. Information was sought regarding seating arrangement, allocation of roles and responsibilities and about class leadership from teachers as well as students.

Seating Arrangement: The data from teachers regarding seating arrangement of boys and girls in the classroom revealed that segregation in seating arrangement was being practiced by most government school teachers. Seventy three per cent revealed that they made girls and boys sit in separate rows, 26 per cent said that they made the children sit together while 1 per cent said that they had separate classes for girls and boys. According to most government school teachers, '*boys and girls talk a lot when they sit together*', 'this *is the system in our school'* or '*boys and girls should not be mixed together as boys are more naughty and do not let the girls study'.* These statements reflect the biased opinions of teachers that lead to their treatment of boys and girls as separate entities. Girls were considered frail and fragile and thus were encouraged to sit in the front rows while boys who were considered as *strong* could sit at the back.

In case of private schools, 87 per cent teachers shared that they followed mixed seating arrangement for boys and girls. Thirteen per cent said that they made boys and girls sit separately in the class. Most private school teachers talked about alternating the sitting arrangement for their students based on rotation of seats on a daily/weekly basis by students. Few teachers talked about making the students sit according to their roll numbers. Some also talked about having special consideration for children with weak eye sight or those who needed more attention were made to sit in front.

Role Assignments: The teachers were asked about the involvement of boys and girls in classroom activities such as fetching water, cleaning, *rangoli* making, helping others, shifting desks, checking homework, shifting desks. Teachers from both types of schools spoke about involving girls and boys equally in all the above assignments. It was observed that in private schools both boys and girls were made equally responsible for carrying out multifaceted tasks – decorating the class/display boards, bringing chalk/white board marker, getting note books, etc. On the other hand, girls were observed to be more involved in various roles in school as they were considered to be obedient and bright as compared to boys who were perceived to be naughty.

Class Leadership Roles: Leadership roles in classrooms were studied in order to explore the trends in allocation of leadership among boys and girls. According to more than one half teachers from the government schools, girls were more responsible, obedient and were therefore made class monitors. Boys on the other hand were often restless, over active and did not conform to the norms. This corroborates the gender stereotype of girls being compliant and the boys being disobedient/non-compliant. Seven per cent teachers from government schools and about 1 per cent from private schools said that they preferred a boy to be the class monitor as boys could show authority and exert control over both boys and girls. Girls according to them were *mild* and *soft* by nature and were 'ineffective' monitors.

School Category wise Disaggregated Data on Leadership Roles (in percentages)

Class Monitor	Government	Private	Total
Girls	31.2	22.0	53.20
Boys	7.3	0.9	8.26
Both	18.3	20.2	38.50
Total	56.9	43.1	100.00

Eighteen per cent teachers from private schools and one fifth from government schools had two monitors in their class – one boy and one girl. This again shows the stark difference in the leadership trends in the two types of schools. A contrast was again found in the explanations by school teachers from the two types of schools for having two class monitors. Most teachers from the government schools reasoned that they had two monitors so that the boy monitor could discipline the boys while the girl monitor disciplined the girls.

Reward and Punishment System

Reward and punishment systems are an integral part of the day to day disciplining of children and play an important role in inculcating moral standards among children. An insight into the prevalent reward system being adopted by the school teachers revealed that most government schools confined to traditional methods of demonstrating appreciation for students clapping, positive verbal remarks. It was seen that most private schools adopted creative and innovative ways for rewarding their children, e.g. star/badge system, point system, leadership roles, etc.

With respect to the punishment system, contrary information was revealed from teachers and children. Most teachers gave socially acceptable answers and shared about not giving any kind of physical punishment to students. Children on the other hand reported about receiving severe corporal punishments by teachers. A contrast in the punishment system was also observed across the two categories of schools. While most government school teachers indulged in severe use of physical punishments where as many private schools were trying to adopt innovative methods of restricting deviant behaviour among children, adopting *negative reinforcements* instead of giving physical punishments to children. A gendered lens unveiled that the incident of corporal punishments were more prevalent among boys than girls. Children narrated instances where girls had walked away with none or milder punishments for the same offence where as boys had been subjected to severe corporal punishment. Interestingly, all students unanimously agreed that the teachers trusted the girls more than the boys. This again corroborates the gender bias where girls are considered docile and soft where as boys are considered naughty and mischievous.

Teacher's Professional Aspirations for Students

Information from teachers with respect to their professional aspirations for their students revealed three emerging trends. One, female teachers are more accepting and forthright as compared to male teachers about women being suitable for *unconventional* professions. Two, private school teachers are much more open-minded with regards to acceptance for both boys and girls for most professions. Three, male teachers from private schools seem to be more free from the gender stereotypes as compared to their counterparts in the government schools with regards to professional aspirations for students.

About two-third male teachers showed preference for girls to take up professions like academics, beauty culture, nursing and considered them suitable for domestic work. They showed increasing preference for boys to take up armed forces, business and plumbing. Higher number of female teachers shared that women were no less than men and could do even better than men in most jobs. This shows a sense of self-confidence and empowerment among these working women.

Children's Professional Aspirations

Children were found to be extremely open and articulate in expressing their opinions and concerns. They strongly opined about their views on different issues and unanimously emphasized that academic performance was not linked to any sex based distinctions. Anyone irrespective of his/her sex, who would work would achieve positive results. The students also showed gendered inclination towards certain professions and this was relatively seen in higher proportions among government school children who conformed to the stereotypical professional choices. Due to their better level of awareness and information, private school children aspired for innovative career choices.

Research Analysis

Analysis of the school practices from a gender perspective reveals several sex based distinctions being followed by schools. It can be drawn from the study of classroom activities that interactions within it seemed to be 'doing' gender among boys and girls in most government schools. Through sex based segregation in seating arrangement, task allocation and in leadership, government schools seemed to be compartmentalizing boys and girls into two separate categories. Children being at an impressionable age are likely to imbibe the gendered classroom practices, thereby accepting the differentiated sex based division of tasks and responsibilities. In other words, government schools through the overt and covert means were translating the commonly accepted gendered beliefs and opinions among the students. Private schools on the other hand, in most cases were more open and adopted innovative methods in carrying out classroom activities. Reward system adopted by the school teachers did not reveal gender based segregation while punishment methods clearly indicated the severity towards the boys. Professional aspirations of school teachers revealed gender stereotypes while children seemed to be more progressive in their thinking. The study recommends a strong need to create a gender friendly social contexts within the classroom and the overall school systems with the objective of bringing about a 'deliberate' change to adopt innovative strategies and do away with the stereotypical compartmentalization of boys and girls. Ongoing gender sensitization workshops for school teachers, inclusion of gender as an intrinsic component in the teacher's training programme and encouraging non stereotypical efforts/activities can be some of the practical means to bring about attitudinal changes among teachers and school authorities.

Building Indo-Canadian linkages: The Emerging Trends

Like India, Canada too has witnessed a lot of research work into classroom pedagogy, co-educational schooling, inequities between boys and girls and the gendered nature of literacy (Heather and Sanford, 1999). While there are a lot of similarities among the range of issues being debated by both countries, there are a few unique approaches being followed as well. Let us attempt to gain an insight into the emerging trends on the basis of evidence of current research and secondary data on gender and school education in both countries:

Girls Surpassing boys

Both India and Canada are witnessing a contemporary situation where girls are surpassing the boys in terms of overall scholastic achievements. Literacy rates for men and women have moved up from 75 per cent and 54 per cent to 82 per cent and 65 per cent respectively from 2001 to 2011 (Census 2011). According to NUEPA (2011), the overall school enrolment of students in India has increased from 101.16 million in 2002–03 to 134.38 million in 2008–09. A comparison of number of students securing 60 per cent and above in primary as well as upper primary levels shows girls securing better grades than boys.

This may be attributed to the intensive efforts being taken by the government towards gender and education with specific focus on enrollment and retention of girls in schools and improving the overall quality of education. Recent studies in Canada too have demonstrated that, during their first years at school and even earlier, young girls do better than boys (Statistics Canada 2006).

Mixed Versus Single Sex Schools

A sundry observation is made with respect to the type of schooling pattern in both countries. While India is questioning the segregation of sexes in its schools, the upcoming trend in Canada seems to be towards creating separate opportunities for boys and girls for harnessing individual talents. Significant among these are single sex schools such as St. Andrew's College for boys, Branksome Girls School, Bishop Strachan Girls School, York House Girls School at Vancouver, British Columbia. These schools claim to teach as per the learning styles geared specifically toward how young men/women learn the best. A distinct step towards this direction is the initiative by the Toronto District School Board (TDSB) having the distinction of being the largest board in Canada and the fourth largest in North America with 595 schools, 16,000 full-time teachers covering 2,57,000 elementary- and secondary-school students. TDSB is creating distinctive environments for their 2,50,000 children under its single-sex schools, called the Girl's Leadership Academy and the Boy's Leadership Academy. According to the board, boys still lag behind girls in literacy and even though the gap in mathematics has been improving, there are concerns about the number of boys who do not graduate from high school. For boys, the focus will be on instructional strategies that will close the achievement gap and get boys more engaged in learning. The Calgary Board of Education is launched an all-boys alternative programme in September 2012 to go alongside their successful all-girls programme.

Role of School Teachers

Both countries are placing a lot of thrust on the role of school teachers in the overall personality development of students. In fact, teacher's training is an area where Indian government is placing a lot of importance both at the levels of pre-service as well as in-service training programmes. The government's 12th Five Year Plan (2012–17) focuses on continuous professional development of teachers, providing them academic support and increasing teacher motivation with an active aim to arrest school dropout, enabling elder girl children to attend primary schools and improving overall quality of education with special focus on girl children. Canada too places profound importance to teacher's training to enable them to face various challenges in the classroom, maintain academic standards and deal with diverse issues related to gender with greater empathy.

Conclusion

Both India and Canada are taking significant steps in view of their national and international commitments towards gender and education. As evident from various research studies and data across the two countries, gender is an integral issue that is given critical importance by both India as well as Canada. Gender based differentiation in the overall education system is observed both overt and covert ways in the present schooling system. Both countries have plunged to take up the issue very seriously and making strident moves in their own unique ways, battling various diverse challenges in through innovative steps. Both are taking initiatives to harness latent talents among young girls and boys and develop their *human* capacities in order to develop young girls and boys into socially responsible, proactive citizens.

References

Blair, Heather and Kathy Sanford, 'Media and the Construction of Gender for Early Adolescents', *Alberta Journal of Educational Research* XLV.1 (1999): 103–105.

Demers, S. and Bennett, C., *Single Sex Classrooms*, Onterio: The Literacy and Numeracy Secretariat, 2007.

Erling, Sally and Jan Reilly, *Single-Sex Schools: A Review of the Literature*, Toronto: Toronto District School Board, 2009.

Gandhi, Anjali, *School Social Work*, New Delhi: Commonwealth Publications, 1995.

Holthouse, David, 'Gender Segregation: Separate But Effective?', *Teaching Tolerance* 37 (Spring 2010): 25–27.

Human Development Report 2013, http://www.undp.org/content/dam/undp/library/corporate/HDR/2013GlobalHDR/English/HDR2013%20Report%20English.pdf Last accessed on 23rd August 2014.

Ministry of HRD, *Elementary Education in India: Analytical Report*, 2005, http://www.educationforallinindia.com/11thfiveyearplanchapteronelementaryeducation.pdf.

Ministry of Women and Child Development (2011), XII Five Year Plan, Report of the Working Group on Women's Agency and Empowerment.

Government of India. Available at http://planningcommission.nic.in/aboutus/committee/wrkgrp12/wcd/wgrep_women.pdf. Last accessed on 23rd August 2014.

NIPCCD, *Statistics on Women in India 2012*, National Institute of Public Cooperation and Child Development, 2010.

NUEPA, *Elementary Education in India: Progress towards UEE*, National University of Educational Planning and Administration and Department of School Education and Literacy, Ministry of Human Resource Development, Government of India, 2014. http://www.dise.in/Downloads/Publications/Documents/Flash%20Statistics2013-14%20.pdf. Last accessed on 23rd August 2014.

Ramachandran, Vimala, 'Gender and Education for All: The Leap to Equality', Background paper for the Education for All Global Monitoring Report, UNESCO, Paris, 2003.

Registrar General and Census Commissioner Report 2011, http://www.censusindia.gov.in/2011-prov-results/data_files/india/Table-2(3)_literacy.pdf. Last accessed on 24th August 2014.

Women in Canada: A Gender-based Statistical Report 2012, http://www.statcan.gc.ca/pub/89-503-x/2010001/article/11542–eng.htm. Last accessed on 24th August 2014.

Index